# *Junior* GIRL SCOUT
# BADGE BOOK

Girl Scouts of the USA | 420 Fifth Avenue | New York, NY 10018

**National President**
Connie L. Matsui

**National Executive Director**
Marsha Johnson Evans

**National Director, Membership, Program and Diversity**
Sharon Woods Hussey

**Director, Program Development**
Harriet S. Mosatche, Ph.D.

**Project Directors**
Harriet S. Mosatche, Ph.D.
Patricia Paddock
Karen Unger

**Authors**
Melissa Algranati, Chris Bergerson, María Cabán, Rosemarie Cryan, Dee Ebersole-Boukouzis, Toni Eubanks, Wendy DeGiglio, Sharon Hussey, Carolyn Kennedy, Sheila K. Lewis, Sarah Lowengard, Ellen Markowitz, Lauraine Merlini, Harriet S. Mosatche, Ph. D, Patricia J. Paddock, Deborah Parker, Karen Unger, Joy Williams

**Contributors**
Glenn Adair, The American Institute of Chemical Engineers (AIChE), Nancy Garfield, Irma L. Marin, Margarita Magner, Amy Messeroll, Joanne Mudhe, The National Geographic Society, Alexandra O' Rourke, Sandy Thomas

**Acknowledgements**
Director of Publishing, Suzanna Penn; Project Editor, Mikki Morrissette; Assistant Editor, Susan Brody; Manager, Creative Design and Production, Christina Cannard-Seward; Marie Kary-Gargiulo, Technical Assistant; Gerri Brown, Director of Sales and New Market Development; Linda LeShanna, Director of Trademark and Licensing; Mindi Rosenthal, Merchandise Manager; Daria Scala, Manager of NES Advertising

**Illustration**
Adam Hurwitz: 5, 11, 13, 17, 21, 23, 25, 33, 35 bottom, 39, 43, 49-51, 56-57, 59, 67, 72-73, 75-77, 79-81, 91, 93, 95,101, 109, 115, 125, 127, 129, 157, 161, 164-167, 171, 174-175, 187, 191, 195, 207, 210-211, 216, 217 top; William Waitzman: 35top, 137, 140, 145; Sara Schwartz: v, vi, vii, 10, 26-28, 30, 34, 38, 46, 58, 60-61, 82-83, 98, 108, 113, 116, 126, 135, 147, 151, 158, 163, 182, 184-185, 206; Karen Stormer Brooks: 89, 98-99, 111, 122-123, 131, 133, 140, 144, 149, 169, 178-179, 181, 189, 201, 209, 217b, 219

**Photography**
The Girl Scout Archives: 2, 3; The Girl Scouts: Lori Adamski-Peek V, V1, V11, V111, 1X, X, X1, 4, 5, 6, 7, 18, 21, 24, 32, 52, 62, 63, 64, 69, 70, 75, 86, 92, 112, 118, 124, 132, 138, 150, 202, The Girl Scouts: Elizabeth Hathon 183, George Kerrigan/Digital Eyes: Cover; all badges, awards, insignia;V1, 9, 97,103,152,162,163,173.

Adstock: Chris Marona, 105; AlaskaStock: Eberhard Brunner 197, Jeff Schultz 196; Allsport/Hulton Deutsch: 85; Animals, Animals: Susan Ley 104r; Corbis: 37br, 38t, Owen Franken 71, Raymond Gehman 29m,123, Michael Gore, Frank Lane Picture Agency/Corbis 29t, Kelly Mooney 84, Richard T. Nowitz 101r, Tim Thompson 45m, Brian Vikander 29b; Earth Scenes: Nigel J.H. Smith198r, Esto: Brad Simmons 130t, FPG: 37, Jeff Baker 74, Paul Boisvert 204, Gary Buss100, Holmes-Lebel 37, Bill Miles 191, Bob Peterson 67, Micheal Simpson 213m, Arthur Tilley V1, 56, 195, VCG 13,14,190, 215; Barbara Koppelman: 143,166; Mountain Stock: Mike Anich 116, Hank de Vre' 90, Anne Marie Weber 107b, David Whitten 205, Bob Woodward 68,101l, NASA: 213l, 218; Omni-Photo: Jeff Greenberg 149, Kim R. Mould 106, Jack Parsons 130b, Shelley Rotner 134; Peter Arnold,Inc.: John Cancaloni 16, Kevin Schafer 198bl, J. & L. Weber 209; PhotoEdit: Davis Barber 107t, Myrleen Cate 31, 44bl, Deborah Davis 44tl, Tony Freeman 81,170, Kathy Ferguson120, Jeff Greenberg 44tr, Richard Hutchings 19, Felicia Martinez 42, Michael Newman 172, A. Ramey 45t, 146r, 147, Rudi Von Briel 146l, 155R, David Young-Wolff 41t, 44br, 53, 78, 88, 110, 115, 142, 168, 194, 198tl; Photo Researchers: Linda Barlett 125, Russel D. Curtis 136, Christine M. Douglas 117, Renee Lynn 177, Lawrence Migdale 54, 55, 66l, Bruce Roberts 180, Jerry Schad 213r, Jim Steinberg 94; PictureQuest; Jose Azel/ Aurora; 156; The Image Works: Bob Daemmrich 43, 66l, 119, 121,127, Eastcott/ Momatiuk 45b, Macduff Everton 155l, Margot Granitsas 155m, Lisa Law 141, NASA/The Image Works, Andrea Dupre, Ronald Gilliland 212, Tim Reese 41b, Tony Savino 114, Ellen B.Senisi 87; The Stock Market: Roger Ball 160, Paul Barton 40, 186, Peter Beck 128, Ed Bock 12, Jon Feingersh 96, LWA-Dann Tardif 65. Roy Morsch 192, Gabe Palmer 208, Adam Peiperl 200, David Pollack 48, Ariel Skelley 57, Tom Stewart 104l, John Tardif 165; Unicorn Stock Photos: Aneal Vohra 91; WaterHouse: Stephen Frink 214, Weatherstock: Warren Faidley 219.

**Design**
Adventure House, NYC

Inquiries related to the *Junior Girl Scout Badge Book* should be directed to
Membership, Program and Diversity, Girl Scouts of the USA, 420 Fifth Avenue, New York, N.Y. 10018-2798.

This book may not be reproduced in whole or in part in any form of by any means, electronic or mechanical, including photocopying, recording, or by any information storage and retrieval system now known or hereafter invented, without the prior written permission of Girl Scouts of the United States of America, 420 Fifth Avenue, New York, N.Y. 10018-2798.

Badge activities for "Making It Matter" on page 208 and "Oil Up" on page 216, include contributions by the American Institute of Chemical Engineers.
"The Food Guide Pyramid" on page 77, is provided courtesy of the U.S. Department of Agriculture.
"Ten Toy Hazards to Avoid" on page 183, is provided courtesy of Toy Manufacturers of America.

Photos on page 4, 5 and 202 courtesy of Pilgrim of Newport, Long Beach, California.
Photos on page 6 and 150 courtesy of California State University, Long Beach, Earl Burns Miller Japanese Garden.
Photo on page IX courtesy of Blue Submarine, Long Beach, California.

© 2001 by Girl Scouts of the United States of America
All rights reserved
First Impression 2001
Printed in the United States of America
ISBN 13: 978-0-88441-620-3
ISBN 0-88441-620-8

29 28 27 26 25 24

For information regarding the CPSIA on this printed material call: 203-595-3636 and provide reference # EAST - 65994

# *Junior* GIRL SCOUT BADGEBOOK

# CONTENTS

**On My Way**
Page 24

## *Girl Scout Basics* — 1
| | |
|---|---|
| Girl Scouting Around the World | 2 |
| Girl Scouting in My Future | 4 |
| Girl Scouting in the USA | 6 |
| The Cookie Connection | 8 |

## *Adventures in Girl Scouting* — 2
| | |
|---|---|
| Business-Wise | 10 |
| Careers | 12 |
| Global Awareness | 14 |
| Humans and Habitats | 16 |
| Lead On | 18 |
| Model Citizen | 20 |
| Money Sense | 22 |
| On My Way | 24 |
| Traveler | 26 |
| World Neighbors | 28 |

## *It's Great to Be a Girl* — 3
| | |
|---|---|
| Becoming a Teen | 30 |
| Being My Best | 32 |
| Consumer Power | 34 |
| It's Important to Me | 36 |
| Looking Your Best | 38 |

III

## 4 Family and Friends

| | |
|---|---|
| Across Generations | 40 |
| Caring for Children | 42 |
| Celebrating People | 44 |
| Communication | 46 |
| Healthy Relationships | 48 |
| Local Lore | 50 |
| My Community | 52 |
| My Heritage | 54 |
| Pet Care | 56 |

## 5 How To Stay Safe

| | |
|---|---|
| Car Care | 58 |
| The Choice Is Yours | 60 |
| First Aid | 62 |
| High on Life | 64 |
| Safety First! | 66 |

## 6 Be Healthy, Be Fit

| | |
|---|---|
| Adventure Sports | 68 |
| Court Sports | 70 |
| Environmental Health | 72 |
| Field Sports | 74 |
| Food Power | 76 |
| Fun and Fit | 78 |
| A Healthier You | 80 |
| Highway to Health | 82 |
| Sports Sampler | 84 |
| Stress Less | 86 |
| Walking for Fitness | 88 |
| Winter Sports | 90 |

## 7 Let's Get Outdoors

| | |
|---|---|
| Camp Together | 92 |
| Earth Connections | 94 |
| Eco-Action | 96 |
| Finding Your Way | 98 |
| Frosty Fun | 100 |
| Hiker | 102 |
| Horse Fan | 104 |
| Horse Rider | 106 |
| Outdoor Cook | 108 |
| Outdoor Creativity | 110 |
| Outdoor Fun | 112 |
| Outdoors in the City | 114 |
| Plants and Animals | 116 |
| Small Craft | 118 |
| Swimming | 120 |
| Water Fun | 122 |
| Wildlife | 124 |
| Your Outdoor Surroundings | 126 |

Pet Care
page 56

Finding Your Way
page 98

Court Sports
page 70

## Create and Invent  8

| | |
|---|---|
| Architecture | 128 |
| Art in the Home | 130 |
| Art in 3-D | 132 |
| Art to Wear | 134 |
| Books | 136 |
| Camera Shots | 138 |
| Ceramics and Clay | 140 |
| "Collecting" Hobbies | 142 |
| Creative Solutions | 144 |
| Dance | 146 |
| Discovering Technology | 148 |
| "Doing" Hobbies | 150 |
| Drawing and Painting | 152 |
| Folk Arts | 154 |
| Jeweler | 156 |
| "Making" Hobbies | 158 |
| Math Whiz | 160 |
| Ms. Fix-It | 162 |
| Prints and Graphics | 164 |
| Puzzlers | 166 |
| Sew Simple | 168 |
| Theater | 170 |
| Toymaker | 172 |
| Visual Arts | 174 |
| Write All About It | 176 |
| Yarn and Fabric Arts | 178 |

## Explore and Discover  9

| | |
|---|---|
| Aerospace | 180 |
| Computer Fun | 182 |
| Globe-Trotting | 184 |
| Let's Get Cooking | 186 |
| Making It Matter | 188 |
| Making Music | 192 |
| Music Fan | 194 |
| Oil Up | 196 |
| Rocks Rock | 198 |
| Science Discovery | 200 |
| Science in Everyday Life | 204 |
| Science Sleuth | 208 |
| Sky Search | 212 |
| Water Wonders | 214 |
| Weather Watch | 216 |

Science Discovery
**page 200**

Theater
**page 170**

v

# Junior Girl Scout

# BADGE BOOK

## INTRODUCTION

Do you love to practice your backstroke in the town pool? Would you love to learn how to make your own jewelry? Do you like to gaze up into a dark summer night and point out the constellations to your family or friends? Do you dream about hitting a home run during your next softball game? Would you like to camp overnight with your Girl Scout troop? Do you enjoy the challenge of a new computer game?

If some of these ideas interest you, then you are going to love doing the badges in this book. By working on the activities in the badges, you will get a chance to learn new hobbies, practice new skills, or improve the ones you already have. Earning badges is one of the truly unique things about being a Junior Girl Scout.

Fun is the most important part of earning a badge. Earning badges shouldn't become a competition with your friends. You don't have to complete a badge if you start it and then discover that it is too hard, or too easy, or just not what you expected. If that's the case, flip through the pages of this book and find another badge that suits you better. The more you enjoy working on a particular badge, the more you will learn. You might find a new hobby that you can continue to enjoy as a teenager and adult.

### On Your Mark, Get Ready, Get Set, Go

The first thing to do is pick a badge that you would like to work on. This book and your *Junior Girl Scout Handbook* have matching chapters. If you enjoyed the activities in the "Be Healthy, Be Fit" chapter of your handbook, you'll love badges such as "Adventure Sports," "Fun and Fit" and "Highway to Health." You could also take on a challenge and explore badges on topics new to you.

You could work on badges with several other girls or with the entire troop or group. Working on the same activities at the same time can be fun. You can laugh together when all goes well and groan together when it does not! When you work together, you could break up a big activity into smaller pieces. Each girl gets one task to do. For example, you and your troop might make the weather game (activity 7) in the "Weather Watch" badge. Some of you could design the game board, while others could come up with the questions and answers. Other girls could create the players' markers. Often, when you work together you can take the activities a step further. For example, if you formed an investment club as part of the "Money Sense" badge, you could track a number of stocks, instead of just one.

## Helpful Hints

Girl Scouts are often very active. You might belong to a sports team, take art classes, take music lessons, and so on. The activities that you do outside of Girl Scouting can be used to earn badges. If you volunteer to take care of younger children during a religious service, for example, you could use it to fulfill a requirement for the "My Community" badge. If you write a terrific story in school, you could use it for the "Write All About It" badge. The scales you learn during your piano lesson could help you earn the "Making Music" badge.

But, you can't do the same project to earn two different badges. So you would not be able to use volunteering to care for a small child as a requirement for both the "My Community" and "Caring for Children" badges. A healthy snack you create for one badge cannot fulfill a requirement to create a recipe in another badge. You'd need to make a new healthy snack or dish.

All activities that contain measurements are footnoted. You can turn to the metric conversion chart on page 235 to convert the measurements into the metric system.

**Fun is the most important part of earning a badge.**

## What's Required?

To earn a badge you must complete at least SIX activities. For some of the activities, you will be required to produce something. For example, you might be instructed to build a small model or plant a garden. Once you have completed the task, you are done with that activity. Or you might be asked to interview someone and ask her five questions. You have completed that activity after you've gotten the answers to your questions.

Other activities are less specific. You can choose how you would like to finish your project. Use the ideas below to complete activities—or come up with ideas yourself, or with your troop, or with your Girl Scout leader.

**1.** Perform it. Show the sports, music, dance, speech, or theatrical skill—such as a puppet show or pantomime, you have learned—to someone else. Plan a party, parade, carnival, fashion show, or other event.

**2.** Make a game of it. Create a maze, challenge, race, outdoor or indoor game, board or computer game for others to play, based on what you have learned.

**3.** Create a work of art. Make a poster, an advertisement, a collage, drawing, model, sculpture, painting, comic or picture book, video, story, poem, or diorama to illustrate your point.

**4.** Document it. Take photographs, keep a journal or diary, make a sketch, record by audio- or videotape, make a newspaper or scrapbook, build a model, or make a graph to document your findings.

**5.** Teach it. Learn your skill so well that you can teach it to someone else.

## Helping Hands

When you work on earning your badges, you can get help and guidance from many different people. Ask your Girl Scout leader. She can tell you to where to get more information, perhaps directing you to books or a Web site. Your family, a librarian, a teacher, a religious instructor, or business people in your community might also be able to lend a helping hand. They could agree to be an audience so you can demonstrate that you've learned a skill. Or they might agree to play volleyball with you so you can perfect your technique, fulfilling a requirement for the "Court Sports" badge.

# The "Our Own Troop's" and "Our Own Council's" Badges

You certainly have many badges to choose from, but you and the girls in your troop may have an interest for which no badge is listed. Or while you were doing a badge, one of the activities might have been so interesting that you wanted to do more on the same topic. That's why you have an "Our Own Troop's" badge. As a troop, you can name the badge, come up with the activities needed, and design what the badge will look like. This badge becomes special for your troop.

## What Do You Do?

1. Check that the subject of your new badge is not the same as that of any other Junior Girl Scout badge.

2. Make sure that the topic you've chosen is in keeping with the Girl Scout Promise and Law.

3. Find out if the topic you want to explore can support at least eight different activities. Even though only six are necessary, you need at least eight activities so girls can find activities to fit their own talents, abilities, and interests.

4. Make sure all the girls in your troop want to do the badge.

## How Do You Create Your Activities?

With other girls in your troop and your leader, brainstorm a list of possible activities. Then look over your list. Ask each other:

• Are the activities safe?

• Are the activities original? As noted earlier, they shouldn't be repeats of ones found in this book.

• Can all the girls in the troop do the activities? If not, can the activities be altered so all the girls can do them?

• Are there people in the community who can help with the activities?

• Are the activities fun and interesting?

• Are there enough options so that everyone's interests and talents can be explored?

• Are the activities free or easily affordable?

• Are the activities challenging enough to be interesting?

• Will all the girls have enough time to complete them?

• Do the activities show respect for all kinds of people?

• Will the girls learn or do something new?

• Is a community service activity included?

Once you can answer "yes" to all these questions, you're ready to design your badge!

This badge becomes special for your troop.

#### Then What Happens?
Your Girl Scout council must approve your badge topic. After your troop chooses a topic and designs the badge, your leader sends a copy to the council. Some councils may ask to see the activities you want to do. Once your "Our Own Troop's" badge is approved, have fun doing it!

#### The "Our Own Council's" Badge
An "Our Own Council's" badge reflects a special quality or resource in your community. Your leader can find out from your Girl Scout council office if it has its own badge. If not, consider creating one and recommending it to your council.

Topics for an "Our Own Council's" badge would take advantage of something unique located in your council's area, like a science museum, a space center, or an historical or geographical site.

An "Our Own Council's" badge is different from a participation patch you might get for attending a council event like a skating party, fitness walk, or holiday celebration. An "Our Own Council's" badge should follow the guidelines of an "Our Own Troop's" badge, but should be broader in scope and opportunities so that all girls in your council can earn it.

## 1 Girl Scout Basics

# Girl Scouting Around the World

As a Girl Scout, you are not only a member of Girl Scouts of the USA, but also a member of the World Association of Girl Guides and Girl Scouts, known as WAGGGS. As a WAGGGS member, you are part of a sisterhood of millions of girls who share many of your Girl Scout values and traditions. This badge will help you discover the global reach of the Girl Scout community.

The Girl Scouts Chalet, Adelboden, Switzerland

Lord Robert and Lady Olave Baden-Powell

## 1. Thinking Day
Thinking Day falls on February 22 each year. Lord Robert Baden-Powell, the founder of Boy Scouting, and his wife, Lady Olave Baden-Powell had the same birthdays on that day, so February 22 was chosen as a time for Girl Scouts and Girl Guides to celebrate international friendship and world peace. Plan a way to celebrate Thinking Day that recognizes your Girl Scout connection to girls around the world.

## 2. WAGGGS on the Web
Check out the WAGGGS Web site *www.wagggs.org* to find out about the different countries that are members of WAGGGS, and the projects that are being sponsored by that organization. Share what you learned with your troop, group, or other girls.

## 3. Show the World
Create a display that shows how Girl Scouts are part of a world sisterhood. Exhibit your display for Girl Scout troops or groups, your Girl Scout council, your school, or a local library.

## 4. Connect with Younger Girls
Create a game or storybook for younger Girl Scouts that will help them understand their connection to Girl Scouts and Girl Guides around the world. Try out your game or storybook at a neighborhood event, at camp, or at a bridging ceremony for younger Girl Scouts.

## 5. Girl Scout Central
Visit Girl Scouting's official online site for all things Girl Scout: Girl Scout Central! Go to *http://www.girlscouts.org/program/gs_central/*. Click on the link to WAGGGS to find out about more about this world-wide organization. Also look at "travel" and check out special international places you and your Girl Scout friends might want to visit.

## 6. Girl Scouting's Founder: Juliette Gordon Low
Find out about the Juliette Low World Friendship Fund. What does this fund do? How do girls all around the world benefit from the money in the fund?

## 7. International Expert
Choose one country where Girl Guiding/Girl Scouting exists. Become an expert on that country and the activities girl members do there. Learn a game, song, craft, recipe, or activity unique to that country and share it with others.

## 8. World Service
Find out about a world problem that affects girls your age. You could think of a problem related to the environment, hunger, poverty, illiteracy, or another issue. Share what you have researched with other girls and think of some ways girls in WAGGGS could help solve this problem.

## 9. Common Roots
Learn about the lives of Lord and Lady Baden-Powell. Also find out how the Girl Guide movement came about. Share your information with members of your troop/group or with a Brownie Girl Scout troop.

## 10. WAGGGS Travel
WAGGGS has four World Centers that any Girl Scout can visit. Find out the following about each of the four centers: Where is it? How can you get there? What types of events and activities can a visitor take part in there? You can find this information online at the WAGGGS Web site *www.wagggs.org*.

## Girl Scout Basics

# Girl Scouting in My Future

**It's great to be a Junior Girl Scout, but it's also exciting to wonder what it will be like to be a Cadette or Senior Girl Scout. What kinds of activities do they do? What trips do they take? Find out with this badge as you look ahead to "Girl Scouting in My Future."**

### 1. Your Own Wider Op

Any event or trip that takes you beyond your normal meeting time and place is a wider opportunity (or "wider op," for short). Plan with the Girl Scouts in your troop or group—or with family or friends—to take your own wider op. Use the Travel Action Plan in the "Adventures in Girl Scouting" chapter of your *Junior Girl Scout Handbook* as a guide.

### 2. Check Out the Silver and the Gold

Find out about the Girl Scout Silver Award for Cadette Girl Scouts and the Girl Scout Gold Award for Senior Girl Scouts. [See the "Just for Girls" section of the Girl Scout Web site *www.girlscouts.org/girls*.] Compare the requirements for earning each of those awards to the requirements for the Girl Scout Bronze Award, which you can read about in the same section and in your *Junior Girl Scout Handbook*.

### 3. Find Out About Wider Ops

In a few years, you will be old enough to go on a national wider op (wider opportunity). Each year,

thousands of Cadette and Senior Girl Scouts attend these special events. Learn about wider ops offered by councils to Cadette and Senior Girl Scouts across the country. Ask your Girl Scout leader to show you a copy of *Wider Ops*, a catalog that describes the events to be held during the coming year. Look through the catalog and decide on three wider ops that you think you might like. Find out the location, age requirements, cost, dates, focus of the program, and the availability of travel scholarships (called "travelships").

### 4. Make a Travel Ad

Cadette and Senior Girl Scouts can travel outside of the United States. Choose a country you would like to visit and find out as much as you can about that country through books, magazines, travel agents, and Web sites. If possible, gather photos, posters, and souvenirs. Share this information by creating an imaginary television or radio commercial in which you tell everyone why your travel spot is "hot" in one minute or less. Perform your commercial before other Girl Scouts, friends, or family members. If possible, record your commercial on video- or audiotape.

### 5. Make Your Own Model Passport

If you become a Cadette Girl Scout or Senior Girl Scout and are accepted to go on an international wider op, you'll need a passport. Look at a passport application. If possible, look at a real passport to see how it is designed. Then, with the information you have gathered, draw a passport OR apply for a real passport with the help of an adult.

### 6. Plan Your Trip to a Wider Op

If you are selected to attend a wider op, what will it take to get there? Select an event from the wider ops catalog that you would like to attend. Then, figure out how to travel there by plane, train, or car. Collect road maps or train schedules, or call a travel agent to ask about plane schedules. You can also find out plane, train, and map information on the Web. Estimate the number of miles you will travel, how much it will cost in gas prices or ticket fares, and how long it will take you to get there.

### 7. Silver and Gold Go Global

Find out what Girl Scouts are doing to benefit our world. Invite a Cadette or Senior Girl Scout who has earned her Girl Scout Silver Award or Girl Scout Gold Award and whose project was about a global or environmental problem to come to your troop meeting. Ask her to share with your troop what she did to earn her award. Prepare questions for her ahead of time.

OR Interview the recipient of a Girl Scout Cadette Silver Award or Girl Scout Gold Award in person, by e-mail, or on the phone. Take notes and share what you learned about her and her project with your troop, group, or family.

### 8. Brainstorm a Service Project

The Girl Scout Bronze, Silver, and Gold Awards all require a service project. With other Girl Scouts, brainstorm ideas for service projects involving sports, safety, health, nutrition, fitness, or other subject areas that interest you. List at least ten ideas. Select one and discuss how you would go about carrying it out. What kinds of help will you need? What kinds of supplies and equipment? How much time will you need? What about donations? Save your list and plans for your Girl Scout future.

### 9. Attend a Wider Opportunity

Camping trips, cookie events, badge workshops, and bridging events are often sponsored by or partially run by Cadette and Senior Girl Scouts. You may be running such an event someday! Attend one and see how an event is put together. Ask the Cadette or Senior Girl Scouts about the preparations they made for the event. Did they coordinate their event with adults? How did they divide the work? Discuss what you learned with your troop, group, or other Girl Scouts.

### 10. Plan Your Own

Design a wider opportunity for a group of younger Girl Scouts. Work with other Junior Girl Scouts and with Girl Scout leaders to plan the kinds of events or activities that younger girls can do. Once you have a design, carry out your wider opportunity for Daisy or Brownie Girl Scouts. Make sure that Girl Scout leaders are involved and that you have the permissions you need.

## Girl Scout Basics

# Girl Scouting in the USA

**There's always something new to learn about Girl Scouting. Become a Girl Scout expert when you work on this badge.**

### 1. On My Honor . . .
The Girl Scout Promise and Girl Scout Law are the foundation of all the activities you do as a Girl Scout. Learn the Girl Scout Promise and Law and then complete the activities about them in the "Girl Scout Basics" chapter of the *Junior Girl Scout Handbook*.

### 2. Daisy's Life
"Daisy" was the nickname for Juliette Gordon Low, the founder of Girl Scouting in the United States. You can read about her on the Web site *www.gogirlsonly.org*, the online site for girls 5-11 years of age. Click on Spotlight and find out about "When Juliette Was a Girl." Discover:

- The type of person she was. Can you think of three or four words that describe her personality? What were her interests?
- The reasons she founded Girl Scouting in the United States. What she was trying to do for the girls of her era.
- Her legacy. What do you do as a Girl Scout today that Girl Scouts in Juliette Low's time also did?

### 3. Ceremonies: A Girl Scout Tradition
One of the special things about Girl Scouting is its ceremonies. A ceremony may celebrate an event, an achievement, or a Girl Scout holiday. Take a leadership role in planning and conducting a Girl Scout ceremony. Look through *Let's Celebrate!* for ideas on how to create and stage your own ceremony.

### 4. Signs, Mottos, and Handshakes
Girl Scouting has unique traditions that Girl Scouts and Girl Guides experience around the world. As a Junior Girl Scout, you will share:

- The Girl Scout sign
- The Girl Scout handshake
- The quiet sign
- The Girl Scout motto
- The Girl Scout slogan
- The friendship circle
- The friendship squeeze
- Special Girl Scout songs

Show that you know all of the above.

### 5. Girl Scouting Close to Home
Find out more about your local Girl Scout council by taking part in a council-wide event.

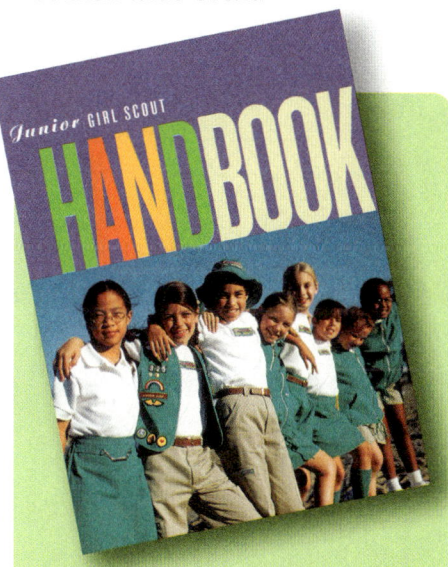

### 6. Check Out Other Girl Scout Books
As a Junior Girl Scout, you are able to do activities from many different program resources written just for you. Your *Junior Girl Scout Handbook* and *Junior Girl Scout Badge Book* are just two of the books available to you. Do activities in two Girl Scout books other than your handbook and badge book.

### 7. More About Junior Girl Scouting
Read about the meaning behind the Girl Scout Membership Pin and the World Trefoil Pin in your handbook and do one of the following activities:

- Plan or participate in a fashion show about the Girl Scouts. If you can, include old and new uniforms and uniforms for the various age levels. You can use a doll, paper doll models, or virtual models on a computer display.
- Start earning an award other than a badge. Some to try are the Junior Girl Scout Leadership Award, the Junior Aide Award, one of the Signs, or a religious award. Read about them in your *Junior Girl Scout Handbook*.

### 8. Careers in Girl Scouting
Girl Scout adults can participate in Girl Scouting as volunteers and as staff members. Find out more about a Girl Scout job (volunteer or paid) that you think you might like to do one day. Do an interview with an adult asking:

- What does she do?
- What skills does she need?
- How does the job support Girl Scouting?

### 9. Girl Scout History
You can find out a lot about the history of Girl Scouts right in your hometown. Talk to women of different ages who are or have been part of Girl Scouting. If you can, find out about some of the books Girl Scouts used in the past and some of the activities that were popular.

### 10. Helping Others
What is the Girl Scout motto? Think of some ways you could live by the Girl Scout motto in your daily routines. Then follow through on this.

## Girl Scout Basics

# The Cookie Connection

Not only are Girl Scout cookies delicious, but the annual cookie sale also supports troops and councils, and teaches Girl Scouts many skills. Whether you are a budding entrepreneur or prefer to help out from the sidelines, you can learn a lot when it comes to cookies! Start with this badge.

You'd be surprised what a Girl Scout Cookie® can build:

 Strong Values

 Strong Minds

 Strong Bodies

 Strong Spirit

 Strong Friendships

 Strong Skills

 Strong Leadership

 Strong Community

### 1. Five Ways to Sell a Cookie

With the help of your Girl Scout friends, figure out five new ways or places to sell Girl Scout cookies. Can you sell them at a community fair, neighborhood recreation center, or holiday parade? With the help of an adult, contact people who can help you find a place for your Girl Scout cookie sale. Remember, Girl Scouts are prohibited from selling cookies over the Internet.

### 2. Cookie Know-How

Good sales people know all about their merchandise (products). Do you know all about Girl Scout cookies? What are the ingredients? How many calories do they contain? How long have Girl Scouts been selling cookies as a way to earn money for their activities? In your troop or group meetings, answer these and other questions that you come up with. Also, be prepared to tell your customers what your troop or group plans to do with the money it earns.

### 3. "Tough Cookies"

Knowing how to deal with the public is an important part of being a sales person. You should always be polite and say "thank you," even if someone doesn't buy anything. With your troop or group, think of several situations that might come up when you are selling cookies and how you will handle them. For example:

- A customer is having a hard time deciding between the different types of cookies.
- A neighbor tells you she is tired of always being asked to buy things.
- A boy says he would like to buy a box of cookies for his mother but doesn't have any money.

### 4. Make Cookie Sales Count

With your troop or group, develop a plan for what to do with the money you earn from cookie sales. Brainstorm several projects or activities. Estimate the costs of each activity by finding out about admission fees, transportation, etc. Figure out how many boxes of cookies you would need to sell to do one of these activities. Work out a plan for reaching your goal and chart your progress. Check out the section on creating a budget in the "Adventures in Girl Scouting" chapter of your *Junior Girl Scout Handbook* for help.

### 5. From Field to Food Shop

With your troop or group, talk about different jobs connected to food, from growing it to packaging and selling it. Some examples are farmer, baker, advertiser, distributor, shipper, graphic artist, truck driver, and dietitian. Invite someone to a meeting to talk about her food-related job and what the job involves.

### 6. Cookies Under Wraps

Be a good neighbor. Buy several boxes of Girl Scout cookies with your troop or group money and wrap them in pretty paper to give as gifts throughout the year. You might take them to senior citizens in a nursing home, or to a family who just moved to your neighborhood. Use this as an opportunity to meet new friends and make them feel welcome.

### 7. Safe Sales

Make a list of safety rules for selling Girl Scout cookies. First, check the *Cookie Sale Activity Guides* from this and previous years, as they have many good tips. Your leader or parents can get those for you. (They are available at Girl Scout council shops and online on the "Just for Girls" Web pages.) Then, brainstorm other safety rules, tips, and ideas. Write them on a poster and hang it where everyone can see it. Review the rules throughout the time you are working on the Girl Scout cookie sale. Here are two rules you might post:

### Safety Rules

1. **Always sell cookies with an adult present.**
2. **Never leave money from cookie sales lying around where it can get lost or stolen.**

### 8. Cookie Creativity

Have a cookie party and get creative! See how many adjectives your group can come up with to describe Girl Scout cookies. Create memorable slogans. For example, try "Sensational Samoas!" or "Think Thin Mints!" Turn your best ideas into posters and advertisements.

### 9. Be Bold

With your troop or group, design a giant poster or display for your cookie campaign that is suitable for a mall, public building, or other place where many people will see it. You will have to get permission from store owners or public officials to do this. Create a design that is colorful and that includes information about the cookies and about the program activities that are supported by selling cookies.

### 10. Cookies Across Cultures

Are cookies as "American as apple pie"? Cookies are very popular in Girl Scouting and in this country. Find out about the kinds of cookies that are popular in a culture other than your own. Are they eaten after school, served for holidays, or reserved for other special occasions? Find a recipe you like from another culture in an international or regional cookbook, and bake a batch of cookies. Sample them with friends and family.

## 2 Adventures in Girl Scouting

# Business-Wise

**Do you want to be your own boss? What does it take to create and run a small business? You need a good idea— along with persistence, patience, and a willingness to learn. Find out more with this badge.**

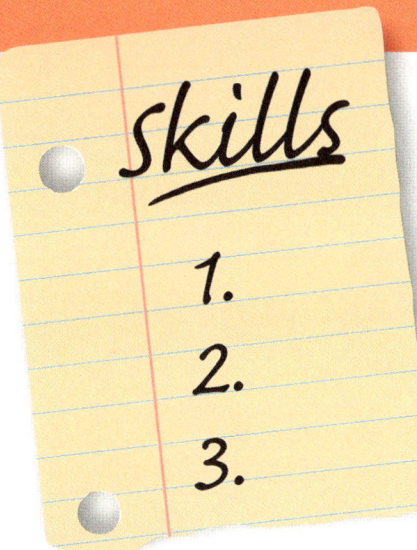

## 1. Talent Scout
Make a list of your skills and interests. Talk to some people in your neighborhood to get ideas about what kinds of products or services are needed in your community. Make a list of businesses that would combine your skills and interests with your community's needs.

## 2. Ask an Owner
Ask a successful female business owner the following questions:

- What was your first business?
- Why did you start your own business?
- What do you like the most and the least about being your own boss?
- What personality traits and skills are needed to run a business?

## 3. Risky Business?
With your troop, friends, or family, debate the advantages of working for yourself, such as making your own decisions. Then consider the disadvantages, such as working long hours.

## 4. Business Plan of Action
Think about a business you could start now, either by yourself or with others. Write your answers to the following questions:

- What product or service will you provide?
- Who will your customers be?
- What will the name of your business be?
- How will you get the money or supplies you need to start?
- How much will you charge for your product or service?
- How will you advertise your product or service?
- How will you keep accurate records of income and expenses?

Your answers make up your business plan. Share your plan with an adult and ask for other suggestions.

## 5. Friends and Money
Talk to a friend who is interested in starting a business with you, and create guidelines that will help to guarantee a successful working relationship. The word "communicate" should be at the top of the list.

## 6. Cost and Profit
Setting prices for your product or service can be tricky. Not only must you cover your expenses, but you must also make a profit! Interview someone who has her own business and find out how she determines her expenses, including materials, office supplies, phone and computer expenses, advertising costs, lighting, and postage. If you are in a service business, ask her to help you determine what your time is worth.

## 7. Be Seen!
Create an advertising campaign for your real or imaginary business using flyers, posters, brochures, or advertisements—or any other means you think will work. How much will it cost to make these items and to place them where customers will see them? Remember to add the cost of advertising to your overall costs.

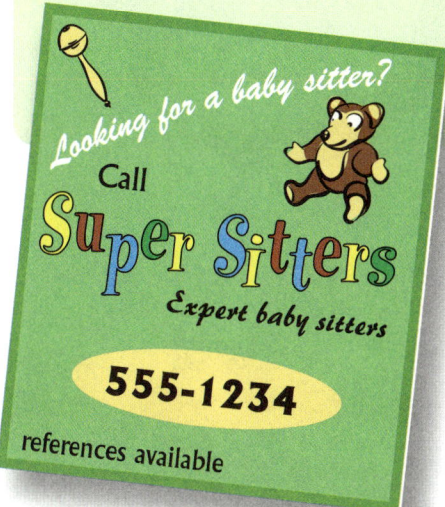

## 8. Practice Makes Perfect
Demonstrate the way you would present yourself and your product or service to your customers. You could do this by trying out your business manners when you meet or greet someone in person or on the phone, or prepare a sample business letter. Prepare a presentation about your product or service for a customer.

## 9. Up and Running
If possible, take part in running a business according to your business plan for at least one month.

## 10. Cash Flow
Find out how to open a savings or checking account for a business. Find out about the services offered by the bank specially for business customers.

## Adventures in Girl Scouting

# Careers

**It's never too early to start thinking about different careers and learning about the skills and education they require.**

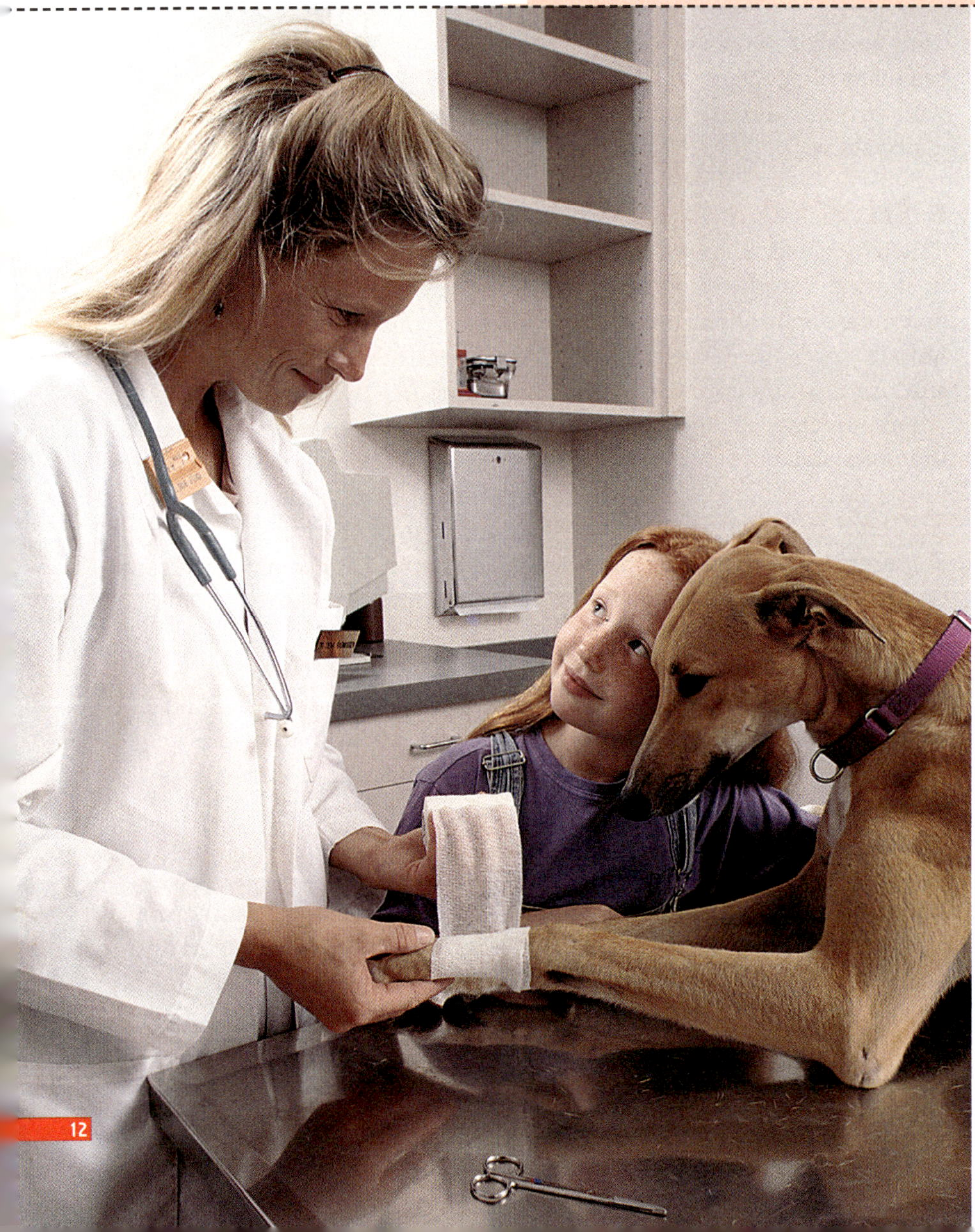

### 1. Check Out the Classifieds
Read three want ads (help wanted ads) from a newspaper or an online job site. What do all those abbreviations mean? What experience or education is needed for each job? How do the salaries compare? Would you like to have any of those jobs? Why or why not?

### 2. Work Is Funny
If you read through the comics in the newspaper, you'll come across many that are written about working life. Find out why work can be funny. If you don't get the joke in a comic strip, ask someone who works to explain it to you.

### 3. Hobbies Can Be Golden
Imagine doing something you love and earning money for it! Your favorite hobby can become a career. Ask five adults whether hobbies they had as children are related in some way to their careers. What did you learn from talking to them?

*lawyer*
*teacher*
*accountant*
*doctor*
*reporter*
*pharmacist*

### 4. A Career for You
Pick a career you might like to have. Find out about the education or special training needed to get a job in that field, and the salary (what you earn when you are starting out and after ten years). What clothes, tools, or equipment are used in this career? Is it hard to get a job in this field? Think of a way to share what you found out with others.

### 5. Thinking on Your Feet
Almost every career requires quick thinking. Try this activity to test how well you think on your feet.

1. Count the number of girls in your group. Then prepare a slip of paper for each girl.
2. On each slip of paper write a word. You can write simple words like "cat," "shoe," "pencil," or "thumb," or more complicated ideas like "friendship," "peace," or "poverty."
3. Fold up the slips and place them in a container.
4. Each girl takes a turn, pulls a slip out of the container, and has to stand up and talk for 30 seconds about her topic. Think 30 seconds is too short? Try it! You'll see how long 30 seconds can be when you have to think on your feet.

### 6. Time's a' Wasting
Time management skills are essential when you work. Find out how to manage time well by reading the time management section of the "Be Healthy, Be Fit" chapter in your *Junior Girl Scout Handbook*. Do one of the activities in that section.

### 7. Interviewing 101
A job interview makes almost anyone nervous. But a good interview—one in which you stay calm, cool, and collected—can get you your dream job. Practice going on an interview to make the jitters go away. Pick a partner, then:

- With your partner, choose a job from the newspaper want ads.
- Decide on the questions the interviewer would ask to find the best person for the job.
- Decide on how the interviewee (the person who wants the job) would answer the questions to make the best impression.
- Role-play an interview. Take turns being the interviewer and the interviewee.

### 8. Role Models
Get information about three women who have successful careers. Interview them to find out about their secrets of success.

### 9. Getting Along in Groups
Almost every job requires you to get along well with others. Read the section about getting groups on track in the "Adventures in Girl Scouting" chapter of your *Junior Girl Scout Handbook*. Ask a working person why conflict resolution skills are important in the workplace.

### 10. Computers on the Job
Talk to people who work about how they use computers at their jobs. Find out at least five different ways computers are used. Share your information with others.

*Adventures in Girl Scouting*

# Global Awareness

**People in the world are becoming closer and more connected—and finding out much more about one another. Take time to learn more about your world.**

## 1. Where in the World
Use a globe or atlas, or go online, and find out about a city or town in a country far away from where you live. What are the similarities between this place and your community? What are the differences?

## 2. The Center of Things
Choose a country you'd like to learn about. Draw a map with your chosen country at the map's center. Now, add the countries that surround it. What geographical features—for example, a river, a forest, or a coastline—does your country have that its neighbors don't? What effect do these geographical features have on the country?

## 3. Show Your Colors
Make or draw the flag of another country. What does the design stand for? Why was the flag designed that way?

## 4. International Friendships
Many cities and towns in the U.S.A. have a "twin" or "sister" city in another part of the world. Does yours? Find out about activities to promote cooperation between cities. If there are activities like these in your area, find out how you can take part in them.

## 5. In the News
How well do neighboring countries get along? Choose a region of the world. Watch TV or look through newspapers for a week and look for any mention of your region. What countries are in that area? How do they get along? What challenges do they face? What are they doing to keep their friendships with other countries strong?

## 6. Be a Diplomat
How do countries work together to address issues that affect them all? Find out! Pick a region of the world. Each person picks one country and becomes that country's representative. Pick one regional issue, such as the environment, the spread of diseases, or the use of illegal drugs. Find out about and talk about how this issue is affecting your country. Can the group come up with a course of action that everyone can agree on?

## 7. Walk in Their Shoes
What would your life be like if you lived in a different part of the world? Choose a country. Find out about a typical day for a girl your age. What would be a typical home? What foods would you eat? What hobbies would you have? What would your school day be like? What cultural, religious, or political rules or guidelines would you follow? Are the rules different for girls and boys?

## 8. Sisters
Go to the WAGGGS Web site www.wagggs.org and pick a WAGGGS country. What are WAGGGS girls in that country called? What does their uniform look like? What is their Promise like? What types of things do they do? Share what you've learned with your troop or group.

Dear Annik,

When my Girl Scout troop visited the Statue of Liberty in New York City we learned that it was a gift from France. This made me want to learn more about your country. I have been reading about some of France's landmarks like the Eiffel Tower, Notre Dame Cathedral, and the Palace of Versailles.

In the United States we also have some important landmarks, such as the Statue of Liberty (of course), the Washington Monument, and Mount Rushmore.

Will you write to me and tell me about your favorite landmarks in France?

How many have you visited?

And thank your country for giving us our symbol of liberty.

Your friend,
Jane

## 9. Write On
Write a letter to an imaginary girl in one of the countries you've learned about. Let her know all the things you've learned about her country. Tell her some things about the U.S.A. What types of things do you two have in common? Celebrate them in your letter!

## 10. Lead the Way
Identify a female leader from another country. She could be a political, religious, business, or cultural leader. How has she become successful? What are her accomplishments?

## Adventures in Girl Scouting

# Humans and Habitats

**How people live depends a lot on the place where they live. Learn more about your world by doing the activities in this badge.**

### 1. Have Home, Will Travel
In some countries, nomadic people (who move from place to place rather than live in one permanent spot) have invented homes that are very portable. Learn out about the types of homes that nomadic people use today and used in the past.

### 2. It's Symbolic
What are some of the symbols used to represent international organizations such as UNICEF, the Red Cross, the World Health Organization, and Girl Scouts? Invent a symbol or flag that could represent your community—its climate, geography, and way of life.

### 3. Farmers Around the World
People almost everywhere grow food. Find out how people farm in two or three different countries. How does farming affect their environments? How are farming tools and other methods different from one country to the next?

## 4. Your Life Would Be Different If . . .
Pick a place with a lifestyle that is different from your own—perhaps a rain forest, a desert, or Antarctica. Look around your home. What items would you have to live without? What items would you need instead?

## 5. Peace of Cake
Since the 1960s, Peace Corps volunteers have lived in countries around the world working with communities on health, education, and other projects. Contact the local Peace Corps recruiting office or go to its Web site and find out more about what Peace Corps workers do. Invite a returned Peace Corps volunteer to visit a troop or group meeting and share her experiences.

## 6. Make a Food Map
Make a list of foods that you typically eat in one day. Research where these products are grown. Then make a products map that shows where the foods are grown. To make a product map, download a world map from the National Geographic Web site www.nationalgeographic.com/education. Draw or make symbols for each food, and make a key or legend for the map.

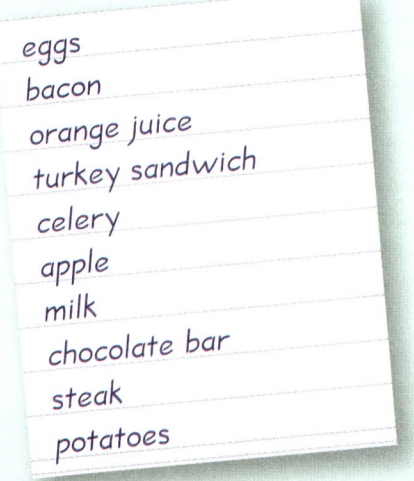

eggs
bacon
orange juice
turkey sandwich
celery
apple
milk
chocolate bar
steak
potatoes

## 7. Break Bread
People all around the world make and eat bread. Prepare one type and taste two others from the list below.

**Flat Bread** *like tortilla, papadum, matzo*

**Filled Bread** *like alu paratha, pastelillo, gyoza*

**Puffed Bread** *like puri, beignet, donuts, sopapilla*

**Fried Bread** *like pakora, fritters, pancakes, johnny cakes*

## 8. The World Close to Home
Do you have many different kinds of restaurants in your town? Pick a certain type of food and find out how it is cooked in two cultures other than your own. Find out how the foods and the recipes reflect the climate and the geography of that country. For example, people in many hot climates cook very spicy dishes. Why? Spicy food makes you sweat, which makes your body cool off in the hot weather. Spicy food also hides the taste of unrefrigerated meat, which can spoil a little in hot weather.

## 9. Take a Look Around You
Become a geography observer in your community. Do this alone or with others. Try to look at the following:

- The kinds of crops and trees you see
- How much land is empty and how much is used
- What is on the land that is used, such as crops for farming, parks for recreation, open space to protect the environment, or buildings used for housing, business, government, shopping, and other uses

Would you keep the land the way it is, or would you make changes? Write a letter or send an e-mail with your ideas to the zoning or planning board in your community, or attend a zoning board meeting.

## 10. What's Best?
How do different living environments compare? Look at living in an apartment building, single-family home, farmhouse, mobile home, or modular home. How are things different in cities, suburbs, villages, and rural areas? In your troop or with others, find a way to show your "dream environments"—your favorite types of homes in your favorite types of communities.

## Adventures in Girl Scouting

# Lead On

**Do you dream of running your own business someday? Maybe you'd like to be the captain of a sports team. Find out how you can be a leader and learn the skills to get you there.**

### 1. Talk Show Star
Create an imaginary TV show in which you are the host. Interview a pretend leader—a mayor, for example. Ask at least five questions about her leadership role. Provide time for your "studio audience" to ask questions as well.

### 2. Let's Welcome . . .
Choose a female leader whom you have read or heard about. Write or tape record what you would say about her if you were introducing her to an audience of Junior Girl Scouts and their families.

### 3. Choose Your Leaders
List at least five leaders, including leaders from your school, community, state, nation, and the world. Choose your favorite leader from the list. With your troop, group, or family, discuss what personal qualities make that person a good leader. Which qualities do you have that are similar to hers?

### 4. Play a Leading Role
A leader should be a role model—someone who practices habits that provide a good example for others to follow. Do an activity with your

troop, group, or family in which you practice being a role model in one of the following areas: safety, sports, or friendship.

## 5. Leading Qualities
One quality that all good leaders have is a sense of responsibility. Make a list of the tasks that you are responsible for on a typical weekday. Ask yourself if you do each of these things without prompting (in other words, without having someone remind you to do them). If you don't, make tomorrow a "Responsibility Day." Keep your list close by and check items off as you do them. Try to finish the entire list without your family reminding you. For more advice on getting things done, check out the time management skills section of the "Be Healthy, Be Fit" chapter in your *Junior Girl Scout Handbook*.

## 6. Follow the Leader
Many games build leadership skills in a fun way. "Follow the Leader," "Simon Says," and "Red Rover" are some examples. Hold an event in which games emphasizing leadership skills are played. Invite younger Girl Scouts, friends, and neighbors to attend. Include games that make players follow directions, such as scavenger hunts and relay races.

## 7. More on Leadership
In a group, identify a community problem and brainstorm actions you could take to deal with it. To guide your planning, use the action plan in the "Adventures in Girl Scouting" chapter of your *Junior Girl Scout Handbook*.

## 8. Team Leadership
Playing sports often provides a good chance to test and improve your leadership skills. Pick a skill you are really good at—such as throwing, batting, volleying, or somersaulting—and volunteer to spend some time teaching it to another girl.

## 9. What Did You Say?
Good communication is important to leadership. Read about communication in the "Family and Friends" chapter of your *Junior Girl Scout Handbook*. Test your communication skills with friends, family, and other Girl Scouts.

## 10. Set a Goal
Decide on one leadership quality you are going to improve over the next month. Write out your commitment, and take at least three actions a week to meet your goal.

*Adventures in Girl Scouting*

# Model Citizen

**As part of the Girl Scout Law, you promise to "make the world a better place." You can help do this by being a good citizen. But what exactly does it mean to be a model citizen? Here are some ideas to help you find out.**

### 1. A Good Neighbor
Citizenship begins at home and in your community. What is a good neighbor? Make a list of ten things that you think make being a good neighbor. Pick one and take action on it.

### 2. Rights and Responsibilities
Rights, as well as responsibilities, are associated with being a citizen of a country. What do you think are some of the rights and responsibilities that come with being a citizen of the United States? Ask different members of the community what they think and compare and discuss the answers that you get.

### 3. Global Citizen
Talk with someone who has been a citizen of another country or who has lived or worked in another country. Ask the person what it was like to live in that country as compared to living in the United States.

### 4. Lawmaker
Design rules, regulations, or laws that might be needed for two of these situations:

- You are the mayor of the first town on the moon.
- An amusement park is being built next to a school.
- A toxic waste dump is being built next to a farm.
- There is a town where everyone owns boats and no one has a car.
- There is a five-story building with no elevators. It has only one inside staircase and one outside staircase.
- A busy highway is built near an elementary school.

### 5. Create a Government
Many board and computer games involve creating a country or city from scratch. They often ask you to make rules for governing the city or country. Try one of these games.

### 6. In Person
Visit a branch of the city, town, or county government that makes policies or laws for your community, or visit a branch of government that enforces the laws of your community. While you are there, find out the names of your state representatives and how they voted on an issue that is of concern to you.

## 10. Paperwork
Help your family keep their identification documents organized and up-to-date. These documents could be residency records, Social Security cards, passports, copies of driver's licenses, birth and marriage certificates, school records, or others. Offer to file or photocopy these important documents. Store them in a color-coded or alphabetized set of folders. You may want to transfer some information to a computer file. Make sure the documents are stored securely—in a fire-proof safe, perhaps—and are ready when needed.

## 7. News Flash
*News flash:* The town board approved building a mega-shopping center instead of a park on the last bit of open green space in town. *News flash:* The city is cutting your favorite after-school program to save money. *News flash:* Your county has approved a new chemical treatment plant. As a model citizen, how do you voice your support or your disapproval of such types of news? Ask adults to tell you three ways that people can legally and peacefully protest in the United States.

## 8. Red, White, and Blue
The American flag is one of the symbols that represents our nation. Read about ceremonies in the "Girl Scout Basics" chapter of your *Junior Girl Scout Handbook* and participate in a flag ceremony.

## 9. Help Out
Design and carry out a small project to show that you are a model citizen in your community. You can do the project on your own or with others.

*Adventures in Girl Scouting*

# Money Sense

**Learning about earning, saving, and spending can help you make your money grow. The activities in this badge will help you get the most out of the money you have—both now and in the future.**

## Troop or Group Budget

### Income

| | |
|---|---|
| Dues | |
| Product Sales | |
| Money-Earning Projects | |
| Contributions (from parents, sponsors, etc.) | |
| Money from Last Year | |
| Others | |
| Total Income | |

### Expenses

| | |
|---|---|
| Supplies | |
| Transportation | |
| Fees (for example, for admissions) | |
| Refreshments (food and drinks) | |
| Awards | |
| Others | |
| Total Expenses | |

### 1. Troop Budget
With your troop, develop a troop budget. Include your expenses, such as equipment, supplies, and the cost of trips and other activities. Also include your income, or sources of money, such as troop dues, proceeds from cookie sales, and money earned through special projects. Then plan for a fun activity. Determine the cost, and figure out how long it will take to earn the money. See the section about managing money in the "Adventures in Girl Scouting" chapter in your *Junior Girl Scout Handbook* for information.

### 2. Best Investments
Find out about the different ways to invest and save money. Learn about three of the following:

- Mutual funds
- Money market accounts
- Certificates of deposit
- Saving accounts
- U.S. savings bonds
- Stocks
- Corporate bonds

### 3. Invest Together
With a group of friends, form an "investment club." Ask an adult for advice. Choose two different stocks or mutual funds. With "pretend" amounts of money, invest equal amounts of money in each. Follow your investments for three months, and then compare how they did.

### 4. Cash or Credit
Sometimes people prefer to use a credit card instead of cash when they buy something. Talk to a banker, an accountant, a financial planner, or another knowledgeable adult about how credit cards work. What are credit card interest rates? Find out how long it would take you to pay for a $250 bicycle if you used a credit card that charged 9 percent interest, 12 percent interest, and 18 percent interest. An adult can help you with the calculations.

### 5. Ups and Downs of the Market
With the help of an adult, follow a stock as it is reported in the newspaper or online for a month. Pretend you own 100 shares of that stock. Have you made a profit? If so, how much? If not, how much did you lose? Think about why you would or would not buy stock in this company, and explain your ideas to your troop or group.

### 6. Careers in Finance
Find out about jobs in the finance industry. Invite someone who works in one of the following jobs to talk about her work. Ask her to explain what her day is like, the training necessary for her job, and what advice she has for someone interested in this type of job:

- Accountant
- Financial planner
- Bookkeeper
- Financial analyst
- Insurance agent
- Stockbroker
- Credit counselor
- Portfolio or mutual fund manager

### 7. Shop Smart
Learn about comparison shopping by spending an afternoon at a nearby mall. In small groups, head for the mall to check for best buys. Be sure to bring a calculator and a notebook. Try to compare the same brand or similar items in various stores. Look for sales, coupon items, discontinued merchandise, and seconds (items with minor flaws). Were there big differences in prices at different stores?

### 8. Reality Check
How much money do you think it takes for an adult or family to live today? With the help of your family, write down all the types of expenses you can think of, including rent or mortgage payments, heat, taxes, electricity, cable television, insurance, phone, water, car payments, food, clothes, entertainment, and gifts. How much would you need to earn to pay these bills?

### 9. Money Doesn't Always Matter
Talk about some good things in life that money can't buy, and make a scrapbook of pictures or drawings of these things. Then have fun for free—take a nature walk, attend free community events, visit a city council meeting, go window shopping with sister troops, or have a picnic.

### 10. How Much Is a Dollar Worth?
That depends on where you are in the world. If you travel to a foreign country, most likely you will have to exchange your American dollars into the currency used by that particular country. In China, it's *yuan*; in Mexico, it's *pesos*; in Italy, it's *lira*; and in India, it's *rupees*. If someone says there is a "good exchange rate," it means you get more for your dollar. Pick two countries and, with the help of an adult, check the newspaper and keep track of the exchange rates for the American dollar in those countries for one month.

*Adventures in Girl Scouting*

# On My Way

**Seeing new places, meeting new people, and exploring your neighborhood and the world are some of the grandest adventures you can have in Girl Scouting and in life. Start your adventures with this badge.**

## 1. Create a Travel Postcard
Choose a place that you would like to visit, and look at pictures of tourist attractions located there. Create two or more postcards about this place that you could send to a friend. Add messages on the back describing the places you have drawn.

## 2. What Would You Do?
With your troop, friends, or family, brainstorm ideas for problem situations in which travelers often find themselves. For example, you might begin your list with "asking for directions when you're lost" and "arriving at a hotel and finding out your reservations have been lost." Put the situations into a hat and take turns acting out the problem, and finding the solution.

## 3. Travel Bug
Choose a spot away from your hometown that you would like to visit for a weekend. Decide how you will get there, the people and places you will want to visit, what you will wear, and what you will take with you. Figure out how much this trip will cost. Then, if possible, go to the place you have chosen.

## 4. International Cooking
Choose a food specialty from a different region of the United States or from a country you would like to visit. Find a recipe for this dish in a cookbook or magazine. Prepare this food and have a tasting party.

## 5. Girl Scouts Statewide
Find out about places Girl Scouts can travel together within your state. Check out camps and other council resources. How would you arrange your visit? What permissions are required? What costs would be involved? How far ahead would you need to plan?

## 6. Plan for a Day
Plan a day trip by completing the Travel Action Plan in the "Adventures in Girl Scouting" chapter of your *Junior Girl Scout Handbook*. If possible, take the trip. After the trip, evaluate what you did. Discuss what went well and what you would do differently on the next trip.

## 7. I'd Take . . .
Imagine spending a weekend away from home. Make a list of ten items that you would take on this trip. Not sure where to go? You could go to a cabin in snowy mountains in the winter, an alligator farm in a swamp in the spring, a city hotel in the fall, or a rafting trip on a river in the summer.

## 8. Life Travel
Check out travel careers. Visit a travel agent or tour guide, or have one visit your troop or group meeting. Find out how she plans trips and tours, what an itinerary looks like, how she uses a computer in her job, how trips and tours are packaged to be more affordable, and what training is needed for this type of career.

## 9. Travel Safe
Be prepared for emergencies when traveling. Review the safety tips found in the "How to Stay Safe" chapter of your *Junior Girl Scout Handbook*. Make up a "Travel Safety Quiz" game. Apply the safety tips that you reviewed to travel situations and use them as questions for your game. Play your game with your troop, friends, or family.

## 10. Pack Up!
Pack a suitcase or backpack for a weekend trip. Make sure that:

- Nothing will leak or spill on your clothes.
- What you need first will be easy to find.
- Your clothes won't wrinkle too much.
- Your shoes won't get your clothes dirty.
- You have all your "personal stuff"—toothbrush, toothpaste, soap, etc.
- You can carry the bag!

*Adventures in Girl Scouting*

# Traveler

**See the world! Meet new people! Whether your trip is around the corner or around the world, preparation is always the key to success. Get going!**

## 1. Stay Safe on the Road
Staying safe is an important part of traveling. With your Girl Scout troop or your family, brainstorm a list of at least eight things you can do to be safe while you are in a new place. Your list might include things like always carrying change for a phone call or remembering not to pull out large sums of money in public.

## 2. Promote a Place
Send away for travel brochures and information on places you want to visit. You can often get information for free by going online or phoning a visitor's bureau or chamber of commerce. Share your brochures with your troop or family. Do they want to go?

## 3. Culturally Curious?
Pick a country or culture, then make or learn about two of the following:

- A traditional article of clothing
- A puppet or toy related to a folk tale
- A traditional craft or folk art
- A musical instrument
- A typical song or dance

Share what you've made or learned with a group of younger children. Tell them about the country or culture, and show them how to make or do something similar.

## 4. Document the Days
Plan and take a trip that lasts a weekend or more. On your trip, keep a diary or log, collect postcards, take photographs, make a video or slide show, or make drawings of your travels. Share them with others when you return.

## 5. Dream Vacation
Create an itinerary for a week-long trip to a country you would like to visit. What is the country most well-known for? How will you get there? What famous sights will you want to see? How will you travel from place to place? What type of money is used in the country? Did finding out about the country make you want to visit it more? Share your dream vacation with a friend. Does she want to come, too?

## 6. Who? What? Where? When? How?
Pretend you are a travel agent or a tour director. Help one of the groups listed below plan a trip to your town or state. Include the transportation they'll need to use, the places they will stay and visit, activities they can do once they get there, and how much you think the trip will cost.

- A sixth-grade class, with four accompanying adults, who want to visit two historic sites in a weekend
- Two people who enjoy the out-of-doors and do not want to damage the environment or waste fuel
- A Junior Girl Scout troop, including two girls in wheelchairs, who want to visit an amusement park in a nearby state

## 7. Careers in Travel
Find out about two of the following careers: conference planner, hotel manager, pilot, flight attendant, train conductor, cruise director, or cruise ship captain. What education or training would you need for the career? What are the average salaries? What other requirements or skills are needed? Invite someone who has worked in one of these careers to talk with your troop. Share your information with others who might be interested in these career areas.

## 8. Girl Scouts Far and Wide
Talk with an older Girl Scout who has participated in a national or international wider opportunity. Find out how she applied and prepared for it, and what her experiences were.

## 9. Entertaining an Alien
Say a representative from a friendly distant planet is visiting the Earth for the first time. You have been chosen to be her host, and you will decide what she will see during her two-week visit. If you could take her anywhere on Earth, what would you take her to see? What are your reasons for the sights and activities on your itinerary?

## 10. Girl Scout Travel Spots
Take a trip to a Girl Scout site: the Juliette Gordon Low National Center in Savannah, Georgia; the Girl Scout national headquarters in New York City; Camp Andrée Clark in Briarcliff Manors, New York; or visit a Girl Scout sister in another city.

*Adventures in Girl Scouting*

# World Neighbors

**Your neighbors are not just the ones who live nearby. Your neighbors are also the people who live all over the globe. Learn about them with this badge.**

## 1. Global Games
Play one new game from another country. Where can you find games that children play around the world? One way is to ask someone whose relatives came from another country. Or look through books like *Games for Girl Scouts*, look on the Internet, or check out information at your local library.

## 2. The Love of Language
Choose two languages, other than your own, and for each one learn:

- To count to ten
- To say "hello"
- To say "goodbye"
- To say "thank you"
- To say "you're welcome"

## 3. Traditions
Find out how one of your favorite holidays is celebrated in another country. What's the same? What's different? Include a different tradition in your next celebration of the holiday.

## 4. World Hunger
Remember a time when you felt hungry. How did it feel? About one billion people in the world are always hungry. Many of these people are children. Try to imagine what it is like to eat just one cup of boiled rice and some water—or even less—all day. Read in newspapers, magazines, or books about some countries where many of the people are hungry. Talk with your troop, group, or friends about world hunger. Think of some ways you can help the hungry, either at home or abroad, and follow through on one idea.

## 5. The World Next Door
Your neighbors (or their ancestors) probably came from all over the world. Find out about groups of people who came to your town, city, or state from different parts of the world. What countries are represented? Why did they come? What social or economic contributions have these people made to your community?

## 6. Without a Home
Many people in the world do not have a home. A lot of these people live in the United States. With your Girl Scout troop or a group of friends, think of some ways you could help the homeless.

## 7. There's No Place Like Home
Different countries have different climates, as well as different local materials to build with. What do houses in another country look like? Pick another country and find out:

- What are the houses made of?
- How big or small are they?
- Why are they made the way they are?

## 8. It's a Small World
Learn more about the history, customs, and heritage of an ethnic group different from your own that is represented in your community.

## 9. Kids Helping Kids
Find out about an organization that helps kids in other countries. Not sure of where to start? UNICEF, Habitat for Humanity International, and Save the Children are just three of them. Find out what you and your friends can do to help one of these organizations. Is there a local project or event you can help with? (Remember: As a Girl Scout you cannot raise money for another organization. But you can help out in other ways.)

## 10. Clothing All Over the World
Find out about the typical or traditional type of clothing that is worn by girls and women in several different countries.

# 3 *It's Great to Be a Girl*

# Becoming a Teen

**The journey you will make to become a teenager is an exciting and challenging one. This badge will help you find the people and resources to guide you on your journey.**

## 1. Get the Facts
Ask a health educator, doctor, nurse, or teacher to visit a Girl Scout meeting to talk about how the body changes in puberty. Before the visit, create a list of at least 10 questions on the physical, mental, and emotional changes both girls and boys your age can expect over the next three to five years.

## 2. Successful Teens
Find out about girls in their teens who have achieved success through an invention, a business, service to others, sports, the arts, or in another way. Why were they successful?

## 3. Read About It
Read or listen to a book that has a teenage girl as the main character. Organize a book swap with your troop or with friends. Have each girl describe a book she has read, then swap her book for another so that each girl gets a new one to read.

## 5. Here's Looking at You!
Set up a personal care schedule and follow it. Include combing, brushing, washing, and taking care of your hair; bathing; brushing your teeth; washing your face; and having regular health check-ups.

## 6. Freedom and Responsibility
Your teen years will bring a lot more freedom and responsibility. Find out from two or three teens how they handle having more freedom, more responsibility, and more decisions to make.

## 7. Today's "Tween"
Look through magazines, read books, or watch television programs and movies that feature girls and boys 9-12 years old. Notice their clothing, behavior, talk, and activities. With your troop, friends, or family, talk about what you see. Are these messages accurate?

## 8. Teen in the Family
Interview family members about what it was like for them when they were teens. You can talk about appearance, school, friends, dating, or any other information that is important to you.

## 9. Celebrate!
In many cultures girls take part in coming-of-age ceremonies that mark their entrance into adulthood. The Japanese celebrate *Seijin no hi Day* on the second Monday in January after a girl turns 20 years old. Many Jewish girls have a Bat Mitzvah when they turn 13, and many Hispanic girls celebrate their 15th birthday, which in Spanish is called *quinceañero*. With a group of friends, and some adult assistance, plan and conduct your own coming-of-age ceremony.

## 10. Teen Habits
Look through magazines or watch some television programs that show teenagers. Make a list of the characteristics and behavior of teenagers as shown in articles, advertisements, or shows. Ask a teenager if your list is realistic.

## 4. Looking Ahead
Find out what's on girls' minds. Check out the questions related to "Growing Up" on the "Ask Dr. M." section of Girls Only Web site www.gogirlsonly.org and read the advice Dr. M. offers.

www.girlscouts.org

*It's Great to Be a Girl*

# Being My Best

**When you have a good opinion of yourself, you take positive risks and avoid negative ones. You make and keep friends, and you're successful in life! Try this badge to build the skills you need for being your best.**

### 1. Set a Goal—and Reach It!

Setting goals and then reaching them boosts your confidence. The best way to reach long-term goals—like improving your grades or saving money for something expensive—is by setting short-term (smaller) goals, such as studying an extra 15 minutes a night or not buying candy after school. Decide on a long-term goal and the short-term goals that will help you reach it.

### 2. Name Your Talents

Boost your self-esteem. Become aware of your talents and strengths. Each day for at least one week, make a list that begins: "I am good at . . ." Then list all the things that you have done well that day, even little things like being patient with your younger brother or sister. Put your list in a safe place, such as inside a journal. Having a bad day? Make a list on that day too, and you'll see that even on a bad day, you're still doing a lot of things well.

## 3. Keep a Journal

Start your own journal—a special book, similar to a diary, in which you can write your thoughts, feelings, and anything else you want. You can be creative and write stories or poems, or draw pictures or cartoons. In your journal, you can be very honest and serious, or you can be happy and silly. Try writing about these topics in your journal:

- What do you like the best about yourself?
- How are you special and different from everybody else?

Write two words that you think each of these people would use to describe you: a neighbor, your best friend, a teacher. Write two words that you would use to describe yourself.

## 4. Find Role Models

Movies and books contain great heroines with self-confidence. Think about a girl or woman in a book you have read or a movie you have seen. What did she do in the book or movie that showed high self-esteem? What do you admire about her? What positive character traits does she have that you would like to develop? Create your ideal role model.

## 5. Think Positively

Turn negative thinking into positive thoughts. Come up with ten things that kids often say that are negative. For each item, figure out a way to turn it into a thought or idea that is more positive. Share your list with friends to show them how to take positive actions.

## 6. Create a "Brag Bag"

With your troop, friends, or family, write positive statements on index cards about each other. Each person should write one positive statement about every person in the group—write one for yourself, too! Collect all the cards that are about you and keep them in a special container. When you are feeling "down," pull out a card and read it.

## 7. Peer Pressure Role-Play

Giving in to peer pressure means going along with the group so you won't feel different or so others won't make fun of you. Create and act out a situation about kids dealing with peer pressure. With your troop, friends, or family, role-play each situation twice. The first time, have the main character give in to peer pressure. The second time, have the main character resist peer pressure. What are some techniques you can use to resist peer pressure?

## 8. Feeling Fit to Be Your Best

Read about health and fitness in the "Be Healthy, Be Fit" chapter of your *Junior Girl Scout Handbook*. Pick one activity from those pages and do it.

## 9. Good Deed

Helping others can help you feel good about yourself. Do a deed for someone else that taps into one of your special skills.

## 10. Award Night

Hold an awards celebration with your friends or your troop at which every girl wins an "I am great at . . ." award.

*Brag Bag*

*You are a fun person to hang out with.*
*You are a good study mate.*
*You are great at sports.*
*You always know what to say to make me feel good.*

## It's Great to Be a Girl

# Consumer Power

**Make your money last: Learn how to be a smart shopper. Use these activities to get the most for your money.**

### 1. Shop Around
Pick an item you'd like to buy. Find out what three different stores, catalogs, or Web sites charge for the exact same item. Which one sells it the most cheaply? Don't forget to add the cost of taxes and any shipping charges that apply.

### 2. Comparison Shop
Different companies make different versions of the same item. Pick something you'd like to buy and compare models made by three different manufacturers. Which one gives you the most for your money? Which one suits your needs the best?

### 3. Stretch That Dollar
Play this game with a friend. Pick a reason to shop: for a friend's birthday present, for back-to-school supplies, or for a holiday gift for a family member. Give yourself a set dollar amount. Then head to the store, armed with a pencil and pad. Who can find the most interesting or useful items for that amount of money?

### 4. Compare Stores
Not all stores are created equal. Pick three stores and compare:

- Which offers the best return policy?
- Which stands by its product if it falls apart a week later? A month later?
- Which treats you with the most respect?

### 5. Your Dollars
Look at two or three different ads that are aimed at kids your age. They can be on TV, on radio, or in print. Name three techniques that they use to get your attention. Are they successful?

### 6. Your Parents' Dollars
Look at two or three ads aimed at adults. Name three techniques that they use to try to get an adult's attention. Do you think they're successful? Ask an adult what they think about the ads.

### 7. Tie-Ins
When a new movie, singer, athlete, or TV show is "hot," other companies use it to help them sell their products. Pick your favorite singer, movie, athlete, or TV show and use it to sell products that you make up.

### 8. Name Game
Pick an item that's good, but not very popular. With your friends, family, or troop, rename it. Give it a name that's guaranteed to get people's attention, and make it popular!

### 9. Pennies Count
Every day for a month, at the end of the day, take the pennies out of your pockets, backpack, or wallet and keep them someplace safe, like a jar or bowl in your room. Whatever you do, don't spend it! At the end of the month, count your pennies. How much money did you "earn?" It really adds up, doesn't it?

### 10. When You Need to Complain
Practice writing an effective complaint letter to a company that makes something you bought. In the letter, explain why the item you bought was disappointing. Try to remain unemotional, using only the facts to support your argument.

## It's Great to Be a Girl

# It's Important to Me

What do Florence Nightingale, Amelia Earhart, Wilma Rudolph and Harriet Tubman have in common? They are famous women who felt strongly about something—they had values that helped them accomplish great things. Want to work for peace, help others, or fight unfairness? Your values—which you will explore in doing this badge—will help get you there.

### 1. The Girl Scout Law in Action
The Girl Scout Law contains important values for girls to live by. Let the words of the Girl Scout Law inspire you daily. Make a Girl Scout Law plaque or wall hanging that highlights the parts that mean the most to you. Use paint, fabric, contact paper, poster board, or other materials to make your plaque or wall hanging sturdy and attractive.

### 2. Values-Based Approaches
Values help you find ways to solve problems. Write a story about how you solved a problem using your values. Or write a short story that shows how a girl your age uses one of her values to solve a problem. If you like, you may draw an illustration for your story.

### 3. Discover Your Values
Check out the section about values in the "It's Great to Be a Girl" chapter of your *Junior Girl Scout Handbook*. Do one of the activities in that section with your family or friends.

### 4. Values Vote
With your troop, group, or family, brainstorm a list of five values. Have everyone copy the list and play "20 Votes." Everyone has 20 votes to cast for the values she thinks are *most* important. You can use your votes all on one value or spread them out any way you like. Without talking, everyone records her votes. Then each girl puts a star by the value she thinks will get the most votes for the group as a whole. Now tally the votes. What was the most popular value? How many people guessed it would be? Discuss with your group why you think people feel it is the most important.

Florence Nightingale

## 5. Values in the News
Find a news report in the newspaper, or on the Internet, radio, or TV that tells about problems people have because they made poor decisions. Decide what value or values could have helped them avoid their problems and why.

## 6. Debate It
When you make decisions, you often have to weigh two competing values. For example, you may wonder: Do I stay loyal to my friend or tell the teacher that she has been cheating on a test? Choose two competing values and have a values debate. With a group, divide into two sides. One group should take one side of the issue and the other group should take the other side. Meet with your group for a few minutes to discuss the major points you want to make and then let the debate begin. Have your troop leader or adult family member serve as moderator.

## 7. Other People's Values
Holidays often reinforce the values of a country or culture. With your troop, group, or family, learn about an important holiday in another country. Learn about some of the traditions of that holiday and the value or values that are a part of that holiday.

Amelia Earhart

Wilma Rudolph

## 8. Secret Sister
A Girl Scout is a sister to every other Girl Scout. Show how you value the sister Girl Scouts in your troop or group. Have a "secret sister" party. Have each person draw a name, and then make something special at home for your secret sister. Bring the gift to your next meeting and give it to her. Remember, don't tell who your secret sister is until it is time to reveal her name at the party. Or you could choose a secret sister at school or in your neighborhood and do something special for her.

## 9. Women of Courage
With your troop, group, or family, name eight courageous women. Discuss what they did and why they were or are courageous. Write the names of the women on slips of paper and put them in a cup. Divide into two teams. Each team takes a turn pulling a slip of paper. The other team may ask five yes/no questions and then guess who they think the courageous woman is.

## 10. Valuing Service
Put the Girl Scout Promise into practice by giving service individually or with your family, troop, or group. Join in a community service project such as a clean-up activity, health fair, or other event. Or volunteer to give service to a community organization such as your school, religious organization, or other non-profit group. Remember: When giving service, Girl Scouts are not permitted to raise money for other organizations.

Harriet Tubman

*It's Great to Be a Girl*

# Looking Your Best

**Looking your best is something anyone can do. Most of all, it involves knowing what is right for you. These activities will help you learn how to look your best.**

Monday  Tuesday  WEDNESDAY

## 1. Collect Tips
Create a "Looking Your Best" booklet, poster, video, or collage that includes the most important tips girls your age need to know to look their best. Get ideas from current fashion and health magazines, from the Internet, and by interviewing people who have information to share. Include health, fashion, hygiene, and nutrition tips.

## 2. A Personal Hygiene Routine
Create a personal hygiene routine that you can follow daily or weekly. Your routine should include caring for your skin, teeth, and hair. Consider how often each action, such as washing your hair, should be done. Learn about products that can help you, such as sunscreen, dental floss, and hair conditioner. Your plans should also include a schedule for washing and mending your clothes. Put your routines on paper and stick to them.

## 3. Aerobic Activities
Select a couple of aerobic activities that you enjoy. Walking, running, jumping rope, biking, skating, and dancing are examples of aerobic activities. For two weeks or more, with a friend, do an aerobic activity of your choice at least three times a week for 20 or 30 minutes. Do different types of activities so you won't become bored. You can substitute a favorite sport, as long as you are moving for at least 20 minutes.

## 4. Skin Care Secrets
Talk to women of different ages and find out about their skin care routines. Do they use just soap and water? Lotions and potions? Have their routines changed as they got older? What secrets can they share for keeping your skin healthy?

## 5. Color Party
Experiment with color. With a friend, collect sizable pieces of fabric or pieces of paper in different colors. Take turns holding different colors up to your face. Decide which colors look best on each of you: lavenders and plums, corals, pinks, reds, blues and greens, or beiges and peaches.

## 6. Organize
Rearrange the clothes in your dresser and closet so you'll have an easier time finding just the right outfits or combinations, no matter how rushed you are. For example, you might pair tops and bottoms or organize by season or color.

## 7. Experiment with Hairstyles
Get together with a group of friends and try different hairstyles on each other. Get ideas from magazines, from the "It's Great to Be a Girl" chapter of your *Junior Girl Scout Handbook*, from older girls or adults—or dream up new hair creations yourselves. Each girl should bring her own hair accessories like clips, headbands, and decorative combs. Experiment with intertwining ribbons, beads, and other decorative items in your hair. Remember not to share brushes, combs, and other hair appliances, so there will be no problems with hygiene. If you can, take instant pictures or shoot a video of your new styles!

## 8. Create Healthy Snacks
Host a troop meeting by preparing a healthy snack to share. Here's a recipe you can try for making Pita Chips. Have an adult around to supervise.

### Pita Chips
1. Separate pita bread rounds into their two halves.
2. Cut each half into six to eight pieces.
3. Spray a cookie sheet with cooking oil for your pita bread.
4. Bake the pita pieces at 350 degrees* for 20 to 30 minutes, until crispy.
5. Sprinkle with garlic powder, cinnamon sugar, chili powder, or grated cheese.
6. Use them as dippers for a low-fat dip.

## 9. Circle of Friends
With a group of friends, possibly girls in your troop, sit in a circle with one girl in the center. Each person will take a turn and give an honest compliment to the person in the center. The person in the center listens without saying anything. After everyone has given a compliment to her, she returns to the circle and the person on her left goes into the center. The activity continues until everyone has had a chance to be in the center.

## 10. Accessory Party
Experiment to see how accessories highlight your features and your outfit. Try different earrings and necklaces—long or short, big or delicate, unusual shapes or colors. How do different belts or the addition of a scarf change your look?

* See page 235 for the metric conversion chart.

# 4 Family and Friends

# Across Generations

Senior citizens have wonderful stories to tell and skills to share. Take advantage of their wealth of information and depth of experience by doing the following activities.

## 1. These Are Their Lives
Interview one or more older adults to find out about their lives. Ask them about dates, special events, or other important days that they remember. Create a painting, time line, or scrapbook showing these important experiences. Give it to the person you interviewed.

## 2. Learn a New Skill
Invite a person who is 70 years old or older and has a special hobby or skill to share it with your troop or family.

## 3. Make a Friend
Visit a person in a nursing home or senior center at least two times. Ask her about her life, share pictures from your life, teach her one of today's songs, or learn a song from her childhood.

## 4. Be a Helper
Find a way to assist an older person in your community. Help an older neighbor with her gardening, help a friend's grandmother with chores, or read to someone whose eyesight is failing.

## 5. Service Directory
With your troop or group, create a list of community agencies, schools, houses of worship, or organizations that help older people. Contact each organization and find out if it allows girls to volunteer. If it does, what commitment is required? Does the organization provide training? Compile this information in a directory. Work with your leader or another adult to make copies of the directory available for people who want to do service projects.

## 6. Girl Scouts Past and Present
Find women in your community who were Girl Scouts from 1912 to 1950. Invite them to share their Girl Scout memories with you. What has stayed the same in Girl Scouting? What has changed?

## 7. Share the Fun
Visit a nursing home, retirement home, or senior citizens' center. Participate in an activity such as singing or a game or craft session. Or create a special activity that you then share with a group of senior citizens.

## 8. Love What You Do
Invite an individual over the age of 65, who is active in her career, to come to your troop or group and discuss what has made her happy and successful in her work.

## 9. What's So Funny?
Find out how humor has changed over the years. Look at cartoons or comic books from 20 or 30 years ago. Ask your local librarian to help you find them. Next, read the funnies in your local paper or your favorite comic book. What's different? What's the same?

## 10. Food Through the Years
Invite a senior citizen to do a cooking project with you. Prepare a recipe she enjoyed as a youngster. Ask her how food preparation has changed. Are some ingredients that used to be easily available now hard to find? What new kitchen equipment has been invented that makes cooking much quicker and easier?

## Family and Friends

# Caring for Children

**Keeping young children happy and safe requires lots of patience and good judgment. Learn some important child-care skills with these activities.**

## 1. Safety First
Make a booklet of babysitter safety measures. Include first aid tips and things to do if a child becomes ill, as well as a list of emergency phone numbers. Leave room to fill in specific family information, such as the doctor's name and number, or the number of an emergency contact person.

## 2. The Danger Zone
Find out what household items can be dangerous for a young child. Make a list of those items and then find out how they are stored in your home. If possible, make a safety check in a home where there is a young child.

## 3. Telling Tales
Children love hearing a good story. Read five books that younger children really enjoy, and choose your favorite two or three to read to a young child. You can also write your own stories to read to children.

## 4. Box of Tricks
Make a "rainy day" activities box for younger children. Include supplies for at least four different types of activities. Make sure the activities are safe for younger children to do. (For example, there should be no small parts that they might put in their mouths.) Do the activities with a child or a group of children.

## 5. Basic Skills with Infants
Invite a health-care professional who works with infants to come to a troop or group meeting. Have her demonstrate the proper way to hold, feed, and dress an infant. Practice each of these skills. *Note:* A lifelike doll can be used for this purpose.

## 6. What Can You Observe?
Plan to spend time with a young child or infant on different days. Keep a written or taped record of your observations of the child's behaviors and moods.

## 7. Planning Ahead
Decide what eight supplies you would need if you were taking a preschooler on an all-day outing. Check with an adult who supervises young children to see if your ideas were right.

## 8. Hungry? Eat Right
What are three healthy snacks you can make for younger children? With the help of an adult, prepare and serve a healthy snack to a Daisy or Brownie Girl Scout troop, or to some other group of younger children.

## 9. The Toy Test
Go through a toy store or catalog and check for toys that would be safe and those that might be dangerous for children under three years old. Share your findings with adults.

## 10. What, When?
Children go through different stages. At each age children develop different skills and interests and are capable of different things. Create a chart that shows what kids can do at each of the following ages: newborn through six months; six through 12 months; 12 through 18 months; 18 months through two years, two years through four years. Use parenting books, Web sites, and conversations with parents and professional care-givers to get your information. Then add a section on what types of things you can do with children at each age. Share it with girls who babysit.

## Family and Friends

# Celebrating People

People speak different languages and have different customs and values. These differences make people special and make it exciting to be a member of a community, a group, or a team. Explore cultural differences with this badge.

## 1. Celebrate the Day
Invite adults from two or three different backgrounds to a troop or group meeting. Find out how weddings and birthdays are celebrated in their cultures or religions.

## 2. Conduct Yourself!
The Girl Scout Promise and Law is a code of conduct (ways of acting). Develop your own code of conduct for relating to other people. You should have at least five guidelines in your code. Live by your code for one week. Was it easy or hard to do so?

## 3. Who Are They?
Imagine that you are a visitor from another part of the universe. No one on your home planet knows about Earth and you must make a report. How would you answer these questions in your report?

- What are the common characteristics of the people who live on this planet?
- What activities do they enjoy?
- What are their beliefs, and what things are most important to them?
- How do they treat their planet?

## 4. One Big Family
Make a "Human Family" collage, poster, display, or booklet. Include photos of people from as many different places around the world as you can.

## 5. Free and Equal
With your friends, write your own "declaration of young people's rights," a document that describes the rights that kids your age should have. Find out about one organization that works to help young people. See how you can assist with the work it does.

## 6. Peace on Earth
Find out about people who are "peacemakers." Identify three people who work for human rights, world peace, or tolerance. Pick one person to learn more about, and share your findings with others.

## 7. Solve It Together
Think of five problems that might occur when people who are different live or work together. Write each of the problems on a slip of paper. In a group, pull out a slip and talk about or act out solutions to the problem. Continue until all the problems have been discussed.

## 8. Include Everyone
People with disabilities can face challenges that people without disabilities may not understand. Find out about ways your school and your community have made it easier for people with disabilities to get around and to participate.

## 9. Reach Out
Watch the news for one week. Look for instances of discrimination or violence against people of other races, religions, or cultures. Discuss with your friends or family what communities can do to combat prejudice.

## 10. It's a Pleasure
Learn four different meeting and greeting customs from around the world and practice them with friends and family.

## Family and Friends

# Communication

Do you ever feel there's a communication gap between what you say and what others hear? Do you know all the ways people can communicate? Try these activities and learn more.

## 1. Get the Message?
Think of a message you want to tell others. What's the best way to communicate your idea? Should you use words, images, colors? Show or read your piece to others. Did they understand your message? If not, what could you change so that they understand your message?

## 2. Signals
Put together a collage or poster with examples of different types of communication, such as semaphore, sign language, signal flags, international road signs, distress signals, or a referee's signals. Learn one set of the above examples and teach it to someone else.

## 3. Communication by the Dots
In the Braille alphabet, a pattern of raised dots represents each letter of the alphabet. A person who is blind can "read" with her fingertips by feeling the raised letters. Below is an alphabet written in Braille. The colored dots represent the raised dots. If you poke a pin through the back of each of the colored dots (on a copy of the chart), you can raise the letters. Try feeling the pattern with your fingers. Now try to write your own coded message using the Braille alphabet.

## 4. Express Your View
Participate in a debate, or prepare and give a two-minute speech on a favorite subject.

## 5. Share the News
Write a short news story about an event in your school or your troop. Submit it to the school newspaper, your Girl Scout council newsletter, or the "Just for Girls" section of the Web site for the Girl Scouts of the USA www.girlscouts.org/girls.

## 6. Play It!
Write a short play. Read a few scenes of your play aloud to others.

## 7. Brand Images
Notice all the advertising and commercial designs you see in a week, such as billboards, posters, signs, and ads on packages. Look at how color, lettering, and empty space are used. Create your own poster, sign, or package that uses what you've discovered.

## 8. Word of Mouth
Listen to several radio shows. Then create a script and sound effects for a news program, music program, talk show, or another kind of program you choose.

## 9. Making It Public
Think about what kinds of communication would be needed to do public relations work, then outline what you would do to promote one of the following:

- A party to open an art exhibit that introduces a new artist to the community
- A tour of your community to encourage businesspeople to open stores
- A presentation to show parents and children a new science center
- A ceremony for an awards presentation in your troop or group
- A conference for international visitors to introduce them to your community

## 10. Words for Life
Find out about careers in communication. Choose one of the following and explain why it could be an interesting job.

- Reporter
- Editor
- Speech therapist
- Interpreter
- TV broadcaster
- Web writer
- Audiologist
- Linguist

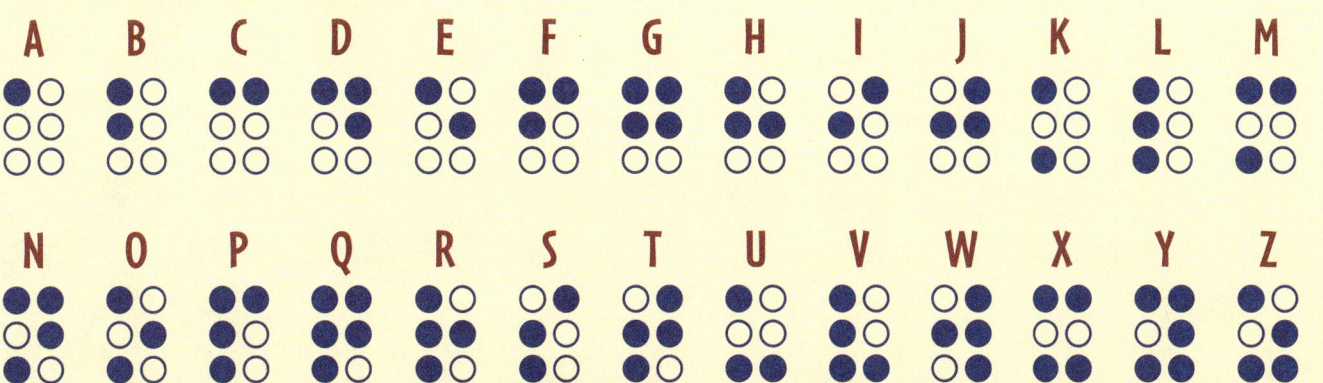

**Family and Friends**

# Healthy Relationships

Learning to get along with people is a skill you will value throughout your life. This badge will get you on the right path.

### 1. Recipe for Friendship
What goes into making a good friend? Take the friendship quiz in the "Family and Friends" chapter of your *Junior Girl Scout Handbook*. Ask three people of different ages to take the quiz, too. Compare your results.

### 2. Story Mazes
Read the decision-making story maze in the "How to Stay Safe" chapter of your *Junior Girl Scout Handbook*. Try creating your own story maze.

### 3. Play the Friendship Game
Put the following questions (and others you come up with) on index cards. Each player takes a turn drawing a card and answering one of the questions.

- What qualities or characteristics do you like most about two of your friends? Don't say which friends, just the qualities.
- What do you expect from a friend?
- Have you ever had to make a difficult choice about a friend? What was it? Don't say which friends—just describe the choice you had to make.
- How do you know when you have a good friend?

### 4. Mum's the Word
Nonverbal communication can be as effective as the spoken word. Write the names of feelings—such as fear, shyness, or happiness—on pieces of paper. Have each person pick a piece of paper. Take turns communicating the feeling to the rest of the group *without talking*. Which feelings were easy to show? Which ones were harder? Why?

### 5. Fun and Games
Make a list of six fun things you can do with friends. Try to think of things that are inexpensive or free. Create your own puzzles, hikes, and challenges. Do one of these each week with friends.

### 6. The Power of Praise
Ask your adult family members about encouraging words they received from family members and friends while they were growing up. How did those words influence them? Make a point to say something encouraging to someone every day for a week.

### 7. It's a Date
Watch a movie or television program or read a book that includes a teenage dating situation. How do the characters handle the relationship? Are there feelings of conflict or peer pressure? Talk with your friends about what each of you would do in similar situations.

### 8. Friendship Club
With your troop, friends, or family, start a monthly friendship club. Each month, another member is responsible for leading a group activity.

### 9. Bridge the Gap
Come up with three ways to improve communication in families. Try one out in your family.

### 10. Be Your Own Role Model
Role-play the situations below so that you can develop positive responses if they ever happen. Find out more about role-playing in "The Choice Is Yours" badge in the next chapter.

- You've been at every practice on time and have tried really hard. However, on the day of the big game, the coach does not allow you to play.
- Your friend is always whispering and sending you notes in class. Instead of scolding her, the teacher sends you to the principal.
- Your friend's pencil point breaks during a math test, and she leans over and asks to borrow a pencil from you. Then the teacher accuses you of cheating!

# Family and Friends

# Local Lore

Every town has a story. Every town had people and events that helped make it what it is today. How much do you really know about where you live? Find out more with these badge activities.

## 1. Word of Mouth
Find out about a story, legend, monument, or landmark in your community. Older residents or your librarian can help. Share your findings with others.

## 2. It's All on the Maps
How has your community changed? Locate a map of your town that's at least 25 years old. Your library, chamber of commerce, or planning commission should have one. Compare that map with one from today. What has changed? What has remained the same? Are all the changes for the better? Which ones would you like to undo? Why?

## 3. From Above
Ask someone from the Soil Conservation Service, the U.S. Geological Service, or a local college or real estate agency if you can see aerial photos of your community made over a period of time. What story do these photos tell about changes in your community?

## 4. Tour Your Community
Take part in a tour of your community. Look for three different examples of architecture from different historical periods. When and why were the buildings or houses built? What types of materials were used? Try sketching, photographing, or writing down information about the buildings.

## 5. Extra, Extra, Read All About It!
Create a one-page poster, newspaper page, or flyer that describes a past period of your community. Include news, ads, or editorials that might have appeared at that time. Share your item with others.

## 6. Sing Someone's Praises
Create a story, song, or poem about the efforts of one person who has had a major impact on your city or town.

## 7. Take a Trip
Visit a local museum, historical society, library, or town hall to learn more about the history of your city or town. What new things did you learn?

## 8. Take Pride
Volunteer at an event, fair, or special occasion in your area. Find an event that brings people together in a celebration of the past; for example, one that highlights important dates in history, or one that recognizes the past contributions of different cultures.

## 9. Walk the Talk
Pitch in on a project that will help preserve the history of your community or something unique about it. Examples would be replanting native plants, or cleaning or fixing up an historical site.

## 10. Focus on the Future
Given how your community has changed in the past 25 years, how do you think your community will change in the next 20, 50, or 100 years? Share your prediction for the future in a creative way—you might use charts, maps, drawings, or a skit.

## Family and Friends

# My Community

Every community has its own special qualities. With this badge, learn more about your community and what you can do to make it even better.

## 1. Show and Tell
Plan a 20-minute walking or bicycle tour of your neighborhood. What are the most interesting, beautiful, or unusual things that people should see? Tape your tour, making sure to give directions to follow as well as the descriptions of the neighborhood features.

## 2. My Favorite Things
What are the best things about living in your community? Write an advertisement, draw a poster, or make up a song that could be used in a commercial that promotes your community.

## 3. Questions and Answers
Have a question or problem in your community? Who do you go to for help? Find out the right places to get information about:

- Sports programs for girls your age
- Reporting a dangerous intersection or road hazard
- Neighborhood clean-up projects
- Services for senior citizens
- Reporting a dangerous animal

## 4. Take a Trip
With your troop or group, visit a community service agency. Find out about the work it does in the community.

## 5. Who's Around?
What are some of the businesses in your neighborhood or community? What do they manufacture, or what services do they provide? Choose one that interests you and find out more about it. Arrange to visit the business or to speak to some of the employees.

## 6. Lights, Camera, Action!
Choose one unique thing about your community—such as a beautiful waterfront, a very old cemetery, or an historical event—and make a videotape about it. Get your family and friends to help out by being in the movie. Premiere your movie at your Girl Scout troop meeting, or at your next family get-together.

## 7. Make It Beautiful
Work with others on a weekend to improve, restore, or beautify a recreational or cultural center for children or adults in your community. Once it's redone, show it off to your friends and family.

## 8. Helping Hands
Everyone needs a little help now and then. Find out what's needed in your community. Toiletry kits for the homeless? Stuffed animals for a children's hospital? For the next couple of weeks, ask store owners and community members to donate materials to whatever cause you decide needs help. Then put the materials together and deliver them to a group that is working with people in need.

## 9. One Small Step
Volunteer to make one improvement in your school or religious community. Can you help with the morning announcements at school or help to watch young children during religious services? What else can you offer to do?

## 10. How It Works
Read in the "Adventures in Girl Scouting" chapter of your *Junior Girl Scout Handbook* about the different types of troop and group government that Junior Girl Scouts can choose. What type of government does your community, town, or city have? How do decisions get made in your community? How would you improve the process?

*Family and Friends*

# My Heritage

**Your heritage is made up of many things: your religious or racial group; your nationality; your family traditions and values. Begin learning about your heritage here.**

## 1. Create a Heritage Scrapbook
Find out more about your heritage. Do you know your family history or the history of other people who share your heritage? Display what you find out, perhaps through a chart, a time line, a family tree, journal entries, a story, or a scrapbook of photographs or mementoes.

## 2. What's in a Name?
See if you can discover the meaning of your first name, your middle name, or your family name. Find out about other people who have the same name. Do they have a heritage similar to yours, or are there other reasons or sources for the name?

## 3. Broaden Your Background
Find out about famous people who share your heritage. What did they accomplish? Why are they famous? Think about an accomplishment that you would like to make someday. Then think of a way you could accomplish this dream, and write a simple plan or time line with your dream as a goal.

## 4. Celebrate Your Heritage
Find a way to celebrate your heritage. What have you inherited that makes you the person you are? How can you show that you are proud of your heritage?

## 5. From Yesterday to Today
Make a toy, cook a special dish, or learn a game, song, or dance that one of your ancestors might have enjoyed.

## 6. Who Said It?
Begin a "wisdom list" of quotations, sayings, and advice that your parents, grandparents, and other older people have shared with you. Put together a booklet that includes your favorite ones.

## 7. Get Together
Ask older people to tell you about their lives, interesting events they remember, or special stories. Can you discover something about your heritage from their stories?

## 8. Your Personal Heritage
Start a diary or scrapbook of your own memories. Write about some important events from your childhood and include important recent happenings. Try to write in your diary at least once a week.

## 9. Memorably Yours
Look around your room or your home and choose one object that you believe you would want to keep with you as you grow up. Why did you choose this object? Why is it important to you? Next, ask older friends or relatives to show you and tell you about an object that they have had for a long time. Why have they kept it? Why is it important to them?

## 10. Host a Heritage Night
Turn one of your Girl Scout troop meetings or events into a heritage celebration. Each girl can share three things about her heritage. Show pictures, read poetry, display artwork, or prepare food that reflects your heritage. You can also teach a game, song, or dance from your heritage.

*Family and Friends*

# Pet Care

Owning a pet can be great fun, but it's also a big responsibility. Find out if that responsibility is what you really want. Do you already own a pet? Find out how to be your pet's best friend with these activities.

## 1. To Have or to Have Not?
Identify four animals that would make good pets for you. Then identify four animals that wouldn't make good pets. Consider each animal's daily needs, how well it would fit in with your home life, the cost of keeping it, and how long it generally lives.

## 2. Be Responsible
Take responsibility for a pet—yours or someone else's—for two weeks. Provide shelter, food, exercise, water, and grooming. Did you spend more or less time caring for the pet than you thought you would? Which tasks were fun? Which ones weren't so much fun?

## 3. Add It Up
What's the cost of owning a pet? Figure this out for a pet you have now, or for an animal you'd like to have as a pet. What does the pet eat? How much does it eat? Does it need a special place to live? What will that space cost? What are its medical needs? Does it require special equipment, like a leash (dogs), a litter box (cats), a saddle (a horse), or an air pump (tropical fish)? Does your community have any laws regarding that animal? Are there fees? Figure out the daily, monthly, and yearly costs for the animal.

## 4. Facts of Life
Is your pet male or female? If female, how many young could your pet produce at a time? How many pregnancies would be possible in a lifetime for your pet? Would you be able to take care of that many animals? Or find good homes for them? What does a vet or an animal shelter recommend?

## 5. Staying Healthy
Find out about illnesses that are common for your pet. How can you prevent them? What are their warning signs? How can they be avoided or treated? Learn how to give medicine to a pet, if possible, and how to seek emergency treatment for your pet.

## 6. Don't Pass It On
Identify two diseases that pets can get or spread, such as tick-borne Lyme disease, tularemia (rabbit fever), or rabies. Find out what is being done to control these diseases and what you can do to prevent your pet from getting them. Do something that will help educate people about a pet disease or help prevent a common pet disease.

## 7. Healthy Diet
What is a good diet for your pet? Collect ads for pet food. What information do they give you about the nutritional needs of your animal? Read labels on pet food containers and compare them for food values.

## 8. Animal Talk
How do you communicate with a pet? How do you show a pet what you want it to do? How does your pet communicate what it wants? Describe some specific behaviors that your pet uses to communicate anger, fear, hunger, and loyalty.

## 9. Book It
Create a scrapbook about your pet. Include pictures from when it joined your family until the present. Write about how you felt when you got your pet. Keep licenses, vaccination forms, and other emergency information in the scrapbook, too. If you don't own a pet, create a scrapbook for the type of animal you'd like to have.

## 10. Other Ways to Be Around Animals
Find out about groups and places that care for pets in your area. Are there rescue societies? A foster care program at an animal shelter? A zoo mentorship program? A bird rehabilitation clinic? Is there a group that fits your interests and abilities where you could volunteer? Share what you've discovered with a parent or guardian.

# 5 *How to Stay Safe*

# Car Care

**You don't have to know how to drive to learn about cars. With an adult partner, find out what makes a car run and how to keep it in good condition.**

## 1. Check It Out
Find out about parts of a car that need to be checked regularly. Include in your safety check the tires, battery, lights, turn signals, emergency flashers, back-up lights, windshield wipers, spare tire, tire jack, flares, radiator, and seat belts. If you live in an area with hot and cold seasons, find out what items you need to check when the weather changes. With an adult partner, use your list to perform a safety check on a car. Show that you can:

- Check the oil level and add the right kind and amount of oil, if needed.
- Check the brake fluid reservoir and add the right amount of fluid, if needed.
- Check the power steering fluid, if the car has power steering.
- Check the automatic transmission fluid, if the car has automatic transmission.
- Check the windshield cleaning fluid level and add some, if needed.

Observe safety precautions at all times. Do not check a car or open the radiator cap while the engine is running. Always make sure the parking brake is on when you do work on a car.

## 2. Write It Down
Pick one of the safety checks from the list in activity 1, and write directions explaining how to do it. You may need to sketch out some diagrams in order to make your instructions clear. Give your instructions to an adult to see if she can follow them. Change your directions if something was unclear.

## 3. On the Dashboard
What are all those lights, buzzers, dials, and gauges on a dashboard for? Ask your adult to help you learn the name of each indicator (many show if something is wrong with the car).

## 4. Keep on Rolling
What are tires made of? Why and how are tires rotated? What causes tread wear? Learn how to check tire air pressure with the assistance of an adult. Discuss the safety issues involved in changing a flat tire for both the driver and passengers.

## 5. Owner's Manual
What are considered special features on a car? What three extra features would you like to have? Why? Find out what those extra features would cost. Look at the owner's manual for a car, visit a car dealership, or do some online comparisons.

## 6. Make It Shine
With the permission of the owner, learn the best way to wash a car or truck. Check the owner's manual to see what type of cleaner to use, then clean the inside and outside of the car. To conserve water, wash the car without letting a hose run continuously. Discuss with your adult partner how waxing a vehicle helps to keep its finish.

## 7. Public Safety
Find out what the safety inspection requirements are in your state. How often do cars have to pass this inspection? Work with an adult partner to find out whether the car you're working on would pass the state safety inspection.

## 8. Driving It
Many people have jobs that involve cars. Visit one of the following at work, or do an interview by phone or at a meeting or event:

- An auto mechanic
- A highway patrol officer
- Someone who drives trucks or other vehicles for a living
- Someone who designs cars or car-related equipment

What is a usual day like? What are some of the tools used? What kinds of safety issues are of concern? Why did she or he enter the profession? What type of training is needed? Would you like to have that job? Why or why not?

## 9. Be Prepared
Find out what you should have on hand for car emergencies. With your family members or guardians, create emergency kits for summer and winter. Put one of your kits in the vehicle so it can be used when needed.

## 10. As We Live and Breathe
Learn about one of the following:

- What devices have been installed in your car to reduce air pollution?
- What parts or products in a car can be recycled? Where would you take them?
- What new designs in cars are being developed to decrease or eliminate the use of gasoline?

## How to Stay Safe

# The Choice Is Yours

**Decision-making is a skill you will use every single day of your life. With this badge you will learn how to make choices that work for you.**

### 1. Share the Experience
In a small group, share a difficult decision you made. What things influenced your decision? What helped you decide? What was the result of your decision? What would you have done differently if you had had a second chance?

### 2. Looking Ahead
Make a list of the important decisions you may have to make within the next ten years. Talk with at least three friends to find out about the kind of decisions they think they will have to make. Compare their lists to your own.

### 3. People Pressures
Create a poster of ways that people pressure or force others to do something they may not want to do. One way might be someone saying, "Everybody's doing it." Share your poster with others and role-play some positive responses to such lines.

### 4. Deciding to Act
With your troop or group, decide on a service project. Make a list of everyone's ideas. Discuss each idea. Come to an agreement about what you will do and put your plan into action. Once your project is complete, evaluate how it went. What changes might you make the next time?

### 5. Learning from Others
Ask family members and other adults how they make decisions. Can you think of some other ways? Decide which ways are helpful and which are not. Make a list of reminders for when you make decisions.

### 6. Computer Game Choices
Play a computer simulation game that has decision-making built into it, such as "The Sims," and discuss with others the consequences of the most difficult decisions you made during the game.

### 7. Try It On for Size
Discuss the following situations and role-play what you would do if:
- A classmate offered you a cigarette on the way home from school
- A group of friends stopped by to visit you when no adults were home (your parents don't permit you to have anyone over when you're home alone)
- Your family planned an outing on the same day as your best friend's birthday party
- A bigger kid tried to bully you in the park
- Some of your friends started teasing a classmate

Make up your own situations and play them out.

### 8. Role Models
Think of the things and people that influence your decisions—for example, friends, school, family, or the media. Star (*) the people on this list whom you can approach when you need help in making a personal decision. What makes these people special?

### 9. Learning by Example
Many children's stories and fables are about people who made the wrong decision and suffered, or who made the right one and were rewarded. Select a story to read to a younger girl, and discuss the decisions in that story.

### 10. There Once Was a Girl . . .
Create a story about a girl who has trouble making an important decision and share it with others.

## Role-playing...
means acting out a situation that could really happen. When you role-play, you try to say and do what the person you are pretending to be would say and do in that situation. This gives you a chance to experience how someone else might feel and act. You should always have a discussion after role-playing to talk about what happened and how everyone felt. When you watch a role-playing exercise, think about what you would do in that situation, and be supportive of the people doing the acting.

**How to Stay Safe**

# First Aid

**Do you know how to act quickly in an emergency? Do you know what is in a first aid kit and how to use one? Become first-rate at first aid with this badge.**

## 1. Learn First Aid
Read the sections on first aid and emergency telephone calls in the "How to Stay Safe" chapter of your *Junior Girl Scout Handbook*. Complete the activities in those sections.

## 2. Ouch!
Learn and practice first aid for cuts, sprains, and fractures. Ask a medical professional—nurse, doctor, emergency medical technician (EMT)—to show you and your troop the right way to treat these injuries. Or ask your family and friends to learn with you.

## 3. Oooh
How would you treat a nosebleed? What would you do if a friend became faint? Ask a medical professional—nurse, doctor, EMT—to show you and your troop the right ways to treat these conditions. Or ask your family members and friends to learn these treatments with you.

## 4. Get Help
Do you know how to get help quickly in your community? Should you dial 911, or some other emergency number? What information would the operator need to know? Read that section in your *Junior Girl Scout Handbook* and practice placing an emergency call. However, do *not* actually dial the emergency number.

## 5. Until Help Arrives
What can you do while you're waiting for help to come? Learn the first aid procedures for a child or adult who: stopped breathing, is breathing heavily, is in shock, has been poisoned, or is choking. Ask a medical professional to show you what to do.

## 6. Share the Messages
Create a four-page first aid and safety book (it could be a coloring book or an activity book) to help educate younger children about basic safety concepts. Important topics to include are emergency telephone numbers, first aid procedures, and warning signs in an emergency. You can use slogans to get your message across. For example, you might promote the American Red Cross slogan, "Check, Call, Care," or create your own slogan.

## 7. Helping Hands
First aid skills are important in many different careers. Identify the types of emergencies each of these professionals might encounter on their jobs: camp director, police officer, firefighter, teacher, lifeguard, and emergency medical technician. What special first aid training do their jobs require?

## 8. Staying Safe
Make a list of all the items included in a basic first aid kit. Use this list to create a kit for your troop, group, or for your family. How would a first aid kit for a home differ from a first aid kit for camping?

## 9. Survivor
With a group of friends, list the top five survival tips you need for very hot or cold weather. Learn about hypothermia and hyperthermia and how to treat each. What can happen if you aren't prepared? How do you treat those conditions? Use your tips to role-play how you would survive outdoors in extreme weather.

## 10. First Aid Challenge
In a group, ask each person to come up with one or more first aid situations. Write them on pieces of paper and place them in a bag or a box. Select a piece of paper and use a first aid kit to demonstrate how to handle the situation. You could create a relay game in which teams take turns acting out the situations that are picked by the team members.

## How to Stay Safe

# High on Life

**Winning a game. Acing a test. Hanging out with good friends. Now those are ideal highs! For this badge you will stomp out harmful habits and get high on life!**

## 1. Natural Highs
With a group of friends, brainstorm a list of ten things in your life that give you natural highs (talking on the phone with friends, exercising, doing a hobby, playing a sport). Pick your favorite activity from your list and do it today!

## 2. It's Your Life
Divide a sheet of paper into three columns. In the first column, write a list of three things you want to accomplish in your life. In the next column, write the approximate age you will be when you expect to achieve that goal. In the third column, write down how using cigarettes, alcohol, or illegal drugs can affect your ability to reach that goal. Include specific things that could happen to you. Share this chart with your troop or group, and also with your family members.

## 3. What Do You Do?
Say you just found out that your best friend has started smoking. How would you bring up the subject? What would you tell her? What do you think her responses would be? What would you say if she asked you to smoke, too? Role-play the situation with your friends, troop or group, or family.

## 4. Share the Information
Get free drug information from the local health department, cancer society, lung association, heart association, or drug agencies. Decide on a plan for helping others in your community know about this information. Carry out your plan.

## 5. Get the Message Out
Create a 30-second or 60-second radio commercial that discourages kids from using drugs. Record it and see if your school will play it on its public address system.

## 6. Get With the Program
Popular media often show teenagers using drugs, alcohol, or tobacco. Watch three of your favorite TV shows or movies. Count how many references are made to these substances. Make a note if the show is promoting a drug-free message or making these substances look "cool." Write to the producers of one of the shows you've watched. Congratulate them if negative consequences are portrayed, or tell them to "get with the program" if the movie or TV show made drug use look glamorous or attractive.

## 7. Media Overload
Magazines, movies, TV, and ads surround us daily. For one week, cut out and collect different ads, comic strips, pictures, or articles that show smoking, drinking, or illegal drug use. Decide what each message or picture is really saying. Develop an anti-substance-abuse poster using these images.

## 8. Spread the Word
Make a drug abuse prevention presentation to younger children. This could be a skit, puppet show, poster demonstration, or audiovisual production.

## 9. The Big Test
Go to your local police station and ask for a demonstration of the Breathalyzer test. How does it work? Is it accurate? What signs does a police officer look for when approaching a drunk driver? What is the penalty for drunk driving in your state?

## 10. Know the Dangers
Talk to your family doctor or school nurse about the proper use of medicine. Why is taking the correct dosage important? What are the dangers of mixing medications—even if a doctor prescribes both? When should medicines be thrown away?

### How to Stay Safe

# Safety First!

**Many injuries at home or away from home can be prevented if you use common sense and practice good safety behaviors. So put Safety First!**

### 1. Safe at Home
Conduct a safety check of your home with your family. Do you have the proper number of smoke detectors? Are they all working? Are all electrical wires safe and out of the way? Correct any hazards that might be dangerous for an infant, a toddler, someone who has a disability, or an elderly person. Then list the following information and post it in a handy spot: phone numbers for the fire department, police, poison control center, doctor, and an ambulance.

### 2. Safe at Any Age
Do an informal survey to find out the most common types of injuries for people your age. Are they from bicycle falls, sports, or just plain carelessness? Write a 30-second or 60-second public safety announcement about how to help prevent these injuries and see if it can be aired at your school.

### 3. Sports Safety
Create a large cardboard cutout of a person wearing a variety of protective gear and equipment for a particular sport or activity. If you created an in-line skater, for example, include kneepads, elbow pads, wrist pads, and a helmet. Use this figure to teach sports safety to your troop, group, or family.

### 4. Campaign for Safety
Create a car-safety poster, videotape, or some other form of media. Include information about the importance of using a seat belt every time people ride in a car, the proper way for infants and toddlers to be buckled into car-safety seats, and why children should not ride in the front seat of a car equipped with airbags.

### 5. Fall Safe
Help prevent one of the most common causes of injuries and death in the United States: falls. Point out where falls can happen easily, such as in bathrooms or on stairs, and show how they can be prevented.

### 6. Look Out!
Take a "hazard identification hike" along a bike path, foot trail, horse trail, compass course, or similar place. As you go along:

- Identify places where you could get hurt or that could cause you trouble.
- Set up some way to warn others of the hazards, or work to remove them.

### 7. Out and About in Public
The Fourth of July—and holiday celebrations like it—can be loads of fun. But don't forget about safety. Choose an upcoming holiday or event, such as a parade, a trip to the state fair, or a local carnival. Talk to the adult you are going with and make a safety plan. What should you do if you get separated? What are the hazards you might prepare for ahead of time, such as: doing activities on water, being in unfamiliar places, being around strangers, having no clean drinking water or shade, being in a sudden storm, traveling in cars or other vehicles, being in crowded places, or being out in the dark.

### 8. It's Not Just a Ride
Learn the basics of bike safety and develop a bike safety checklist. Include topics such as protective gear, how to see if your bike is in proper working order, and rules for riding on the road. Talk to a local bike shop employee, police officer, or other resource person for help.

### 9. Show the Way
With your troop, friends, or family, plan a way to help younger children learn about safety. Include topics like crossing the street, safety in the kitchen, and getting help in an emergency. You can use the "Safety Sense" Brownie Girl Scout Try-It to help you plan.

### 10. Fire Safety
Knowing what to do in case of a fire saves lives. Plan, talk about, and practice fire escape routes for your home, troop meeting place, or school. Learn what to do by checking out the information in your *Junior Girl Scout Handbook,* going online to find resources about fire safety, or talking with a firefighter.

# 6 Be Healthy, Be Fit

# Adventure Sports

**Hiking, mountain biking, kayaking, rock climbing—if the thought of exploring these high-adventure sports gets your heart beating, this is the badge for you! Adventure sports are fun and exciting—once you've learned the skills necessary to do them safely.**

### 1. Get Strong
Adventure sports require strength, flexibility, and balance. When you're not actually doing the sports, prepare for them by doing:

- Squats and lunges
- Wall presses and push-ups
- Walking, running, and skipping

Go to the "Just for Girls" Web site to see how to do lunges, squats, wall pushes, and push-ups. Playing hopscotch, jumping rope, skating, and skateboarding will also keep you fit and ready for any adventure.

### 2. Picture It
Create a scrapbook of adventure sports. Tear out pictures and articles of kids doing just what you want to do.

### 3. Kayak
Grab your paddle and learn how to:

- Get in
- Keep your balance
- Paddle
- Roll (un-swamp your kayak)
- Turn
- Get out

## 4. Rope It

Go to a ropes course and have a blast! Learn how to get yourself and your friends:

- Over the wall
- Up the line
- Down the Zip line
- Through the web

## 5. Ride the Waves

Learn how to windsurf. Or try your hand at surfing with a board. Learn how to:

- Get up
- Keep your balance
- Judge the water
- Make a turn
- Get off safely

In order to do this activity, you must know how to swim. You must keep your PFD (personal flotation device) on at all times!

## 6. Mountain Bike

Mountain biking differs from road cycling. When you mountain bike, you are usually riding over unpaved, bumpy roads—where rocks, logs, or other obstacles can get in your way. Learn how to:

- Shift gears
- Brake safely
- Keep your balance downhill
- Ride over bumps and ditches
- Turn sharply

You must have your bike helmet on at all times!

## 7. Impact Free

Adventure sports pit you against nature: mountains, rocks, and water. Playing adventure sports can destroy the natural environment needed for the sport. How can you keep your fun from eroding away? Pick a sport and find out what type of impact it has on the environment. What can you do to lessen that impact?

## 8. Adventure Obstacle Course

Create an obstacle course for you and your friends. Use your imagination, and whatever's around (hula-hoops, rope, and empty soda bottles filled with water or sand are good places to start). Come up with ways for people to:

- Jump high
- Jump long
- Test their balance
- Zigzag
- Use their arms
- Run
- Slide

See who can get through the obstacle course the fastest, or the most creatively.

## 9. Gear Up

Adventure sports require specific equipment—both for the sport and for your own safety. Pick an adventure sport and find out:

- What pieces of equipment are needed and how they work
- How much equipment costs to buy and maintain
- What type of safety gear is used and how to maintain it

## 10. Climb the Walls

Try your hand at rock climbing. Go to a gym or recreation center that has a climbing wall and find out:

- How to put a harness on properly
- How to tie a figure 8 knot
- How to belay
- How to climb
- How to rest without coming down
- How to rappel

## Be Healthy, Be Fit

# Court Sports

**Explore sports that are played on a court, such as basketball, tennis, and volleyball. With this badge, you will learn more about these sports, improve your skills, and get in the game!**

### 1. Warm Up
It is important to warm up before you take part in sports and fitness activities. Develop a warm-up and cool-down routine (at least five minutes long) to use before and after playing. Learn three stretches for your upper body and three for your lower body.

### 2. Juliette On the Court
Did you know that Girl Scouts have been playing basketball since 1912? What did they wear when girls couldn't wear trousers or shorts in public? How were rules or equipment different?

### 3. Keeping Track
Learn how to keep score in a court sport. How are points earned? Attend a game in your area and keep your own score of the match or game. Watch the official scorekeepers at work. Or watch a match on TV and see if you agree with the official scorers.

### 4. Practice, Practice, Practice

Great athletes regularly practice the basics of their sport. Choose a sports skill you'd like to improve. For example, you could practice your volleys, serves, spike shots, free throws, or forehand. For one week, spend 30 minutes a day practicing and notice how much you improve.

### 5. Play Ball

Play a court sport two days a week for three weeks. Practice with a friend, play at school, or join a local team. After the three weeks, you'll know if this is a sport for you. Like it? Great! Not a good fit? Try another one.

### 6. Same Sport, Different Court

Some court sports, such as tennis, can be played on different court surfaces. What are the three surfaces tennis is played on? How are they maintained? How does the surface affect the players' game? If possible, play tennis on two different types of courts.

### 7. Tell It Like It Is!

Be a sportswriter. Watch a high school, college, or professional women's court sport. Take notes during the game so you can write a short article about it. Who won? What was the score? What were the exciting moments? Who were the stars? Think of a fun title for your story. If possible, compare your story with a newspaper article about the game and see what you can learn from the pros in the media.

### 8. World of Sports

Court sports are played all over the world. Some sports, such as badminton and squash, are popular in other countries but may not be as well known in the U.S. Pick one of these not-so-common court sports. Find out all about it—a brief history of the sport, the countries where it's popular, and women who are star players. Try playing it if you can.

### 9. Be a Role Model

Choose a professional female athlete you admire. Pretend you are that athlete and give a 15-minute talk to a group of Daisy or Brownie Girl Scouts. In your presentation, talk about:

- Who you are, what sport you play, and why you are here today
- One of the highlights in your career
- Three reasons why sports and fitness are good for girls
- One of the most important skills of your sport

The more you can learn about the athlete you have chosen, the more interesting your talk will be!

### 10. A Winning Combination

Many court sports can be adapted so that people with special needs can play, too. Find out if your recreation or community center offers court sports for players with disabilities. Talk to the coach or instructor to find out if and how the court and the rules have been adapted. If you can, volunteer to help at a session.

## Be Healthy, Be Fit

# Environmental Health

**Staying healthy is about more than just eating an apple a day—it's also about understanding your environment, taking care of it, and not getting too much of a good thing. Start with these badge activities.**

### 1. Sun Sensations
A sunny day is often the sign for outdoor fun. Before you go out, protect yourself. Have a sun safety fashion show with a group of friends. Include items like sunscreen with UV protection of at least 15, lip balm, sunglasses that protect from UVA/UVB rays, umbrellas, a wide brim hat, and a cotton shirt as part of the show. When developing your "sun safety look," be stylish and creative. Almost anything goes as long as it helps protect you from the sun.

### 2. The Sun Squad
Create a "Sun Squad." Find young people with whom to go out in the community and educate people about sun health. Create a "sun sense" quiz: provide people with the facts about sunscreen and other ways they can protect themselves from the damaging rays of the sun. With an adult, patrol beaches, lakes, or pools to get the word out.

### 3. Water Water Everywhere
You need water to live. Learn the different ways to conserve water. With a group of friends, develop a Top 10 list of different ways you can conserve water and keep it clean, such as recycling water from fish tanks by using it to water plants.

### 4. Goin' Fishing?
With an adult, find out if the fishing spots in your area are clean. Look for warning signs posted around the area. Or call your local or state Health Department or the Environmental Protection Agency and ask which waters are safe. Find out about the kind of testing done on the waters. Share your findings with your friends and family.

### 5. Get the Word Out
Create a commercial that encourages people to focus on environmental health. Pick one of the following topics: sun safety, noise pollution, water health, safe waste disposal, or air quality. Create a catchy slogan and provide information on how to find out more about that issue.

### 6. "Block the Spread of Lead" Relay

A "lead blocker" is a food that is high in calcium and iron, such as spinach or milk. These help protect your body from the harmful effects of lead. Try this game to learn more about "lead blockers:"

1. Divide into two teams and give each team a basket or bucket.
2. Place at least ten food items, some high in calcium and iron, and some low in these nutrients, around the room.
3. The game begins when someone shouts, "Block the spread of lead!"
4. The first person for each team grabs the bucket and races to pick up one item that she thinks is a "lead blocker." Then she races back and hands the bucket to a teammate.
5. The game continues until the players think they have all the "lead blockers."
6. A team gets one point for each "lead blocker." A team loses a point if they have a food product high in fat, like chips. The team with the most points wins.

### 7. Environmental Times

With a group of friends, brainstorm a list of important environmental issues in your community. Create an environmental newspaper. Ask an environmentalist, a reporter, or an editor to help you with your paper. Share your paper with family and friends.

### 8. Smoke Free

Second-hand smoke affects the air you breathe and puts your health at risk. With your troop or group, work on a "smoke–out" day for your community. Contact organizations like the American Cancer Society, Tobacco-Free Kids, or The American Lung Association and find out what's planned for your area. Or try a "smoke-out" day with your family if one or more of your family members is currently a smoker.

### 9. Every Breath Counts

Asthma is a condition that causes a person's airways to get smaller and makes it difficult to breathe. Environmental conditions such as second-hand smoke and pollution can trigger an asthma attack. Come up with a list of at least five other things that can cause an asthma attack. How can you improve the environment to help reduce asthma triggers? Talk to a doctor or to someone who has this condition, or go online for more information.

### 10. Get the Lead Out

Find out about the dangers of lead. What are the three biggest sources of lead poisoning? How can lead poisoning be prevented? How can it be treated? Contact the Environmental Protection Agency, the Center for Disease Control, or your local doctor to get information.

## Be Healthy, Be Fit

# Field Sports

**Get out on the field and play! Soccer, softball, field hockey, track and field events, and lacrosse are all popular field sports. Get ready to get in the game with this badge.**

### 1. Warm Up
Warm-ups prevent injuries and help you play better. Start with a two-minute walk, then pick up speed for three more minutes. Slow down gradually. Take two minutes to do some slow stretches. Show your walk and stretch routine to someone else.

### 2. Play Ball!
Play a field sport at least six different times. What do you like about playing the sport? What do you dislike? How have you improved? What is your goal for getting better?

### 3. Pump It Up!
Music can make you feel pumped up and psyched for the game. Plan and make a tape with at least four songs that you think would prepare a team for a big game. Play it for your Girl Scout team, family, or friends.

### 4. Scores and Stats
Choose a field sport that interests you. Learn how to keep score. What other statistics are important in the game? Attend a local match or game and watch the scorekeeper at work. Keep your own score for the game. Did you and the scorekeeper agree? No one playing this sport where you live? Watch a match on TV.

### 5. Feet and Cleats
Why do certain field sports require special shoes? Look at the footwear for three different field sports. What is the special feature of each? How do shoes for one game differ from shoes for the other two games? Not sure where to start? Visit a sporting goods store, look through catalogs, or go online to sites that sell shoes.

### 6. The Right Stuff
Choose a field sport and learn about the equipment needed to play. With a friend, list all the equipment that's needed. Then pick three of the pieces and find out:

- Why are they made the way they are?
- How do they work?
- How do you maintain them?

You can find out by talking to your gym teacher or someone from your town's Parks and Recreation Department, visiting a sporting goods store, looking through catalogs, or by going online.

### 7. Drink Plenty of Liquids
The recommended daily amount of water a person should drink is six to eight cups.* While there are many liquids, water is the best for you and usually, the least expensive (especially if you get it from the tap). Try to drink six to eight cups of water a day, every day for three days. Did you do it? What helped/got in the way of reaching your goal?

### 8. Work It, Girl!
Find one woman with a sports career and interview her about her work. What does she like about her job? What training did she have to get? What advice does she have for young girls interested in that career? Don't have anyone local? Watch interviews of women in that field on TV, read about them in magazines, or go online. The "Just for Girls" Web site can be a good place to start. www.girlscouts.org/girls

### 9. Team Up to Win!
There are many different types of people and personalities on a team. Think about your favorite team or a team you play on. What are three things that help make that team a success? For one week, work on one quality that will make you a better team player.

### 10. Be a Fan
Choose a female athlete in a field sport you admire. Why do you admire her? Is she a good role model for girls? Design a sports trading card for your athlete.

* See page 235 for the metric conversion chart.

## Be Healthy, Be Fit

# Food Power

**Eating a properly balanced diet helps you do your best. Poor eating habits can make you tired, cranky, and even sick! Score some points for good nutrition by doing this badge.**

### 1. Track It
Check whether you are eating the balanced diet you need. Record everything you eat for one week. Keep track of the food groups, the number of servings you had from each group, and those you missed. How could you improve what you ate for one meal each day?

### 2. Keeping It Balanced
Keeping healthy and fit is a balancing act. The "healthy pyramid" outlines healthy habits that can put you on the right track for health. Create your own healthy food pyramid. Make one section for eating right, another for fitness, and a third one for healthy living habits. Cut out pictures from magazines or draw your own pictures that represent each category. Glue these pictures into the appropriate boxes of the pyramid.

### 3. Create a Food Advertisement
Design an ad for a healthy food. Your ad can include a catchy slogan about the benefits of the food that people will remember. Show your ad to others.

### 4. Understand Food Labels
Food labels can help you make healthy decisions about what to eat. Create a chart to track three items found on food labels. The chart can include: calories, fat, or vitamins. Gather three labels from different brands of the same type of food. What are the differences in those items, if any, among the three different brands?

### 5. Messages
Watch several hours of children's television programming. (Saturday mornings are a good time.) Count the number of food commercials that are shown. In what ways do commercials teach good or poor eating habits? Find out which advertised products are nutritious and which are not.

## 6. It's All About Choice
Try this fun way to eat healthier foods. With at least two other friends, brainstorm a list of healthy food categories. For example, your list might include foods high in vitamin C or calcium, green foods, or healthy snacks. Write each category on a separate piece of paper and fold them up. The first player draws a piece of paper and reads the category out loud. Using a timer, give each player one minute to write down as many items as they can that fit into that category. Players get points for each correct answer.

## 7. Balanced Lunch?
Look over your school's lunch menu for a week. Is there a mix of dairy, meat, poultry, veggies, and grains? Are foods fixed in a variety of ways—baked, fried, deep fried, steamed, or served raw? Write a letter to your school principal letting her/him know what you discovered. If the menu is well-balanced and tasty, congratulate the menu planners. If not, give your school suggestions.

## 8. End Hunger
Do a service project to help fight hunger. Around the world, children, women, and the elderly are the most likely to live with poor nutrition and hunger. Here are a couple of ideas to try out with the members of your family or friends:

- Collect canned or boxed food. Find a local food pantry, soup kitchen, or international organization to donate to. Include manual can openers for canned food!
- Volunteer to help distribute food in a soup kitchen.

## 9. Speak Your Mind
What advice would you give the President of the United States to end hunger in this country? Speak to your friends and family about this, then write the President by letter at: Mr. President, The White House, Washington, DC 20505, or send an e-mail (*president@whitehouse.gov*).

## 10. Scavenger Hunt
When looking at food labels, note how much of each nutrient is present. In each serving, if there's 5 percent or less of the recommended daily allowance of a nutrient, that food is not considered a significant source for it. If the food contains 20 percent or more of the recommended daily serving, it is considered a major source. Identify five nutrients that are important for your health, such as calcium, zinc, vitamin C, protein, and carbohydrates. With a friend, go on a scavenger hunt in a grocery store or in your own cabinets. Your goal is to identify foods that provide the highest percentages of those important nutrients.

**Eating Healthy…**

## Be Healthy, Be Fit

# Fun and Fit

**Have more energy. Sleep better. Study better. Feel great! You can be fit by making the right choices every day and by adding fun exercises to your week. Start your fitness routine with this badge.**

## 1. A Little Each Day

Walk to school. Ride your bike. Take the stairs. Think about how you can change your routine just a little to add more fitness to your day. On your own or with your troop or group, come up with seven ways you can make fit choices throughout the day. Pick one and add it to your next week's schedule.

## 2. Chart the Race

Make a large troop activity chart. Record every girl's name down the side of the page, and list five or six activities across the top. Place a start banner on the left and a finish line on the right. Identify physical activities that each person can do. For the next three weeks, each time you or one of the girls in your troop takes part in an activity, put a footprint in the appropriate square. Who will cross the finish line first? Not in a troop? Race with your family and/or friends!

## 3. Warm Up

Warming up before you exercise or play a sport helps get your muscles ready to move. Spend five to ten minutes warming up. Plan a warm-up activity to get you ready—use movements that are similar to the sport or fitness activity that you will be doing, like arm circles for swimming, high knees for soccer, or small jumps for basketball. Start your warm-up by walking around slowly. Add the movement you've chosen. Slowly pick up the speed. For fun, use music or sing a song to get you moving. Create a warm-up routine for your favorite sport.

## 4. Cool Down

After a sports or fitness activity, it's best to slowly cool down. A cool-down is just like a warm-up, but instead of gradually getting faster, you go slower. For example, once you are finished in-line skating, you could skate slowly, and take really long strides. Create a cool-down routine for your favorite sport.

## 5. S-t-r-e-t-c-h

Stretching keeps your muscles and joints loose, reduces your chance of injury, and helps you relax. The best time to stretch is after you exercise, when your body and muscles are warm. Show your troop, friends, or family how to do three of the following stretches:

- Front of thigh stretch
- Back of thigh stretch
- Calf stretch
- Back stretch
- Chest and front of shoulder stretch
- Stomach stretch

## 6. Get Moving

Aerobic exercises—jumping rope, dancing, walking fast, and swimming—are exercises that make you breathe faster and deeper. They help your heart and lungs work their best. For the next two weeks, do aerobic exercise three to five times a week. You'll need to do them for 15 to 20 minutes to get any health benefit. Don't overdo it, though. Make sure you are working out just hard enough by taking the "talk test"—you want to feel slightly out of breath but still be able to talk while exercising. Start slowly at first. Include a warm-up and a cool-down. Try a variety of activities so you don't get bored!

## 7. Know No Obstacles

Read about the international games in the "Be Healthy, Be Fit" chapter of your *Junior Girl Scout Handbook*. Learn one and teach it to younger girls.

## 8. Strengthen Up

Strong muscles will help you run faster and jump higher. They will also help reduce your chances of getting injured. For the next two to three weeks, do strength-building exercises two to three times a week. Work out for at least 15 minutes. Learn the right way to do squats, lunges, push-ups, and sit-ups. You can ask a gym teacher or athletic coach.

## 9. If the Shoe Fits, Wear It!

Wearing shoes that don't fit can really hurt your feet! They can also hurt the way you walk, ride a bike, or play sports. How do you know if the shoe fits? Try this activity: Stand on a piece of paper and trace your bare foot. Put your shoe on a piece of paper and trace your shoe. Cut out both shapes. Hold them together, sole to sole. Are they about the same shape? Is your shoe a little longer in the toes? If not, it's time for new shoes!

## 10. Fancy Footwork

Flat feet need shoes that give extra support. High arches require shoes with extra cushioning. See if you have flat feet or high arches by taking the watermark test. You will need a bucket, water, and a brown paper bag. Don't forget some towels for cleaning up.

1. Take your shoes and socks off. Put your bare feet, one at a time, into a bucket of water. Place each wet foot on the brown bag. You should have just enough water to leave a footprint, but not so much as to make a mess.

2. Reading your footprint: If your footprint looks like a pancake with toes, you have flat feet. If there is little or no connection in your footprint between the front part of the foot and the heel, you have a high arch.

## Be Healthy, Be Fit

# A Healthier You

**Develop good habits now for a fun and healthy life. This badge is a good place to start.**

### 1. Healthy Bones
Strong bones are important for a lifetime of health. Eating calcium-rich food can make the difference. Find seven different foods that are calcium-rich. For one week, try to eat at least one calcium-rich food at each meal.

### 2. Strong Bones
Doing physical activity for a half an hour a day helps build strong bones. The best activities for bones are called weight bearing, like walking, running, skiing, or jumping rope. For one week, do some type of weight-bearing physical activity for at least 30 minutes each day.

### 3. Talk to Me

Find out about eating disorders. Learn the answers to these questions:

- What are the signs and symptoms of anorexia and bulimia?
- What are some of the health problems that can result from these illnesses?
- How can you help someone who is suffering from an eating disorder?

### 4. Tell Me What You Think

Some girls and women see a distorted picture of how they look. With at least one other friend, develop a survey of five questions that asks how satisfied girls your age are with the way they look. Ask some friends to complete your survey. Do you see them the way they see themselves? How do they see you? Do you agree?

### 5. Getting the Message Out

With a group of friends, create a "healthy habits" skit that can help educate girls about what they can do now to increase their chances for a healthy and active future. Come up with a catchy title and take the show on the road.

### 6. Preventable or Inevitable?

Examine one of the following: skin cancer, osteoporosis, heart disease, AIDS. Write the illness on a sheet of paper. Divide the paper in half. On one side, list causes of the disease that can be prevented. For example, you can prevent osteoporosis by eating foods rich in calcium. On the other side, list causes of the disease that cannot be prevented. For example, more women than men suffer from osteoporosis—and they can't do anything about that. Look at the list of causes that are considered preventable. Using your list, come up with three healthy tips for that disease that young people can follow to lower their chances of getting sick.

### 7. Ways to Help

Many organizations nationwide promote and bring awareness to women's health issues. They run events to help educate people about the dangers of various diseases. Pick a health issue, and participate in an event.

### 8. Get Well Soon

Get permission to visit or write to a person who is in a hospital, nursing home, or hospice, and send him or her your warm wishes. Be creative.

### 9. Keeping Track

Create a way to track your progress over a one-month period toward a healthier you.

### 10. Relay for Sun Safety

Protecting yourself from the harmful effects of the sun is a year-round job. Try the following game to learn more about protecting yourself from the harmful effects of the sun:

1. Create at least two relay teams.
2. For each relay team you will need your sun safety gear: a hat with a wide brim, sunglasses, sunscreen, and an extra-large T-shirt.
3. Define the relay starting and ending lines.
4. Each team lines up in a straight line behind the starting line with the first person holding their safety gear in their hands.
5. When the signal is given to start, the first girl in each team must put on a T-shirt, hat, sunglasses, and put some sunscreen on her nose. Holding the sunscreen in her hand she runs to the finish line, and turns around and heads back to the starting point.
6. When the first girl returns to the starting point, she passes the sunscreen to the next racer, removes all the "sun safety gear" and passes it to the next person. Teammates can help.
7. That person then repeats the course, and she passes everything to the next person.
8. The race continues until everyone on each team has had a turn.
9. The team that finishes first wins.

## Be Healthy, Be Fit
# Highway to Health

**With this badge you will learn to listen to your body and what it's trying to tell you—it's the best way to be on the highway to health!**

### 1. Sincerely, Your Body
What would your body say if it had a chance to talk? Write a letter to yourself as if your body were doing the talking. It could say things like: "If you want me to have energy to do all my homework, dance, play soccer, and hang out with friends, then I need to get more sleep!" Or, "What were you thinking, eating all that junk food before a test!"

### 2. Healthy Steps
With a group of at least three friends, brainstorm a list of five healthy habits. Then brainstorm a list of five unhealthy habits. Write each habit on a piece of paper and place it in a bag.

1. Mark a starting point on the floor, using tape or a rope. Players start with their toes on the line. Pick a piece of paper out of the bag and read it aloud. Is it a positive habit—and something you do? Take one step forward. Don't do it? Take one step backward. Is it a negative habit—and something you do? Take one step backward. Don't do it? Take a step forward.

2. After you have read each habit, notice where everyone is standing. Discuss steps to take to improve healthy habits and try three of them for a month.

## 3. Sleepy Head
If you don't get enough sleep, you won't have the energy to make it through the next day. Find out what happens to your body when you sleep and what happens when you don't get enough sleep.

← Get enough sleep

## 4. Germ Busters
Germs cause disease. Learning how to keep your hands clean is one way to stay healthy. (Germs are often found on your hands.) You need at least three other friends to do this with you. You will need cooking oil, cinnamon, access to a sink to wash hands, and measuring spoons (teaspoon and tablespoon).

1. Rub one tablespoon* of cooking oil all over your hands.
2. Sprinkle one teaspoon* of cinnamon all over your hands. The cinnamon represents the germs.
3. Wash your hands briskly for 20 seconds as follows:

Girl #1: washes hands with cold water and no soap
Girl #2: washes hands with warm water and no soap
Girl #3: Washes hands with warm water and soap

Which is the best way to wash your hands if you want them to be germ free? What was the most surprising thing you learned about washing your hands?

## 5. Eating on the Run
Look through your *Junior Girl Scout Handbook* for healthy snack recipes and try making some. Or get some recipes from a cookbook or online.

## 6. Don't Explode
Fighting with your sister, moving to a new place, or a divorce in your family can cause stress. How can you fight stress? Do this group activity to find out.

1. Each person gets an empty balloon. The balloon represents your body. One at a time, share what makes you feel stress. Every time someone mentions an item that you find stressful, blow once into your balloon, holding the end closed with your finger.
2. Next, each girl shares four things that help her to relieve stress. If someone mentions something you do to help reduce your stress, let some air out of your balloon for the amount of time it takes you to say "chill." Then hold the end of the balloon again with your finger.
3. Do you have air in your balloon at the end, or is it empty? What does an air-filled or empty balloon mean?

← Clean Hands

## 7. Stress Relief
Read the section about stress management in the "Be Healthy, Be Fit" chapter of the *Junior Girl Scout Handbook* and pick one way to help you relieve stressful feelings.

## 8. Mirror Mirror
You can make a mirror using a paper plate, glue, and aluminum wrap. Cut out a circle of aluminum wrap and glue it onto the center of the plate. Make sure you glue the aluminum wrap with the shiny side up so you can see your reflection. Decorate the edges of your plate. After you make your mirror, look into it and say the following, completing the last sentence:

*Mirror Mirror, in my hand,
I want to be the healthiest
in the land.
To live the life that is good for me,
I will tell you what's the key.
One way I am healthy is*

_____ .

(Fill in the blank with your healthy idea and write it on the back of your mirror.)

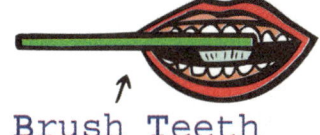

Brush Teeth

## 9. Take Care of Your Teeth
Because you've been brushing your teeth for many years, you may think you know how to do it perfectly. But most people don't. Ask a dentist or dental hygienist for some tips on the proper way to brush and floss, and the amount of time you should spend every day. Start better dental health habits today!

## 10. Check Out Healthy
Regular check-ups by a doctor help you grow up healthy and strong. Make a colorful poster about the importance of regularly visiting a doctor. Find out how often girls your age need to have a check-up and include this information on your poster. Display your poster where young people and their parents can see it.

\* See page 235 for the metric conversion chart.

## Be Healthy, Be Fit

# Sports Sampler

**Playing sports is fun and it helps you build a strong body and a quick mind. Learn about different sports and activities with this badge, and discover the ones you like best.**

### 1. Stretch It Out
A proper warm-up before you take part in sports and fitness activities will help reduce your chances of getting hurt by increasing the blood flow to your muscles and preparing them for exercise. Create a five-minute warm-up and a five-minute cool-down. Learn three stretches for your upper body and three for your lower body. Do them before and after you play—every time!

### 2. Practice Makes Perfect
Choose a sport that you want to learn or improve on. Pick three skills that you want to practice, either with a friend or on your own. With a coach, teacher, or parent, set some improvement goals. Then spend at least an hour a week practicing for the next three weeks.

### 3. Play Time
Participate in a sport by taking part in a tournament or play day, or become a member of a club, team, or intramural program. Discover two ways you can improve your play.

## 4. Try Something New
Playing the same sport over and over again can stress your body out. So try a new sport in addition to your regular favorite. In-line skating, volleyball, tennis, snowboarding, cycling...you make the choice. Spend at least six sessions at the sport. Decide if you like it or not.

## 5. Safety First
Safety awareness is vital when you play a sport. Still, accidents can happen. Learn how to treat two of these basic injuries that might happen when you are learning or practicing a new sport: skinned knees, nosebleeds, blisters, ankle sprains, and muscle strains. Can you think of ways to avoid these injuries in the future?

## 6. See and Tell
For one week, look through the sports section of your local newspaper. Compare articles about sports with male players and sports with female players. The sports can be played by professional, high school, or college teams. Write a letter to the sports editor of your newspaper complaining if sports weren't covered equally or congratulating if they were.

## 7. You Go Girl!
You can almost feel like you are participating in a sport by cheering for someone else. Write a cheer—with at least two verses—for your troop or favorite team. If you want, you or a friend can make up a movement routine to go along with it. Show your cheer to your troop and encourage them to perform it with you at a local girls' or women's sports event.

## 8. "HerStory" of Sport
Pick a sport you would like to know more about. Trace the role of women in the sport's history. When did women start playing it? Were the rules changed for women? How did it become popular among girls and women? Do many girls and women play this sport? Do famous women athletes compete in this sport?

## 9. Spread the Word
Some people can't play certain sports because they don't have the proper equipment. With some friends, find a group in your community that needs help with its sports program. Ask what the group needs and what you can do to help. For example, you could start a sports equipment drive for the group. You might need to work with someone from a sporting goods store, or another adult, to collect equipment. Make sure the equipment is safe and in good working order.

## 10. Sport Search
Find out about two sports that are new to you. Are they played or taught in your community? Check out the local Parks and Recreation Department, community centers, or the yellow pages. Collect the following information about these sports. Where can you play them? How do you start learning? What are the fees? What equipment do you need? How many people do you need to play? Share your findings with your troop and see if anyone wants to learn a sport with you!

*Be Healthy, Be Fit*

# Stress Less

Being stressed out stinks! Unfortunately, you can feel stressed out over many things: moving, starting a new school, fighting with a friend, listening to the news, even being out in bad weather! Help is here. Find out about some of the ways you can relax. (One of them is to laugh!)

## 1. Create a Personal Stress Kit

Let your personal "stress less" kit rescue you from stressful events! Make an attractive container. Carefully stock it with things that will help you relax, laugh, dream, or put you at ease. Be sure there are at least six items in your kit. You might include books, cartoons, photographs, music, a card or letter from a friend or relative, or a picture from a magazine of a place that looks peaceful. Think about how each item helps you relieve stress. Remember to pull out your kit when you need to de-stress.

## 2. Stress Less Writing

One way to let go of feelings that are stressful is to write in a journal or notebook about what's on your mind. Start a "stress less" journal for those times when you need to release some tension.

## 3. What Are You Feeling?

Learning how to identify and describe your different moods and feelings is an important part of dealing with stress. Keep a feelings diary for a day. How many different moods did you experience?

## 4. Do for Others

One of the best ways to lessen your stress is to focus on someone else. For one afternoon or evening help someone with a project or problem.

## 5. Move That Stress Away

Physical motion can release the tension in your body. (Make sure your motions aren't harmful to you or anyone or anything else.) Make a list of ten actions you can take to reduce stress. Some examples are running up and down the stairs a few times, dancing around to your favorite song, or jumping rope. Look at your list when tension starts to rise. Do one of your motions!

## 6. Listen to Music

Listen to five of your favorite songs. Decide which one is most relaxing to you and why. Play your song for two other people and see if they think it is relaxing. Find out what music they would choose to relax.

## 7. Pass It On

Ask three of your friends or classmates how they deal with stress. Collect the five best techniques. Remember to try one of them yourself the next time you're feeling stressed.

## 8. Read and Relax

Read a book. Following a character's adventures can help you forget about your stress. With other girls, come up with a list of especially relaxing books.

## 9. One at a Time

Are you stressed because you are trying to do too much in too little time? Maybe you need to practice some time management. Read about time management in the "Be Healthy, Be Fit" chapter of your *Junior Girl Scout Handbook*.

## 10. Practice Elevator Breathing

Deep, focused breathing can refresh your mind. Imagine that breathing in and exhaling out is like an elevator moving up and down the floors of a building. Practice these exercises.

- Inhale slowly through your nose. Feel your breath travel all the way to the basement (the bottom of your spine).
- Exhale slowly through your mouth.
- Put your hands on your belly and inhale, taking your breath up one floor to your navel. Exhale.
- Put your hands on your ribs and inhale, taking your breath up a second floor, to your chest. Exhale.
- Put your hands on your face and inhale up to the attic— your throat, cheeks, and forehead. Feel your head fill with breath. Exhale and feel all your tension and worries leave your body and go out the elevator door.

## Be Healthy, Be Fit
# Walking for Fitness

Did you know that walking is the easiest way to stay fit? All you need are good walking shoes, a little free time, and a buddy. So grab a friend, and point your shoes north, south, east, or west…whichever way suits you best!

## 1. Warm Up
Learn three stretching exercises to do before and after walking. Practice warming up before you walk, and cooling down after.

## 2. Make a Plan
Develop a personal walking program and follow it for three weeks. Each week, try to increase your speed and distance. Need help developing a realistic plan? Talk with a coach or fitness instructor.

## 3. Best Foot Forward
Visit a store that sells walking shoes. Ask a sales person what to look for in a walking shoe. Compare several brands of shoes. Be able to explain which brand you would buy and why.

## 4. Keep Track
Make a list of interesting sites within walking distance of your troop meeting place, school, or home. With a family member, friend, or Girl Scout troop, walk to at least two of these sites.

## 5. Be Prepared!
Create a simple first aid kit to take on walks. Learn how to care for sunburn, insect bites, heat exhaustion, heat stroke, and blisters.

## 6. Fast Food
Plan and pack a well-balanced, easy-to-carry snack for an extra-long walk. Don't forget to take along a filled water bottle.

## 7. Weather It Well
Put on a walker's fashion show with your friends. Show that you would know the right ways to dress for the weather when you walk in cold or hot weather. Be sure to explain the importance of dressing in layers.

## 8. Lend a Hand
Take part in a weekend project to clean up a walkway or trail in or near your community.
OR
Help at a charity walk by cheerleading, passing out water or snacks, or giving directions.

## 9. Add It Up
Keep track of your car or bus trips for one week. Write down the mileage and the time it took to travel that distance. Could you have walked any of your trips instead of riding?

## 10. Find the Way
On a walk, use a street or road map to arrive at a new destination. Know which side of the road to walk on and how to walk safely in a group.

*Be Healthy, Be Fit*

# Winter Sports

**Fill your winter with adventure, fun, and fitness with this badge. Learn to ski, sled, snowshoe, and skate. If you live where winter days are too warm for snow, don't worry—there are several winter sports that you can try, indoors or out.**

## 1. Material Girl!
Winter fun can make you sweat! Which fabrics will keep you warm and dry? Try this experiment to find out: Take one wool sock and one cotton one. Soak them both in water and then wring out the water. Hang the socks to dry. After one hour, check on your socks. Which feels drier? Which sock would you rather wear in the cold? Got something made out of a wonder-wicking fabric? Repeat the experiment using that item, too.

## 2. Get Ready for Skiing or Snowboarding
Prepare for skiing before you hit the trail or slopes! Learn about the difference between snowboarding and cross-country or downhill skiing. Learn how to clip into and out of bindings. Compare different types of equipment. Find out what works best for you. Learn at least two different exercises to help you get ready for using those ski and snowboarding muscles!

## 3. On the Slopes
On the slopes, learn how to turn, stop, walk uphill on your skis, and recover from a fall. Learn how to safely and properly get on and off a ski lift. Learn how to get back into your bindings if your boots pop out. Don't forget: Warm up your muscles first so they are ready to ski. Remember—never ski alone.

## 4. Distance Traveling
People have used cross-country skis, snowshoes, and sleds to travel long distances in snowy climates. Use a winter form of transportation to follow a marked trail or path. Learn how to use the equipment, including how to stop and start. Travel with a well-trained adult and winter survival gear.

## 5. In-Line Skating
Downhill and cross-country skiers, speed skaters, figure skaters, and hockey players train all year round. You can, too. In-line skating uses and develops the same muscles used for winter sports! First, learn about in-line skating safety gear that is necessary to wear—helmets, wrist guards, kneepads, and elbow pads. Next, learn the basic skills of in-line skating (how to start, stop, turn, and most important, how to fall and get back up). Practice for at least one-half hour.

## 6. Don't Forget Your Sled!
Plan a sledding outing with a group. Learn what makes a good sled hill and what is involved in safe sledding, including what protective gear to wear. Find out about the different types of sleds available and which ones are the safest. Learn to steer, slow down, and stop.

## 7. First Aid for Cold
Learn how to recognize the signs of wintertime health hazards, such as windburn, hypothermia, and frostbite. Learn what to do about each.

## 8. The Winter Olympics
Visit the library or the United States Olympic Committee Web site *www.usoc.org* to find out about one of the following sports:

- Bobsled
- Curling
- Luge
- Speed skating
- Ski jumping
- Biathlon

## 9. Balance, Coordination, and Agility
Practice these moves on ice skates, or do them wearing in-line or roller skates on a smooth surface. Remember to wear protective gear and to skate with a buddy.

- Glide while balancing on one foot. Alternate balancing on your right foot, then your left. See how far you can glide while balancing.
- Skate backwards.
- Cross over. Crossing one skate over the other lets you turn quickly. Start skating slowly. Pick up your right skate and take a giant step over and across your left skate.
- Skate an obstacle course. Set up several cones or plastic soda bottles filled with sand. Skate around these as quickly as you can. Try crossing over or even skating on one foot.

## 10. Ice Hockey Anyone?
If you are attracted to the ice, learn the basics of ice hockey and become a team player. Discuss the importance of playing fair. Learn why protective gear is so important. If possible, attend a women's ice hockey game.

# 7 Let's Get Outdoors

## Camp Together

**Hike or bike, sing or stargaze, watch a sunrise or sunset, sleep in a tent or in a cozy cabin. Round up your friends or family and head to the great outdoors! To earn this badge, you must do activities 1 and 2.**

## 1. Make a Plan

Help plan a group camping trip to a troop house, cabin, tent unit, or cottage for at least two nights. Create a budget for your trip. Then plan what to eat, what to take, and how to get there.

> Budget Items
> Food
> Cleaning supplies
> First aid kit
> Program supplies
> Rental of facilities
> Charter of bus
> Gasoline, tolls
> Other travel expenses

## 2. Safety First

Do each of the following:

- Learn to recognize hazards such as cliffs, poisonous plants, insects, animals, or unstable footing that could be a danger. Discuss with others how to protect yourself in such situations.
- Establish a buddy system, group boundaries, and a signal for gathering the group in case of an emergency.
- Establish a "lost plan," or what a girl would do in case she is separated from the group.
- Review the fire and evacuation plans posted at the site. Learn what you should do and practice an evacuation.

## 3. Walk Softly

Learn about "leave no trace" camping. Find out how poor camping and outdoor recreation practices can cause damage to the campsite and environment. Show what you have learned about three or more of the following: erosion; fire, air or water pollution; feeding wildlife; not removing garbage; and destruction of plant or animal habitat. Explain or show how you can prevent each of the ones you choose.

## 4. Dress Right

Develop a list of group and personal clothing and equipment to take with you on your trip. Help to pack and carry the equipment and supplies.

## 5. Fueling and Cleaning Up

Plan a day's worth of nutritious camping menus: breakfast, lunch, dinner, and snacks. Plan for any health or religious needs regarding food. Cook one meal over a camp stove or use a solar oven. Decide on nutritious foods that you can bring when doing outdoor activities. Learn how to clean up and dispose of garbage.

## 6. Challenge Yourself

Learn a new outdoor skill such as how to pitch a tent, use a map and compass, rappel, dry food, bird-watch, purify water, or cook outdoors.

## 7. Pitching In

Before you go, make a schedule for activities, free time, bedtime, meals, clean-up, and setting up and closing camp. Make a kaper chart that gives each girl a turn at the different jobs.

## 8. Natural World

Plan an outdoor activity that helps you learn more about your natural surroundings through observation. Perhaps plan a nature hike or scavenger hunt.

## 9. The Outdoors at Night

Do one of the following, after discussing nighttime safety:

- Take a starry night hike or stargaze from an open spot.
- Go to an area where everyone can sit quietly. Listen to the night sounds for a while, then write a poem about what you heard or experienced.
- Or plan your own activity that captures the night.

## 10. Learning from Experience

(Do this activity last, after you've returned from your trip.) As a group, make a list of camping tips to share with new campers. Decide what worked for you and the group and what you would change for the next camping trip. Share what you discovered about yourself and the outdoors and what you'd like to do your next time out.

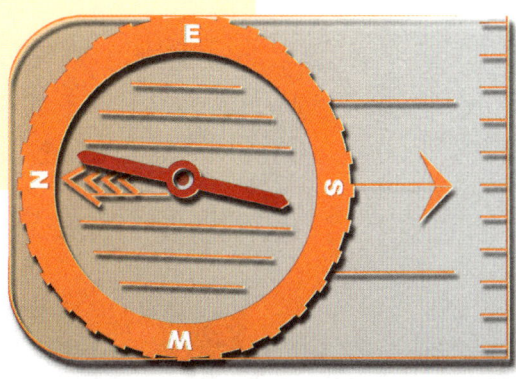

*Let's Get Outdoors*

# Earth Connections

Ecology is the study of plants and animals—including people—and their environment. If you love nature—trees, animals, plants, raindrops, whatever—then you'll love the activities in this badge. You must do activity 1 in order to complete this badge.

### 1. Be an Ecologist: Your Study Area

Visit a natural area near where you live, such as a park or campsite. Mark out an area that is no larger than 20 paces square. This will be the "ecosystem" or community that you will study.

- List the plants and animals you observe in your ecosystem. Or count the number of different types present. Determine if you have different levels of plant life in your ecosystem, such as groundcover, shrubs, and trees. How do you think the different levels affect each other?
- Using a thermometer that measures air temperature, or your hand, take or feel the temperature at ground level and chest level in at least three different places within your ecosystem. Where is it the warmest, the coolest? What causes differences in temperature?
- Dig a small hole in the soil and note the different layers of soil. Feel and find out if there are differences in what the soil is made of and how it feels.

### 2. Traveling Through Time

Ecological succession—when one community replaces another over a period of time—is a natural process of change. A pond might fill in to become a meadow or a meadow might grow into a forest. Think of yourself as a time traveler. Draw what you might see in the future for two of the following sites:

- Lake or pond that has a marshy area at one end
- Fallen tree
- Vacant lot or a meadow
- Burned forest

### 3. Identify That Tree

Learn to identify ten tree species using leaves, seeds, fruit, and bark as a means of identification. Describe the kind of ecosystem where each is likely to be found.

### 4. Reading the Rings

Find a tree stump where you can read the growth rings. A year's growth consists of a light and a dark ring. In order to figure out how old a tree was when it died, count each dark ring and add five to the total number (for the early years when growth is hard to see). Look for years of rapid growth (the wider rings) and years of slow growth. What might have caused the differences in growth years?

### 5. Eco-Games

Help others understand relationships within an ecosystem by playing a game that shows how plants and animals depend upon each other. *Games for Girl Scouts* might help you.

### 6. Saving Animals and Plants

Visit a zoo or game preserve. Find out why the zoo or preserve exists, and if the zoo or preserve is doing any research to learn about and preserve species.

### 7. Adapt or Perish

Look for some examples of ways that plants or animals have developed or adapted in order to survive in their habitat. You might consider environments with little water or lots of water, those that are very hot or very cold, or even those environments that have been changed by humans.

### 8. Plants and People

Learn to identify five different plants that are native to your area. Find out if American Indians or early pioneers used these plants for food, medicine, or something else, such as bedding or fuel. *Note:* Do not pick or eat any plants that you are studying without the supervision or permission of an adult.

### 9. Observing Change

Find out how animal or plant groups change. Make observations over a period of time by doing one of the following:

- Return to your study area during a different season and make the same observations. Look for examples of change.
- Keep track of the kinds and numbers of birds coming to a feeding station or special spot over several months. Are there differences at different times of the year?
- Choose a tree in your area. Record the changes you observe during a school year. Include signs of change, visitors, and anything else you notice.

### 10. Earth as an Ecosystem

Most environmental problems don't stop at state or country boundaries. Consider one of the following problems and learn what is being done in this country and abroad to protect the earth's ecosystems:

- Air pollution
- Mass cutting down of trees in rain forests
- Oil spills
- Over-fishing
- Running out of landfill sites for garbage

Come up with some ideas about what you might do as a creature in the earth's ecosystem to help ensure the survival of your habitat, and act on one of them.

*Let's Get Outdoors*

# Eco-Action

**Eco-action means doing things for the environment that will help people, animals, and plants stay healthy and the air, soil, and water stay clean. This badge will help you take action.**

## 1. Green Team
Start your own eco-action club with friends and family members. What simple things can you do to reduce pollution? Use less water or electricity? Produce less garbage? Damage the environment less? Create an eco-action pledge and decide on a way for everyone to do two of these Earth-friendly things over a two-week period. When the two-week period is up, club members should meet to share their experiences and renew their pledges to help the environment. Continue to meet as long as you like working on Earth-friendly projects.

## 2. Plant a Tree
Trees not only look beautiful, they also provide shade, act as a wind or sound break, add oxygen to the air, prevent soil erosion, and provide food and shelter to many animals—including humans. Take part in a tree-planting activity. None scheduled? With permission, plant one or more trees in a place where someone agrees to take care of them, such as your backyard, your schoolyard, or at a community center.

## 3. Every Drop Counts
People, plants, and animals need clean water to survive. Do something to conserve water, such as:

- Distribute free water-saving devices for showerheads, toilet tanks, or faucets to people you know in your community. Get these from a local government conservation agency.
- Ask your local fire station to provide fire hydrant sprinkler caps so that the kids in your neighborhood can cool off in the summer without wasting too much water.

## 4. What's Watt
Just how much electricity do your family appliances use? Look at the wattage information on each appliance you use—it's usually on the back or side of the appliance. Then multiply the wattage by the number of hours your family uses the appliance each day. Don't forget to count the watts used by light bulbs. Do this for three days. Which appliances use the most electricity?

## 5. Start the Presses!
With a group of friends, give people the scoop on environmental issues in your neighborhood by publishing a newspaper. You'll need reporters, a photographer or artist, a designer, and an editor to make sure the copy is interesting and accurate. Create a name for your newspaper. Work with your "staff" to cover stories that are important to your community.

## 6. Trashy Art
People produce tons of garbage every day but cities are running out of places to put it. Help reduce the amount of garbage you produce. Make a work of art by using some of the stuff you would ordinarily throw away. Get creative! Let your imagination turn things such as bottle caps, old game pieces, milk jugs, and packaging into "masterpieces." Want to do more for the environment? Hold a trashy art show with pieces made by your friends, family, or troop members.

## 7. Paper Rules!
Plastic takes about 500 years to break down, yet paper takes only six months. Encourage your community to use less plastic by creating an advertising campaign on brown paper bags. Collect at least ten large brown grocery bags in good shape. Decorate each bag with an environmental message. Donate the bags to a neighborhood store so that they can be reused.

## 8. Clean and Healthy
Make a difference. Improve the environment in your community by doing an Earth-friendly service project, such as:

- Joining or starting a project to label storm drains that empty into streams and rivers.
- Helping to control soil erosion in a park.
- Educating the community about noise pollution.

## 9. You "Auto Know"
Many states require that vehicles be tested for emissions—what comes out of the tailpipe—to make sure they are not polluting the air more than the law allows. If you live in one of those states, go along when your family car is inspected to find out what and how auto emissions are monitored.

## 10. Women's Work
Learn about a woman who was or is a champion of the environment. Find out how she became interested in helping the Earth, what she did, and how she prepared herself to reach her goal. Ask a librarian or teacher for help locating books and videos on women who have helped the environment. Don't forget to "surf the Net," too.

## Let's Get Outdoors

# Finding Your Way

It's no fun getting lost. That's why it helps to know how to read a map or use a compass. They are easy to use, once you learn how—which is what this badge is all about. Use a compass or a map to get you where you need to go!

### 1. Know Your Maps
There are many different kinds of maps. There are maps that show you travel routes, landmarks, or bus routes, and topographical maps that describe the terrain of a portion of land. Collect three different types of maps or charts that include the place where you live or an area you would like to visit. Be able to explain what kinds of maps they are and the information each gives about the area.

### 2. North, South, East, West
A compass is a tool that is used to help you find north, south, east, and west. Show that you know how to use a compass by:

- Explaining how to adjust a map for the difference between true and magnetic north.
- Taking a compass bearing from a map and following it.
- Sighting an object, walking to it, and returning to your starting point.

### 3. How Long and How Far
Maps can help you figure out how much time you will need to get to a specific place. This helps when you are planning a trip, whether it's a walk to the park or a drive to a relative's house. First you need to find out how far away a place is. Using the scale of your map, figure out how many miles or kilometers it is to your destination. Now determine how long it would take to drive to this place. Don't forget to factor in some time to deal with things like traffic, terrain, and weather, etc. Check your calculations by using a map site on the Internet or ask an adult to look them over.

## 4. Walk the Distance
Find out how long it takes you to walk one mile (or kilometer) comfortably over fairly level ground. Then figure out how long it should take you to walk the distance between two points you have marked on your map. When calculating your walking time, don't forget to consider the type of terrain and your walking speed. (It usually takes longer to walk up hills than it does to walk on a flat surface.) Walk the distance and see if your estimate was correct.

## 5. Map Maker
Has anyone ever asked you how to get someplace? One way to help is by drawing a map. Draw a map of your route to school, to a shopping center, or to a favorite spot. Ask someone else to test your map by following it. Be sure to include a legend or key which explains the symbols you used and the compass directions.

## 6. Map of the Place
Maps aren't just for roads. Sometimes once you have arrived at your destination, you need a different kind of map to tell you where things are located at that particular place. For example, you may need a map of the inside of a local museum to find out where the dinosaur display is. Draw a map to scale of a specific place (a local park or inside your school), locating major landmarks and other important features. Include a legend or key, which explains the symbols you used, a scale, and compass directions.

## 7. Make a Model
Make a three-dimensional model of a portion of a topographical map to show contour intervals of the hills and valleys.

## 8. Finding Your Way Without Map or Compass
What would happen if you found yourself lost without a map or compass? Could you find your way back to safety? Learn how to look at the sun, the stars, and the nature around you to show you the way home. For example, to find which way is north, locate the North Star in the night sky or look for moss, which grows on the north side of a tree. Show your troop or group that you know how to find north, south, east, and west by using the sun, stars, and other natural signs. Describe to the group what natural signs lost hikers could use to find their way back to camp.

## 9. Trail Signs Traffic
One way to find your way while walking or hiking is by leaving trail signs. These are made by arranging rocks, grass, and sticks in a specific way to indicate a direction. Learn about as many different trail signs as you can. Use your knowledge of trail signs to set up a mini-trail in your backyard, park, or schoolyard. Teach the various trail signs to your troop or group and then set the group loose to follow your mini-trail. Perhaps you could include a hidden prize at the end of the trail.

## 10. Bus and Train Maps
Some maps don't list roads, they list routes—bus and train routes that is! Learn how to use a local bus or train map, or the bus/train map of a city you would like to visit. Choose a place within that city and map out how to get there using public transportation. Don't forget that some destinations require you to transfer onto another bus or train. If it is possible, with an adult, put your route to the test by taking the bus or train to your destination.

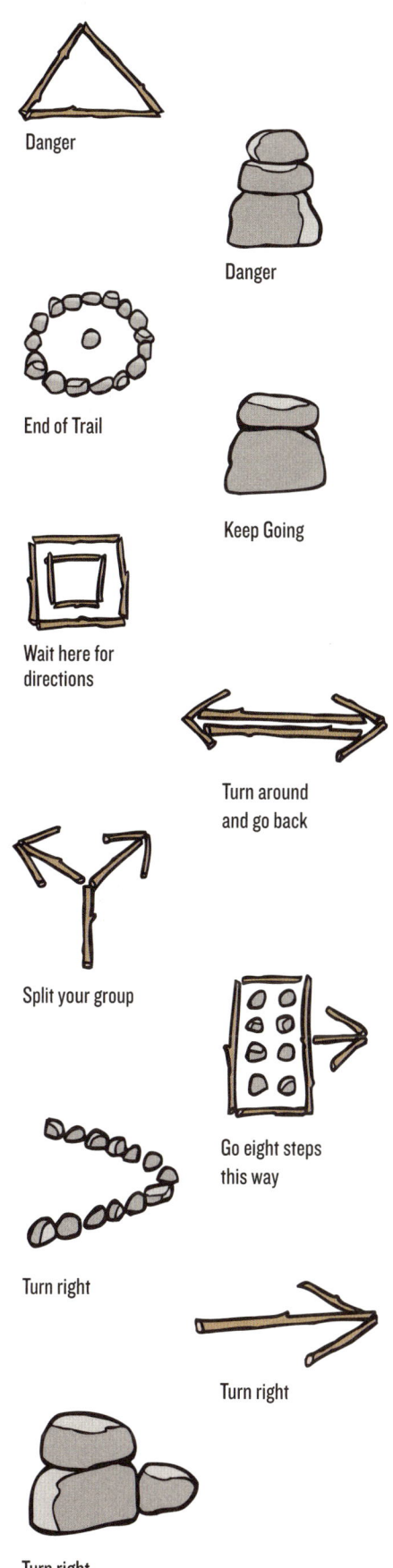

*Let's Get Outdoors*

# Frosty Fun

**Got the winter blues? Think it's too cold to go outside? With this badge you can find tons of things to do this winter with your family and friends.**

### 1. Dress Cool
Hold a fashion show to demonstrate a "cool" way to dress for the winter. Make sure the outfits show the proper way to layer clothing. Include fabrics that help you stay dry and items that protect the head, face, hands, and feet from the cold.

### 2. Snow Sculptures
Did you know that you can make wonderful snow sculptures by using different things to mold the snow? Try cookie cutters, margarine tubs, juice cartons—anything that will leave a shape in the snow. Show off your masterpiece, or have a snow sculpture contest with friends and family.

### 3. Flaky Fun
Are all snowflakes different? Find out by doing the following: Collect snowflakes on black cloth or paper, then take a close look at them with a magnifying glass. Show what you have learned by drawing at least six different snowflakes or by cutting their shapes out of paper.

## 4. Snow Painting

You don't need paper to paint in the winter—snow works just fine!

**What You Need**

- A plastic squeeze or spray bottle for each color
- Bottles of food coloring
- A refrigerator (optional)

**What You Do**

1. Fill each spray bottle with cold water.
2. Place a few drops of food coloring in the bottles (one color in each bottle). The more drops you add, the darker the color will be.
3. Place the spray bottles in the refrigerator to chill or leave outside for a few minutes. The water has to be cold so that it won't melt the snow.
4. Spray the colors on the snow to create your snow painting.

## 5. Serious Fun

Learn about hypothermia (low body temperature) and frostbite. For each condition, learn how to recognize it, avoid it, and how to help someone who has it. Using what you have learned, find a way to teach younger Girl Scouts about both conditions.

## 6. Snow Detective

Find three different animal tracks in the snow and figure out which animals made them. Can you tell what they were doing by the clues left in the snow?

## 7. Snow Travel Savvy

Prepare a snow-storm emergency kit to keep in your family's car during the winter. You'll need:

- Package of kitty litter or sand—this can help a tire move off snow or ice
- Shovel
- Flashlight with fresh batteries
- Sleeping bags or blankets to keep warm
- Food that won't spoil, such as crackers, granola bars, and peanut butter
- Matches in a waterproof container
- Candles to melt snow (have an adult help you)
- Clean can in which to melt snow
- Piece of brightly-colored cloth (such as a red bandana) to tie to the antenna

What else should you include? If your family has a cellular telephone, be sure its batteries are fully charged before you head out.

## 8. Ice Safety

Outdoor ice-skating, ice hockey, or ice fishing can be loads of fun if you do it safely. Before you walk onto a frozen pond, find out:

- How deep the ice must be for the activity you want to do
- How to dress
- What to take with you
- What to do if someone falls through the ice

To answer these questions, arrange to have someone from your local parks or fire department do an ice safety and ice rescue training for the girls in your troop.

## 9. Be a Sport

Keep in shape in the winter by learning and practicing a new winter sport, such as figure skating, snowshoeing, cross-country skiing, or snowboarding. Learn:

- What equipment you'll need
- How to choose the equipment for your size and skill level
- Three basic skills

Practice your chosen sport at least once a week for two to three weeks.

## 10. Natural Insulation

How do harbor seals, walruses, and polar bears keep warm in icy waters? They have a layer of blubber, or fat, that keeps them warm. Prove that fat can insulate by doing this:

- Place the same amount of water and ice cubes into two same-size containers.
- Thickly coat one finger of one hand with something that has a lot of fat, such as vegetable shortening or peanut butter.
- Place the fat-coated finger into one container of ice water. Now place a clean finger from your other hand into the other container of ice water for a few seconds. Which finger feels cold first?

## Let's Get Outdoors

# Hiker

**Hiking or walking outdoors lets you explore your surroundings, and enjoy the scenery—it's good exercise, too! To earn this badge, complete activities 1 and 10. You must also take at least two all-day hikes or an overnight backpacking trip.**

### 1. Safety First
Discuss the following for each hike you plan to take:

- What to do in an emergency and how to get help.
- What to include in your group first aid kit.
- How to set a pace that's comfortable for everyone.
- What your "lost plan" would be if anyone becomes separated from the group.
- What hazards you might encounter where you are going—like poison ivy, snakes, or rocky trails—and how you can avoid them.
- What to do in case of rain, wind, lightning, a snow white-out, or sudden change in the weather. Find out when to seek or make shelter, or when to turn back.
- How to make sure you stay hydrated (get enough water).

## 2. Comfort and the Right Stuff

Plan and show how to dress and what to take along on a day hike or a one-night backpacking trip. Show what clothing works best for different seasons and different kinds of weather. Plan what you should take to avoid sunburn and glare from sun, water, or snow. Show how to dress and prepare for tick, chigger, or mosquito country. Dress your feet with both the right kinds of shoes and two layers of socks—a light pair and a heavier pair. Find out what to look for when purchasing a fanny pack, daypack, or backpack. Consider comfort, weight distribution, padding, and durability. Demonstrate what you've learned with a skit, a fashion show, a game, or by making a poster or collage.

## 3. Know Your First Aid

Help put together a first aid kit for your day hikes or backpacking trip. Demonstrate how to give first aid treatment for common hiking problems such as blisters, sunburn, and insect bites. Also, learn to recognize signs of hypothermia, frostbite, heat exhaustion, heat stroke, and shock.

## 4. Give Back to the Sport

Organize or take part in a trail building or maintenance project. This could be on a wilderness trail, an urban trail, an interpretive nature trail, a jogging path, a physical fitness trail, a wheelchair-accessible trail, or a trail for the blind.

## 5. A Different Kind of Walk

Use a compass and a topographical or orienteering map to lay out a cross-country hike. Or follow an orienteering course set up by an orienteering group.

## 6. March Forward

Take part in a Volksmarch, a noncompetitive walk, sponsored by a Volkssport club.

## 7. Be an Explorer

Be an explorer on a trek into "unknown" territory. Carry a small notebook, a pen/pencil, and art materials. In your notebook, write a detailed description and make a sketch of three animals or plants that you observe. After your return, check some animal and plant field guides that include your area of the country. See if you can find the names of the animals and plants that you recorded.

## 8. Hiking Is Worldwide

Walking for pleasure and fitness can be a way to see the world, and trails can be found in many countries. Use the Internet or your library to discover where you would find one of the trails listed below. Plan your dream trip to one of the sites here or abroad, and describe what you might experience as a traveler.

- Appalachian Trail (Appalachian Mountains, U.S.A.)
- Grande Traversée des Alpes (France)
- Haleakala Crater (Maui, Hawaii, U.S.A.)
- Inca Trail to Macchu Picchu (Peru)
- New Milford Track (New Zealand)
- Pacific Crest Trail (Cascade Mountains, U.S.A.)
- South Kaibab Trail (Grand Canyon, Arizona, U.S.A.)
- West Highland Way (Scotland)

## 9. Share the Fun

Find a way to share the fun of hiking with others. For example, you could take photographs, write a poem, or create a song or short skit about what fun hiking is.

## 10. Happy Trails to You

Help your group plan and go on two all-day hikes or an overnight backpacking trip to a council-approved site. Plan where to go, what to wear, and what to take. Follow safety procedures. Do each of the following to make your trips successful ones!

- Find out about hiking trails near you. Find out as much as you can about the area beforehand. Do you need a permit or a reservation? Is there a limit to group size?
- Determine the distance you will travel. Do you want to complete the entire trail or just part of it? How much time do you estimate you will need to complete the hike?
- Are there any hazards? What are the fire regulations for the area?
- Are there special stops to look for, or something that you can learn about beforehand, such as something about the history or the wildlife in the area?
- For each hike, plan nutritious snacks and meals.
- Make a list of personal and group gear needed. Divide up the group gear fairly. Learn to pack smart and carry no more than 15 percent of your body weight.

After each hike, discuss what went well and what you need to change to ensure safety and fun another time.

Let's Get Outdoors

# Horse Fan

Horses are majestic and graceful animals. Some people keep them as pets. Others use them to farm. Still more ride them in parades, festivals, and sporting events. If the sound of a neigh makes your day, this badge is for you.

## 1. On the Trail
Find out where you can ride horses in your community. Ask each group or facility how much it charges for membership, riding, or riding lessons. Find out whether its specialty is English or Western riding. Find out which groups provide instructions, which require you to own your own horse, which have indoor and outdoor rings, and which have riding trails.

## 2. Caring for Horses
Visit a stable. Find out from the owner or manager what is involved in the care of a horse. Find out how much and what kind of food a horse needs daily, acceptable treats for horses, everyday care in a stable, and how often a horse needs to be shod and why. If possible, watch while a farrier pulls and resets a shoe.

## 3. Fashion and Function
Show the correct and safe clothing for horse shows, Western trail rides, and your group's equestrian activities. You can model the clothes yourself, or use pictures. Point out to others the safety features to look for in the footwear, pants, jackets, and safety hat you wear when riding.

## 4. Horses Through History
Make an illustrated booklet about the history and development of the horse. To do this you can draw your own pictures or use photographs that you find in magazines and other places. Be able to point out and name the principal parts of a horse.

## 5. Song of the Horse
Listen to cowboy ballads and teach one to your troop.

## 6. Make a Career of Riding
There are many careers associated with horses. Explore at least three of them. You might begin by finding out the type of training and experience your instructor needed before she could begin to teach others, for example.

## 7. Ease with Equipment
Learn the parts of a saddle and a bridle. Find out how each part contributes to the comfort of the horse and rider. Learn how to take care of a saddle and a bridle and how to keep them in good repair. If possible, assist with the saddling and bridling of a horse.

## 8. Horse "Tales"
Learn about famous or legendary horses. Tell a horse story to your troop or another group.

## 9. Horse Stories
Read one or more books about horses. These might include books on horsemanship, information on related careers, stories about famous horses, or stories of adventure on horseback.

## 10. Showing Off
Attend a horsemanship event at camp. Can't find one close by? Then watch a live or televised performance by show riders, such as a rodeo, a local horse show, or a draft-horse pulling contest.

*Let's Get Outdoors*

# Horse Rider

**Riding a horse can be a thrilling experience. Learning to ride takes time and practice. This badge will give you a "leg up" on your riding skills.**

### 7. Horse Anatomy
Name the principal parts of a horse. Find out from a veterinarian or horse trainer what can be done to prevent the common ailments or diseases of horses.

### 8. New Skills
Identify two new riding skills you want to learn. Then work with an instructor to learn and practice.

### 9. Perfect Your Form
Take riding lessons to learn the basics of riding: lead a horse before and after riding, mount and dismount, start, stop and back up, ride at a walk and trot, and guide a horse while riding and with supervision. Already know the basics? Then demonstrate to others how to mount and dismount, and ride at a walk and a trot. Show others how to groom a horse and how to care for a horse after exercising.

### 10. See for Yourself
Take a trip to a state or county fair to see a horse show. If possible, enter a show class that is right for you and your horse.

### 1. Get Ready to Ride
Saddle and bridle a horse by yourself. Explain the care and use of each part of the tack and the importance of correct fitting. Hitch a horse at the correct height when bridled, using a halter, a suitable knot, and the correct length of lead rope.

### 2. Equipment Expert
Visit a harness or tack shop or obtain a harness catalog and become acquainted with different styles of saddles, bridles, and bits. Find out the advantages of each type and know the approximate cost of each type. Teach someone else how to clean and care for tack.

### 3. In Good Form
Show that you can do the following in good form:

- Mount and dismount correctly
- Turn and stop a horse, at both a walk and a trot, and on command

### 4. Clips, Combs, and More
Examine the tools used to groom a horse. Discover the purpose of each. Learn to use the brush and currycomb. Learn how to brush a horse before and after saddling. Practice safe stall and barn behavior.

### 5. Ride On
Plan and take part in a ride with others that includes a trail breakfast or other meal, group skill riding, or a cross-country ride.

### 6. Horses, Safety, and You
Explain to your troop, friends, or family the safety regulations for riding, and equestrian etiquette. Show how to give proper hand signals when riding on public roads and how to do an emergency dismount at halt and at walk. Tell what to do if your horse rears, trips, bucks, stops, or bolts.

*Let's Get Outdoors*

# Outdoor Cook

**Some of the best camping memories are made sitting around a campfire—or camp stove—eating the meal you've prepared outdoors. Try the activities in this badge to make some new memories (and some great food, too).**

## 1. Bon Appetit!
With a group, help plan, prepare, and serve an outdoor meal. Help do at least one of the following: plan the menu, make shopping and equipment lists, shop, pack, take care of food at the site, prepare and serve food, or clean up.

## 2. Bean There, Done That
Find three recipes that use a common food such as beans, rice, or potatoes. Prepare at least one of those recipes during a cookout. Save the other recipes for future trips.

## 3. Cook It
Find out how to use at least two different cooking methods from the list below:

- Propane stove
- Butane stove
- Gas stove
- Charcoal
- Canned heat
- Solar energy

## 4. Don't Let the Fire Go Out
Show your ability to maintain a cooking fire in windy or wet weather.

## 5. Cooking On a Camp Stove
Show how to use a backpacker's stove or camp stove safely by preparing a meal on it for yourself and your group.

## 6. Keep It Clean
On one of your cookouts, take a lead role in the clean-up process. Show that you can do two of the following:

- Put out a fire
- Remove the ashes
- Extinguish the camp stove
- Wash, sanitize, and store the dishes
- Dispose of the trash, wet garbage, tin cans, and glass without endangering or damaging the environment

## 7. No Cooking Tonight
Help plan and prepare a tasty, easy-to-pack, lightweight, high-energy dinner for hot weather or emergency use that requires no cooking or refrigeration.

## 8. Mix It Up
Experiment with making and packaging your own dry mixes for use on your next camping trip.

## 9. All Dried Up
Sun-dry or oven-dry some fresh fruit, vegetables, or seasonings to use on a cookout.

## 10. Test the Waters
In camping areas where the water has not been tested and approved by the local health department, you will need to know how to purify the water before using it for drinking or cooking. Show your ability to purify water using one of the following methods:

- A commercial water purification kit
- Water purification tablets

Water purification tablet

Solar Oven

*Let's Get Outdoors*

# Outdoor Creativity

**Poets, writers, artists, and musicians have been inspired by nature to create some of their most famous works. Let nature inspire you by trying some of the activities in this badge.**

### 1. Many Ways to Be Creative
Use nature as your inspiration and create a drawing, painting, sculpture, or other work to share with others. Talk about why your subject appealed to you and what you hoped to show in your work.

### 2. It's Famous
Find a famous creative work that was inspired by the natural world. You can choose a piece of music, a painting or sculpture, a poem or story, or another work. Learn a little bit about your choice and the person who created it. Share the work and your knowledge with others.

### 3. Nature in Three Lines
Try writing the kind of poem known as a haiku. Haiku is a form of poetry that originated in Japan. A haiku doesn't rhyme, and has 17 syllables—five in the first line, seven in the next, and five in the last. A haiku usually mentions one of the four seasons—either by name (winter) or by reference (snow). Two examples are to the left.

*Girls in a circle*
*Summer campfire glowing*
*Sparks stories and song.*

*Snow falls softly swift*
*Flakes swirling and dancing like*
*Tiny ice skaters.*

## 4. Capture a Piece of Nature

Capture a season in full bloom by pressing flowers.

**What You Need**
- Two sheets of cardboard
- Sheets of newspaper
- String or rubber bands
- A flat, heavy weight (a large, thick book would do nicely)
- Flowers (Do not pick wildflowers—use flowers that you have permission to pick from a garden or yard. Flowers that are flat dry better than flowers that are very round and dense.)

**What You Do**
1. Lay out your flowers. You can keep the stems and leaves or remove them.
2. Put down a sheet of cardboard and top with two sheets of newspaper.
3. Place some of your flowers on the newspaper. Make sure they don't touch each other.
4. Place two more sheets of newspaper on top.
5. Continue layering flowers and sheets of newspaper.
6. Top with the other piece of cardboard.
7. Carefully tie string or put rubber bands around your stack of flowers and papers.
8. Place your stack in a cool, dry place where it can remain undisturbed for two weeks.
9. Place a weight on top of the stack.

In two weeks, very carefully check your top layer of flowers to see if they have dried. If they have not, leave them alone for another week. After the flowers are dry, you can use them for many types of artistic creations.

## 5. Celebrate Nature

Plan a creative outdoor event—on your own or with a group. Include activities in which the audience can participate, such as songs or skits. You can have poetry readings, readings of traditional legends about nature and the environment, and other activities. Include an activity that particularly celebrates the natural environment in the spot you are holding the event.

## 6. Your Own Garden

Plant a garden of your own. If you don't have space for a large garden, you could participate in a community garden or you could use a large planter. You could choose plants that fit a special color scheme, plants that flower, plants that are mentioned in a favorite book, or herbs that you could use to make lotions or bath oils. Get advice in choosing plants and caring for plants.

## 7. A Garden Tour

Gardening can be a very creative pastime. Take a tour of a community garden, a botanical garden, or a number of gardens in your neighborhood. You can also tour gardens online. Look at the plants that are growing when you visit and ask about the succession of plants that will bloom the rest of the season. Notice the arrangement of the plants, the plants that need sun and those that need shade, those that are scented and those that aren't, and those that have other uses (such as herbs for medicine or cooking). Decide what you would plant in a garden of your own.

## 8. A Girl Scout's Own

Plan a Girl Scout's Own ceremony that takes place outdoors, celebrating the special relationship Girl Scouts have with the outdoors. Make sure each person attending has an opportunity to participate.

## 9. Starry, Starry Night

Participate in a night watch when you are on a camp-out. Choose a special spot outdoors. Arrange for one-hour shifts through the night, signing up in pairs. Let yourself become part of the outdoors at night by keeping silent. How is the night world different from the day? What happens to your senses?

## 10. Diversity in Nature

Find two very different outdoor spots in which to express your creativity. Choose the same medium in which to be creative—writing, painting, or song, for example—and create two works that represent your feelings about the two different places.

## Let's Get Outdoors

# Outdoor Fun

**Part of the fun and tradition of being a Girl Scout is becoming involved in activities outdoors. Try these badge activities and have some outdoor fun. You must complete activity 1.**

## 1. Get Going
Help your troop, group, or family plan and carry out two outings. They should each be one half-day or longer. Plan activities specific to the sites you choose to visit. Find out what types of equipment and facilities are already on each site. Then make a list of additional group and personal equipment you will need to take.

## 2. Outdoor Emergencies
Do you know what to do during outdoor emergencies? People can get lost or hurt. A bad storm can come up—anything can happen. Pick three emergencies and role-play what you should do.

## 3. Eating Out
With others, help plan, buy, pack, carry, prepare, and serve a different meal or snack for two outings. You may plan one that requires no cooking, one that requires each person to cook her own food, or one that requires you to cook for the group. Prepare a menu and kaper chart—remember to include clean-up chores.

## 4. Build a Fire
Show that you can build a basic fire, prepare food on it, put it out, and leave the fire site "without a trace" of use. Use only enough wood or charcoal to get your job done.

## 5. A First Aid Kit
Help plan, assemble, and pack a first aid kit that is appropriate for your outdoor activities. Demonstrate your knowledge of the uses of the items in the kit. Know first aid and prevention practices for burns, cuts, and cold or hot weather-related illnesses.

clean and sanitize cooking equipment

take all trash with you

## 6. Protect the Environment
Know how to dispose of waste water and garbage without damaging the environment. Learn how to sanitize and keep your dishes clean in the outdoors.

## 7. Sing Around the Campfire
Plan songs, games, and activities for each of your outings that are suitable to the season and the site.

## 8. Tied Up in Knots
Demonstrate how to tie a square knot and several ways it may be useful when on an outing. Learn another knot as well, like a bowline, and its outdoor uses.

## 9. Clean Up
Help unpack, clean, and store your group's equipment after each outing. Discuss the trip, what you learned, and what you would do differently the next time.

## 10. Looking Ahead
Make plans for the next trip outdoors. Figure out how to make the next trip different from the last one—maybe you will stay overnight instead of going on a day trip, or camp in a tent or a cabin.

## Let's Get Outdoors

# Outdoors in the City

**Some people think that being outdoors means being in the country, but you can have a lot of fun being outdoors in the city, too. Check out the activities in this badge and discover how to find adventure and excitement in the city.**

### 1. What Can You Do?
Find out about three outdoor activities your city has available for kids your age. Not sure where to begin? Try these for starters:

- Call or visit your city's Parks and Recreation Department to find out about programs offered year round.
- Find out about recreation sites that are free and those that cost money to use.
- Find out about sports programs, gardening, or urban ranger programs.
- Find out about day camps or other activities offered by schools, youth-serving agencies, government organizations, and houses of worship.

### 2. Safety on Wheels
Organize a safety clinic for younger kids on roller-skating, in-line skating, or scooter or bicycle riding. Help younger kids improve their skills and learn basic safety rules.

### 3. Urban Wildlife
Find out what kinds of animals are in your city and where they live. Look for different habitats and spend some time observing wildlife in more than one habitat. Check out parks, trees, roof gardens, and schoolyards. Is there wildlife that lives year round in your city? Are there birds that pass through your city during fall or spring migration? Is there wildlife in your city that can be harmful to your health?

### 4. Do You Double-Dutch?
Learn how to play an outdoor game that kids living in the city have been playing for generations. Try:

- Double-dutch jump rope
- Hopscotch or potsy
- Stick or stoop ball
- Handball or punchball

### 5. Group Walk
Plan a guided walk with a group. Look for interesting sites in your city. Map a route that includes these sites and some rest stops. Organize a group to follow your route.

### 6. Cook with City Sun
Use the city sun to make sun tea and sun jam.

### 7. Urban Art
Find a spot outdoors in your city that you think is especially beautiful. Create a piece of art that reflects your feelings about this spot.

### 8. Tackle a Community Service Project
Participate in a community service project that tackles a community environmental problem or help with a community event that involves outdoor recreation. For example, you could help spruce up a city park or work at an aid station at a city-sponsored marathon.

## Sun Tea

**What You Need**
- A clear gallon* jar with a lid
- Four tea bags
- Cool water

**What You Do**
1. Fill the jar with the water.
2. Drop in the tea bags (you could use herbal tea or bags of different teas to create a unique flavor).
3. Close the lid and let the jar sit in a sunny spot all day or until the water darkens and the tea is brewed.
4. Pour your sun tea over ice and enjoy.

## Sun Jam

**What You Need**
- 1-1/2 pounds* of ripe strawberries, blueberries, or blackberries
- 1 cup* of sugar
- 2 teaspoons* lemon juice

**What You Do**
1. Wash the fruit well.
2. Remove stems and mash slightly.
3. Mix all the ingredients in a pan and boil for five minutes without stirring.
4. Remove and let cool for 30 minutes.
5. Pour into a 9" x 9"* baking pan.
6. Cover with plastic wrap.
7. Place outside in a sunny spot for three to eight hours so the mixture will thicken.
8. Pour your jam into a sterilized jar and keep in the refrigerator or use it right away spread on bread or as a topping for ice cream or frozen yogurt. Yum!

### 9. A City Garden
Become involved in a city garden. Help with an established community garden plot or start one. Plant a rooftop garden, window boxes, or planters. Share the fruits of your gardening labors with a neighborhood food bank, community center, or senior center. (You can supplement the meals if you are growing vegetables or decorate tables if you are growing flowers.)

### 10. Kites and Frisbees
Find an open spot and practice flying a kite or tossing a Frisbee. Invite an expert in kite flying or Frisbee tossing to speak to or perform a demonstration for your group, friends, or family.

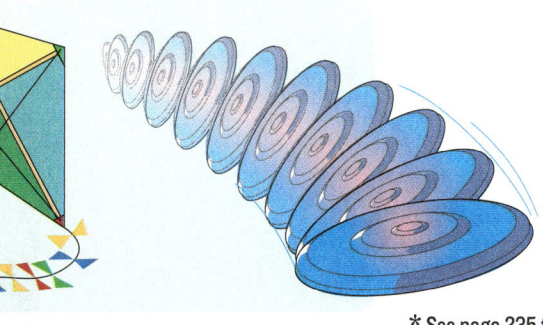

* See page 235 for the metric conversion chart.

## Let's Get Outdoors

# Plants and Animals

**Are you aware of how big a part plants and animals play in your everyday life? From the eggs and toast you have for breakfast to the feather pillow and cotton sheets you sleep on at night, you depend on plants and animals to get you through the day.**

### 1. Plants Here, There, and Everywhere

Play a game in which you try to find as many plant products as you can in your local market. For safety, play this game in teams. Here's how: Using a certain amount of time, each team must find (and write down) as many things that are made with or of plants. The team with the longest list wins.

### 2. Garden Gifts

Gardeners use different plant parts to propagate (make more) plants. Grow your own greenery from one of the following:

- Seed, such as avocado, orange, or sunflower seed
- Root, such as a sweet potato or ginger root
- Leaf, such as jade plant or African violet (stick the leaf stalk into the soil)
- Stem, such as daffodil bulb or crocus corm (bulbs and corms are two kinds of underground stems.)

### 3. Creature Teacher

Are you cut out to be an animal trainer? Find out by teaching a dog, a cat, or a bird a trick or a new behavior. Always work with an animal you know is friendly, and ask an adult to help. Figure out how to get the animal to do what you want without making it feel scared or uncomfortable. It might take a while for the animal to catch on, so be very patient. Remember to reward the animal each time it does what you want.

### 4. Wild Relatives

Animals such as dogs, cats, pigs, and chickens were domesticated (tamed) long ago. How are they different from their wild relatives? Find out by observing the same domesticated animal at least twice to see how it behaves. Next, watch a TV program or video, or read a book or a magazine about one of its wild relatives. Note the things these "cousins" do that are the same and those that are different.

Lynx

## 5. Creature Clusters
Scientists like to group things according to the characteristics that they have in common. Create your own animal groupings by cutting out 15 to 25 pictures of different animals. Group the animals in at least two ways such as: how they look, what they eat, where they live, how they move, or how they bear their young. Explain your reasons for the groupings.

## 6. Veggie Voyagers
Pick one fruit and one vegetable grown in another country that you have never tasted. Prepare a dish with each one for your friends, family, or troop. Get recipes and cooking tips by consulting a cookbook, a magazine, the Web, a relative, or a friend.

## 7. Seed Art
People around the world use seeds to make decorative items, such as jewelry and mosaics. Use at least two kinds of seeds that people eat to make your own work of art.

## 8. Living Sculpture
Imagine being able to make sculptures that are alive! Gardeners do just that when they train and trim plants into shapes such as baskets, balls, hearts, or even giraffes! This is called *topiary*. Create your own plant sculpture by using bushy, trailing, or flowering plants. Try using thick wire, metal clothes hangers, wooden sticks, or plastic strawberry containers to create your topiary frame. Tie the plant to the frame with plastic covered twist ties or string. Use a hand pruner to shape your plant, but ask an adult to help with this.

### Some FRUITS to try...

Prickly Pear Cactus

Lychee Nuts

### Some VEGGIES to try...

Tomatillos

Celery Root

## 9. What a Pest!
Some plants and animals are considered pests because they damage crops, cause diseases, and harm other plants and animals. Learn about one plant and one animal that are considered pests in your community. Find out why they are considered harmful and how they are being controlled. Here are some examples of pests you might investigate: deer tick, rat, cockroach, Mormon cricket, flea, kudzu, poison oak or ivy, and leafy spurge.

## 10. Go on Safari
At a zoo or using your favorite animal books, go on a "world wildlife safari." Find the name of animals that:

- Have a thick fur coat for a cold climate
- Have long fingers for grasping branches
- Have bright colors for attracting a mate
- Have long legs for wading
- Have a dark color for living in shadows
- Have a tongue that reaches in hard-to-get places
- Have big ears that help to cool their blood in hot climates

**Let's Get Outdoors**

# Small Craft

Whether paddling, rowing, sailing, or just drifting, being on the water can be a lot of fun and great exercise. Choose your craft and perfect your skill—it can keep you floating for a lifetime. To earn this badge, you must complete activity 1.

## 1. Staying Afloat

Show that you can select, use, and care for a PFD (personal flotation device). Be able to:

- Adjust a life jacket or life vest to fit
- Know if a PFD is in good condition
- Throw a buoyant cushion or life ring
- Float, swim, and do HELP (Heat Escape Lessening Position) and huddle in a PFD
- If you are a swimmer, put on a PFD while in water that is over your head

## 2. All Hands on Deck

Be ready for boating emergencies. With a knowledgeable adult, talk about what to do if three of the following things happen:

- You fall overboard
- Someone else falls overboard
- The wind rises (or, if sailing, dies)
- You see a storm approaching
- The boat swamps or capsizes
- It gets dark or foggy
- There is a fire on board

## 3. From Bow to Stern

Learn nautical terms for the major parts of a boat and use them correctly. Identify three kinds of water craft.

## 4. Permission to Board

Be able to trim your craft (maintain a balanced position of a boat in the water by moving around passengers and gear). Show that you can:

- Board properly
- Stow things and move weight around safely
- Change places safely

## 5. Shove Off

Show that you can handle a small craft safely. Demonstrate in a rowboat, rowing shell, kayak, or canoe that you can:

- Stow the paddle(s) or oar(s)
- Get underway
- Make turns and go straight
- Speed up, slow down, and stop
- Dock or land
- Secure the craft

## 6. Hoist the Sails!

Show that you can handle a sailboat. Demonstrate that you can:

- Get underway
- Raise and lower the sail(s)
- Sail straight ahead
- Tack and come about
- Speed up, slow down, and stop
- Dock or land
- Secure the craft

## 7. Full Speed Ahead!

In a boat with a motor, show that you know how to:

- Get underway
- Start the engine, change speed, and stop
- Use the oars, if the boat has them
- Make turns and go forward and backward
- Dock or land
- Secure the engine and the craft

## 8. Thar She Blows!

Learn to keep a sharp lookout. Show that you practice rules of the water by knowing how to:

- Keep away from swimmers, divers, and people fishing
- Look out for other craft, floating objects, or hazards under the surface
- Spot landmarks or navigational aids such as buoys or lights or read a navigational map
- Help someone in distress, and signal for help yourself
- Cross wakes correctly

## 9. Red Sky in the Morning, Sailors Take Warning

Be a water and weather watcher. Check to see if it is safe to be out on the water by keeping track of the following:

- Wind direction and speed
- Waves, tides, currents, or water releases from dams
- Cloud formations
- Weather signals and reports

## 10. Swab the Deck!

Do your share to keep a boat shipshape. Do at least three of the following:

- Unload or stow gear or rigging
- Wash down, bail out, or sponge off
- Sand, scrape, or chip
- Paint, patch, or fix up
- Tie knots, splice, or whip lines

*Let's Get Outdoors*

# Swimming

Swimming: Great exercise, great fun! Whether you swim indoors or out—in a pool, pond, lake, or ocean—know the basics and swim safely. You must complete activity 1 to earn this badge.

## 1. Know Water Safety
Show that you know when and how to:

- Select and wear a PFD (personal flotation device)
- Keep afloat using clothing and other flotation devices
- Cooperate with someone who is trying to rescue you
- Use good sense in cold water, in deep water, in a current, and in rough water
- Tread water

## 2. My Buddy and Me
Swimming with a buddy is more fun than swimming alone, and it helps keep you safe. Create and practice a "buddy check call" so that you and your buddy know if either of you need help. Use it every time you swim.

## 3. Like a Fish
Learn to snorkel. Show that you can choose a mask that fits your face, put it on so it won't fog, breathe through it, and clear the mask. Practice your snorkeling skills by swimming 25 yards* along the surface parallel to the shore. Show that you can surface-dive, swim 15 feet* underwater, resurface, and clear your snorkel and mask.

## 4. Go Swim!
Show that you can swim by doing each of the following:

- Glide six feet*
- Kick 25 yards*
- Swim the crawl 25 yards*
- Do two of these strokes for 50 yards* each—crawl, elementary backstroke, sidestroke, or breaststroke

## 5. Helpful Swimmer
Show that you can help another swimmer who:

- Has a cramp
- Is shivering from hypothermia
- Has a sunburn or heat exhaustion
- Is tired

Read the first aid section in the "How to Stay Safe" chapter of your *Junior Girl Scout Handbook* for more information.

## 6. Check It Off
Make a water safety checklist that includes ways to avoid:

- Underwater hazards
- Falling through ice
- Falling in water accidentally
- Overestimating your swimming ability
- Polluting water that you swim in
- Swift currents

## 7. Underwater Swimmer
Swim under the surface of the water. Show that you can do a surface dive, a deep dive, or a jump, and then swim underwater and bring up something from the bottom.

## 8. Diver
Perform two different dives from a low board, platform, or deck. First, be sure an adult who is present has checked the water depth and hazards, and they have said it is safe to dive.

## 9. Going for the Gold!
Get involved in a swimming competition.

- Join a swim team to build your speed and endurance.
- Learn about swimming stars and their records.
- Be able to follow the rules in competitive swimming for starting, turning, timing, and scoring.

## 10. Water Moves
Look at ways other living things move through the water. Watch for creatures that have tails that act as rudders, feet that paddle, or fins that flutter. Imitate animal actions in a water game you make up.

\* See page 235 for the metric conversion chart.

## Let's Get Outdoors

# Water Fun

**Traveling near a lake or stream? Going to the ocean or sea? Why not explore the wet and wonderful world of water. To earn this badge, you must complete activity 1.**

---

The HELP position

### 1. Safety First

Show how to use a PFD (personal flotation device). Refer to the American Red Cross Web site *www.redcross.org*.

- Put it on, adjust it to fit, and fasten it securely.
- Jump into the water with a PFD on.
- Float and swim with a PFD on.
- Practice the HELP (Heat Escape Lessening Position) and the huddle position to keep warm.

### 2. Picture It

Increase your awareness of different water habitats by doing three or more of these activities:

- Listen to the sounds of moving water by the ocean, along the shores of a lake, or by a swiftly running stream.
- Watch waves in salt or fresh water.
- Watch a leaf float in running water.
- Smell the air near salt water, running water, or a swamp or bog.
- Look for signs of life on a beach walk.
- Feel a breeze while on the water or fly a kite along the shoreline.
- Watch a sunset or sunrise reflected in a large body of water.

Find a way to express your feelings about your experience through the arts or participate in a Girl Scout's Own ceremony that celebrates water as your theme.

### 3. A Balancing Act

Show how to get in and out of a small craft safely. Keep the boat in trim (balanced) as you:

- Load gear
- Stow things
- Sit down and stand up
- Move around and change places

*Note:* This can be done in a small boat, sailboat, canoe, or two-person kayak.

### 4. Get in the Swim of Things

On a swimming trip to a pool, pond, or lake, show an adult how you can:

- Float on your back for one minute.
- Tread water for two minutes.
- Do two different swim strokes.
- Use your best stroke and swim 50 yards.*

Remember: Use the buddy system at all times.

### 5. Water Games

Make up and play a game in the water to show you understand and can use the buddy system.

*See page 235 for the metric conversion chart.

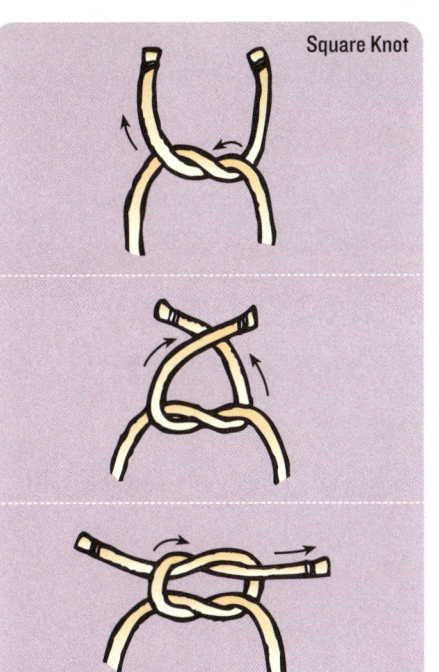

Square Knot

### 6. A Sailor's Life
Do at least two of the following:

- Tie a fancy knot.
- Sail a model boat.
- Learn a song about the sea and sing it.
- Learn something about life on the water or under it.

### 7. Precious Water
Brainstorm ways that you can conserve water. Also think of how not to add to water pollution in your community, or in an area that you are visiting with your family or group. Then, start the habit of being a clean water saver.

### 8. Look Closely
Plan a discovery trip to a lake, stream, or salt-water environment. See how many exciting discoveries you can make about this aquatic habitat. Find out:

- What plants and animals live in the water and on the land nearby.
- Whether the water is warm or cold, clear or murky.
- What the bottom surface is like under the water.

### 9. Let the Games Begin
With a friend or family member, attend a water event, such as a canoe or kayak race, swim meet, surfing competition, fishing derby, parade of sail, synchronized swimming event, or water polo game. Learn the rules of the event.

### 10. Jobs on the Water
Tour a place where people go to have fun on the water, such as a marina, pool, cruise ship, party boat dock, or boat landing. Talk to someone who works there and find out what they do that helps others enjoy and be safe on the water.

*Let's Get Outdoors*

# Wildlife

**From the dandelion growing in the crack of a sidewalk to the blue whale that calls the ocean depths its home, wildlife can be found in almost any part of the world. Try your hand at observing and helping some of the wildlife that lives in your community.**

## 1. Wildlife Symbol Party
Every state in the U.S.A. has a state bird, flower, and tree to represent it. Which were chosen by your state? Why? Have a wildlife symbols "party" at which each person chooses an animal or plant that best represents her. Everybody then takes turns trying to figure out why the other person chose her symbol.

## 2. It's All in the Details
Field scientists often sketch, draw, or photograph the plants and animals they study. Try your hand at drawing or taking pictures of a plant or an animal you can easily observe. Use your pencil or camera to capture details, such as the shape of a flower, the color of a bird's eye, or the design on a butterfly's wing.

## 3. Creature Feature
All birds have a beak, but the shape and size of it depends on what the bird eats. For each of the following, choose something from your kitchen or from a toolbox that best matches how each bird uses its beak as a tool to eat its food.

- Hawk (tears meat)
- Flamingo (strains water for tiny creatures)
- Hummingbird (drinks nectar from long flowers)
- Woodpecker (picks larvae hiding under tree bark)
- Goldfinch (cracks seeds)

## 4. We Are Family
Scientists group all organisms (living things) according to characteristics that they share. Pick two of the wildlife groups listed here and learn what characteristics all of its members share: amphibians, birds, fish, insects, mammals, reptiles, plants.

## 5. Touch-Me-Not!
Have you ever touched poison ivy or seen a scorpion use its stinger? If so, you know firsthand how plants and animals use poison to protect themselves or catch a meal. These poisons can hurt or even kill people. Learn to identify one or two poisonous plants or animals in your area. Where are you likely to run into them? What should you do if you touch, or are bitten by, one of them?

## 6. Staying Alive
Find two animals or plants in your state or region that are considered endangered (in danger of dying out). Why are they endangered? What's being done to protect them? Participate in a project that helps wildlife in your community.

## 7. Take a Closer Look
People use different tools to help them get a closer look at plants and animals. Use two of the following items to see a plant or animal up close: binoculars, magnifying lens, microscope, spotting scope, zoom camera.

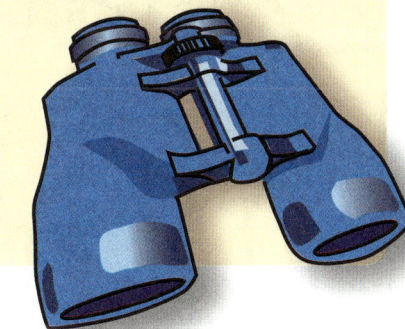

## 8. Animal Watcher
Scientists and nature lovers use field markings (special patterns, marks, or shapes found on the animal's body), behaviors, and the song or call of that animal to identify animals and birds. Use these three things to identify at last three kinds of birds or other animals in your neighborhood.

A tree growing through the crack of a sidewalk.

## 9. Nature's Remedies
Many medicines, home remedies, and beauty aids are made with plants. Find out the healthful properties of three of the following: aloe, ginger, chamomile, peppermint, ginseng, hot pepper, garlic, coriander, foxglove, and chocolate. Ask a librarian, a pharmacist, or someone at a health food store, or go online if you need help.

## 10. How Was Your Day?
Field biologists learn a lot about animals by observing them doing everyday things, such as eating. Pick a wild animal that you can easily observe in your backyard, a neighborhood park, a zoo, an aquarium, or a wildlife preserve. Watch the animal for a while to try to discover three of the following: what it likes to eat, where it spends most of its time, how it gets around, how it keeps clean, how it communicates, and how it cares for its young.

*Let's Get Outdoors*

# Your Outdoor Surroundings

**Do this badge to get a taste of the many different ways to have fun outdoors, from exploring nature, to hiking, to protecting the environment.**

## 1. What Would I Need If . . .
Find out about the best fabrics and products for different types of weather conditions. Find out about the various types of equipment used in camping, trekking, and traveling. Visit an outdoor store, look through an outdoor catalog, or visit an outdoor equipment company's Web site.

## 2. Pack It Up
Plan a trip to an imaginary site. What equipment would you absolutely need to bring to survive? What would you bring to make your travels more comfortable?

## 3. What Does Minimal Impact Mean?
What is the definition of minimal impact? Read about it in the "Let's Get Outdoors" chapter of your *Junior Girl Scout Handbook*. How could you practice this on one type of outdoor trip, like backpacking, troop camping, a day trip, or a trip to a park?

## 4. To Protect the Environment
In a troop, group, or with other girls, brainstorm a list of ways you can help the environment. Look in your *Junior Girl Scout Handbook* for ideas.

## 5. An Outdoor Hobby
Learn about an outdoor activity that can become a lifelong hobby. You could learn to ski or hike, do outdoor photography, try orienteering, backpacking, or bird-watching. Find someone who is an expert in the hobby to teach you the basics.

## 6. Classifying Outdoor Objects: the Artist and the Scientist
Art and science are often related when you are outdoors. Look around a park, backyard, or other outdoor space and find a number of different objects. Then use the following list of words to describe how each object looks:

- Shape—circular, square, oval, cone-shaped
- Size—inches, feet, meters, centimeters
- Texture—rough, smooth, slick, gritty
- Directions—right, left, up, down, in the middle, bottom left
- In relation to—parallel to, horizontal to, smaller than, wider than
- Color—shaded, intense, lighter, darker

## 7. An Outdoor Career
Learn about a career that is spent mostly outdoors. Find a woman who is working in that career. Invite her to speak with your troop, friends, or family. Or see if you can visit her at work. Don't know anyone who works outdoors? Check out the "Just for Girls" section of the Girl Scouts Web site.

## 8. What Do You See?
Do this activity with a group.
1. Each person collects an assortment of natural objects that can be held in the hand. For example, a pine cone, a shell, a feather, a leaf, a rock, a twig, or a flower. Each person does not show her objects to anyone else. Each person also has a pad and a pencil and chooses a partner.
2. Partners sit back-to-back—one is the artist and one is the scientist. The scientist holds one of her objects and describes it to the artist without saying what the object is. The artist tries to draw the object from the scientist's description.
3. Compare the drawing with the object. How well was the object described? How accurate was the drawing?

## 9. Take a Nature Hike!
There are tons of hikes you can take! Try a color-palette hike where you look for as many colors as you can while you hike. Or hike to find shapes in nature. At night, go for a spider-eye hike where you shine your flashlight beam parallel to the ground in grassy places and look for those red spider eyes.

## 10. Outdoor Fun and Games
Collect different outdoor games to play with other Girl Scouts or friends and family. Plan an "Outdoor Fun and Games Day" in which each person gets a chance to lead some of the games and play in others. Create wild and wacky prizes and have healthy snacks on hand to keep your energy up.

# 8 Create and Invent

# Architecture

**Learn about different styles of architecture and get started designing your own spaces. Here's a chance to let your creativity out.**

### 1. Building Tour
Walk in your community (or a place you are visiting) with a friend or family member. Find examples of architecture that you like and don't like. Record your observations in a sketchbook or with a camera so you can talk with your walking partner about what you liked and didn't like.

### 2. Making Their Mark
Learn about a well-known architect and visit one of her projects in person or online. Find out why this person is known for her work.

### 3. Down to Scale
An architectural plan is a drawing of your project that uses a scale measurement, such as 1 inch = 1 foot*, to represent the actual size of the object on paper. Make your own plan of a room to scale, using graph paper or a computer software program.

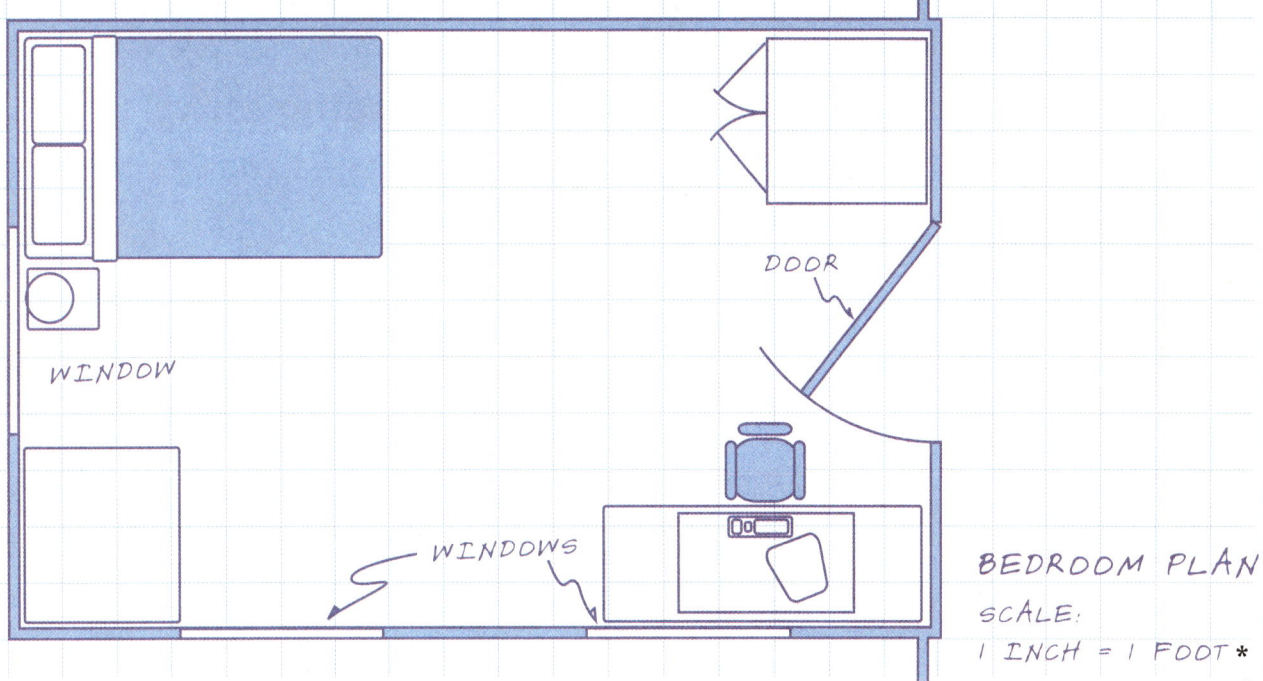

### 4. Conserving Energy
Find out what kinds of laws exist in your state or community that encourage energy conservation in building structures.

### 5. Nature's Design
Design a garden—a children's garden, a living maze, a special theme garden, a public garden for flower or vegetable plots, or a Japanese garden. Include artwork, plantings, structures, walkways, and other things you could use to make it a special place. Sketch a plan or do a scale model.

### 6. Making Your Mark
Participate in a project that helps restore a public space or building in your community. Document the changes that happen by taking before and after pictures.

### 7. Architecture Around the World
Create a way to show the architecture of different countries. What makes the architecture distinct? How have climate, culture, natural resources, or lifestyle shaped the architecture? What do the homes and buildings tell you about the people who live there?

### 8. Idea File
Create a notebook, file box, or computer file to keep your favorite architectural ideas in. Use this file as you do other activities in this badge.

### 9. From Airports to Zoos
In a group, brainstorm a list of buildings or combination of buildings you would love to design if you were an architect. Decide who will use them, what activities will happen in them, and how people with disabilities will use them.

### 10. House of Sticks
Create a structure out of twigs, small pieces of driftwood, toothpicks, coffee stirrer sticks, or a combination of small sticks. Use glue, string, and tools appropriate to the materials.

* See page 235 for the metric conversion chart.

*Create and Invent*

# Art in the Home

**Add art to your home using simple household or store-bought materials by doing this badge.**

### Gourd Decoration

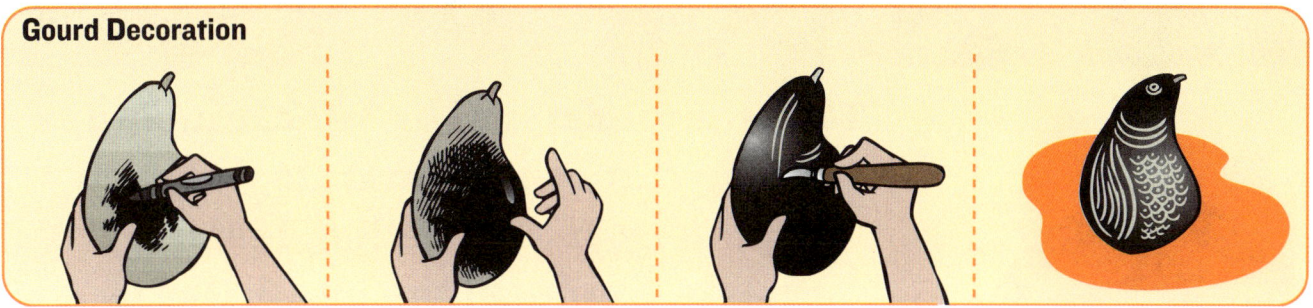

### 1. Art in Style
Collect pictures of different rooms showing different styles of furniture, rugs, wall coverings, decorations, and lighting, and different color schemes. Using your collection, do one of the following:

- Decide which furniture style you like best and why.
- Look at the patterns in the rooms. How many patterns are there—on the floor, walls, windows, and furniture? Do they go with each other or do they clash?
- Look at the colors and how they are used. Do different colors give different feelings? How are colors used together?

### 2. Measure Up
Measure a room in a house. Draw it on a large piece of paper in scale, 1 inch = 1 foot.* Indicate doors and windows. With colored paper, cut shapes to scale for furniture, rugs, storage units, etc. Move the cut pieces around on the scale drawing and then place them where they look best to you. Look for ways to improve the use of space. When you're satisfied, glue the shapes in place.

### 3. Create a Dream Room
Cut out pictures of furniture, accessories, wallpaper, and rugs that you like. Arrange them in a shoe box to create your "dream room." Glue into place and show your room to others.

### 4. A Dried Gourd Decoration
Dried gourds are used throughout the world in places such as Mexico and Central and South America, as bowls and containers. Try making your own gourd decoration.

1. Start with a gourd that has a smooth surface. If it is not already dried, it will have to dry out for a long time before this project is completed, perhaps six to eight months. It will feel much lighter and the seeds will rattle when it is dry. Clean it after it is dry.
2. Using heavy pressure, cover the entire surface of the gourd with black crayon except for the areas where you want the color of the gourd to show.
3. Smooth the crayoned gourd to a glossy shine with a tissue.
4. Study the shape of the gourd and decide on a design. A gourd with a long neck might make a nice goose. A round gourd might suggest a small animal.
5. Using blunt scissors or a knitting needle, scrape through the crayon to expose the gourd underneath. Scrape, but don't cut, the skin of the gourd. If you don't like your design, cover over the surface once again with black crayon and begin the scraping process over again.

### 5. Say It with Flowers
Visit a store that sells plants and flowers to see a variety of arrangements. Then make your own floral arrangement or centerpiece.

### 6. Home Arts: Home Business
You can make home arts, and then sell them as part of a home business. Visit at least two shops that sell things for the home that are made by people at their homes. If possible, arrange to speak with someone who creates home art for sale.

### 7. Budget for the Future
Visit a store that sells furniture, rugs, china, table linens, curtains, and other household items or look through mail order catalogs or on the Web. Select items that you think you would like to have in your home someday. List them and find out the prices.

### 8. Design Your Own Room
Make two plans for your own room, including what you need for sleeping, storage, relaxing, homework, and hobbies. Make one plan as if you had an unlimited budget; the other plan as if you had very little money to spend.

### 9. Holiday Decor
Make a decoration, such as a harvest wreath, a dried flower arrangement, a flag, or a table centerpiece, to add a festive look to your home during a holiday.

### 10. Accent on Beauty
Create something that would make your home nicer, such as a basket, wall hanging, or quilt. For ideas, look through how-to craft books or at other badges with art activities.

* See page 235 for the metric conversion chart.

Create and Invent

# Art in 3-D

**Three-dimensional or 3-D art includes sculpture, mosaics, murals, origami, and pottery. In this badge, learn to translate your designs into 3-D art.**

### 1. In the Fold
Origami is the ancient Japanese art of paper folding. Make an origami paper crane, a symbol of peace and hope. After each girl in your troop or group has made one, use the cranes as decoration for a Girl Scout event celebrating world friendship.

### 2. Mold It
Mold clay or other modeling material. Your work can be something that is useful or something that is purely decorative.

### 3. Past Masters
For centuries, art students have tried copying the styles of famous artists. Look at art online or in museums. Search online using key words such as "sculpture," or the names of specific artists. After reviewing the work of three artists or sculptors, try your hand in the 3-D medium and style of one you admire.

### 4. Negatives Are Positives

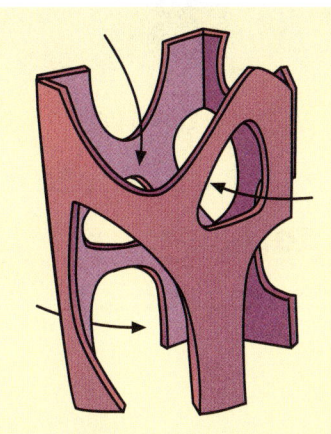

In sculpture, the positive space is the solid part of the work and the negative space is the air space that is still considered a part of the design. Create an abstract sculpture using boxes, crates, pieces of wood, cardboard, or polystyrene. Include negative as well as positive space in your design.

### 5. Carve It

Explore the art of woodcarving. How-to books and wood carving tools and kits are available at most arts and crafts stores. Many stores offer classes on how to use the tools and kits. Ask your art teacher or another adult for help. Keep in mind safety issues and be sure that an adult is around whenever you are sharpening your skills. After practicing for a while, make a wood carving, either realistic or abstract in design.

### 6. All Around the Town

Look for examples of three-dimensional art in your community. Try to find at least five examples.

### 7. Art That's Me

Every culture expresses itself through art. Create a piece of art in 3-D that represents your heritage.

### 8. Art as Therapy

Arrange to visit a site where people with different abilities and special needs are creating art. Find out if local schools, hospitals, or nursing homes have an art therapist on staff. Ask if you could be allowed to talk to or observe one of them at work.

### 9. It's Mobile

Find out about mobiles and stabiles and try creating one of your own.

### 10. Wire It

Create a three-dimensional design by twisting, cutting, and/or coiling wire. Use tools appropriate to the heaviness of the wire. Add other materials as needed for your design.

## Origami

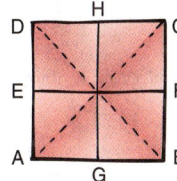
1. Fold square as shown; solid lines form peaks, dotted lines form valleys.

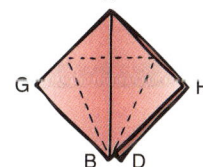
2. Bring ABCD together to form small square. Bring F and G to center fold. Repeat on other side. Fold down top to form triangle.

3. Unfold to small square. Pull B up over center point X, pulling in G and F. Repeat with other side.

4. Fold outside points to center on dotted line. Repeat on other side.

5. Make diagonal creases on neck and tail.

6. Fold up neck and tail.

7. Unfold tail. Push into wing, reversing center fold at the same time. Repeat for neck.

8. Fold head on dotted line. Push into neck, again reversing center fold.

9. Spread wings gently, holding bottom and pushing down on X.

**Create and Invent**

# Art to Wear

What you wear says a lot about who you are. If you are interested in fashion design or the history of clothing, or if you just want to change your fashion look, read on.

## 1. Fashion Through the Ages
Collect pictures of fashions from three periods of history, dating about 20 years apart. You can check the fashion picture collection at a library or museum, online, or in issues of fashion magazines or paper doll books. Draw pictures of what you find and arrange them attractively on a poster or in a booklet. What do you like or dislike from different eras? For instance, you might like how the hoop skirts from the mid 1800s look, but not like how they keep you from playing sports.

## 2. Fashion Friendship
Make a friendship anklet (see the "Create and Invent" chapter in your *Junior Girl Scout Handbook*) or an accessory for a friend, such as a vest, belt, or scarf, using a technique that you have learned, such as sewing, knitting, crocheting, or embroidering.

## 3. Fashions From Afar
Create a poster of the traditional dress of countries from three continents. Explore libraries, museums, and magazines, talk to family and friends, or look online to find out how the garments or decorations reflect the culture and lifestyle of the people.

## 4. Show Your Flair
With an adult's help, make an item of clothing or alter one you already own. Show off your creation at a troop or group fashion show. With others who are interested, plan the fashion show to kick off or conclude a fabulous season in Girl Scouting. Invite the public. Give the show a theme, such as "Girl Scouts Dress Globally," "Spring Fever," or "Roaring Twenties."

## 5. Pattern-maker
Some fabric designs or patterns are made by batik, tie dyeing, silk screen, or embroidery. Try your hand at creating a pattern. Select a method and create the pattern. Use it on a plain piece of fabric, a shirt, or other item. Display your item in a troop or group fashion show, or wear it on a special occasion.

## 6. Fashion Add-ons
Create a clothing accessory for yourself, such as a jacket, vest, belt, scarf, or hat, in a technique that you have learned—sewing, knitting, crocheting, or embroidering.

## 7. Sell Fashion
What careers or hobbies in fashion interest you? Explore that question in your troop or group in one of two ways:

- Invite people in your community—shop owners, art students, designers—to talk about their careers. Talk to them one on one, or as part of a panel.
- Visit a flea market and talk to people who display their art to wear, from belts to boots and hats to jewelry.

## 8. Doll Clothes
Collect dolls from your home or from friends and give them a fashion tune-up. Design jackets, dresses, pants, or other fashion components for one or two dolls.

## 9. The Old Is New Again
Look at jewelry from two to three different decades. What was popular? Are any trends from the past popular now? What's the newest trend? Draw or create a piece of jewelry that you think will be a future trend.

## 10. Decorate Your Wears
Dress up a plain or old garment with a small decorative item. For instructions on making the item, consult crafts or sewing booklets available at specialty shops or online. Check the following for ideas: embroidery, crocheting, lacework, quilting, appliqué, braiding, beads, buttons, costume jewelry, tassels, fringes, and pompoms. Model your finished creation for friends and family.

Create and Invent

# Books

What would the world be like without books? How else would you find out about the past, visit distant places and planets from your armchair, or become involved in a good story? Read on.

## 1. It's a Wide World

Read two folk tales, stories, or poems from a culture other than your own. Share what you have learned in any of the following ways:

- Act out one or more of the stories or folk tales.
- Learn more about one or more of the writers.
- Read one of the stories, poems, or folk tales to your Girl Scout group or another audience.
- Create puppets and put on a puppet show, based on one of the stories, for a group of younger children or Girl Scouts.

## 2. Picture This!

Select one or two picture books and do one of the following:

- Read the books to younger friends or Girl Scouts. Ask what they like about the illustrations and the stories.
- Create two book covers to go with your selected books.
- Create your own picture book in the same style.

## 3. Be a Tape Worm!

Make an audiotape of a book, short story, magazine article, joke or riddle collection, play, or poetry collection that you can give to someone who cannot read. You could, with your troop or group, make tapes at a local agency that serves people who are blind or visually impaired. Practice reading aloud so that your tape will sound polished and smooth.

## 4. Be a Reading Helper

Some children and adults have trouble reading. Find out from a reading specialist, teacher, librarian, or another adult about different types of reading difficulties or disabilities. Then, with the help of adults as needed, do one of the following:

- Put together and distribute a list of places to go in your community for reading help. This information is available at most libraries.
- Be a reading buddy. Find out if there is a place where you can help a younger child who is having reading trouble. Check with your teacher or leader, or ask your librarian if there are literacy or reading organizations in your community. Volunteer to spend at least one-half hour a week for at least a month with your reading partner.

## 5. The Living Past

When you read about something that happened a long time ago, you make the event come alive again in your mind. Read a story, poem, or folk tale that reflects past life in the United States.

## 6. Read and Review

In a newspaper or other source, read reviews of new books for your age level. Check one of the books out of the library, read it, and decide if the review was right.

## 7. How To? Read On!

Become an expert in a subject by reading about it. You might read about the subject matter of another badge in this book. For example, read a book about dance, music, the life of a famous woman artist or sports hero, horses, cooking, the environment, or an historic event. Review the book in writing or discuss it with your troop or family.

## 8. Build a Library

Share your love of reading with others in your community in one of two ways:

- Set up a schedule with other Girl Scout members to bring library books in large print, in Braille, or on tape to someone who will enjoy them.
- With the help of an adult, collect books and magazines for specific age levels and donate them to a library, camp, nursing home, youth shelter, pediatric office, clinic, day-care center, or other facility.

## 9. Books for Life

Find out about careers for people who like books. If you can, visit with an author, poet, illustrator, editor, librarian, bookstore owner or book publisher, or invite any of those professionals to visit your troop or group.

## 10. Your Library's Treasures

Explore your local library's resources. Prepare a poster to encourage greater use of the library, or an advertising flyer to let the community know about all the library's treasures. Some libraries sponsor readings by local poets and authors, or concert series. What kinds of classes or lectures are available at yours?

*Create and Invent*

# Camera Shots

**Are you a camera bug? Do you love taking videos? Lights! Camera! Action! Start shooting with this badge—you're on a roll.**

### 1. Camera Shop
Learn about three different types of still or video cameras and three different kinds of film, and about other ways of recording or shooting pictures.

### 2. Portraits
Have friends or family members pose for you. Take:

- Action shots
- Full-body poses
- Close-ups of their faces

How do your photos or videos show the personality of their subject?

### 3. Be a Sports Photographer
To capture a sporting event or athlete, you need to get as close as you can to the action. Practice shooting friends as they jump rope or snowboard, or play softball or soccer. Take at least ten pictures or videotape for ten minutes. Try to learn the best ways to take pictures or shoot a video when things are moving quickly.

### 4. Landscape
Take at least five photographs that focus on the environment: sunsets, storms, water, trees, hills, buildings, skylines.

### 5. The Basics
Learn to use a video camera. Find out how to turn it off and on, where to put the battery and to how to recharge it, how to insert and remove the tape, how to record, how to view what you have taped, and what special effects your camera has.

### 6. Show Time
Select one of your best photographs—enlarge it and create a special frame for it. Or select one of your best videotapes—edit it, record music or dialogue to accompany it, and show it to friends and family.

### 7. Get Ready, Get Set
Learn how to maintain and clean your still or video camera. Also find out how to remove a completed roll of film or tape, insert a new roll or tape, or transfer digital images onto a computer.

### 8. Tell a Story
Take at least five pictures or create a videotape to tell a story or to illustrate a children's book or poem.

### 9. Screen Test
Directors and camera people check their work every day at a screening called "dailies." They can see what worked and what has to be reshot. Try your hand at videotaping a family or Girl Scout event—a party, a conversation, or a sport. Then have a screening party with some of your friends and family. What worked? What didn't? What might you do differently the next time?

### 10. Getting It in Shape
Visit a video editing facility or spend some time with someone who knows how to edit videotape. Find out what kinds of computer hardware and software can be used for editing and special effects. Learn what is involved in editing, dubbing, adding titles, and creating special effects. Do some simple edits and titles for your own video production.

# Create and Invent

# Ceramics and Clay

**You can use clay to make beautiful art. To create objects that last a lifetime, dig in, coil up, and fire away.**

## 1. Make It with Clay

With the help of a skilled artist or teacher, practice two or more of the clay-building techniques below and finish at least one piece:

- **Pinch pots**
- Slab work (used for tiles, chimes, or decorations)
- Wheel thrown pieces
- Modeling/sculpting in clay (such as a figurine)

**Make a Pinch Pot**

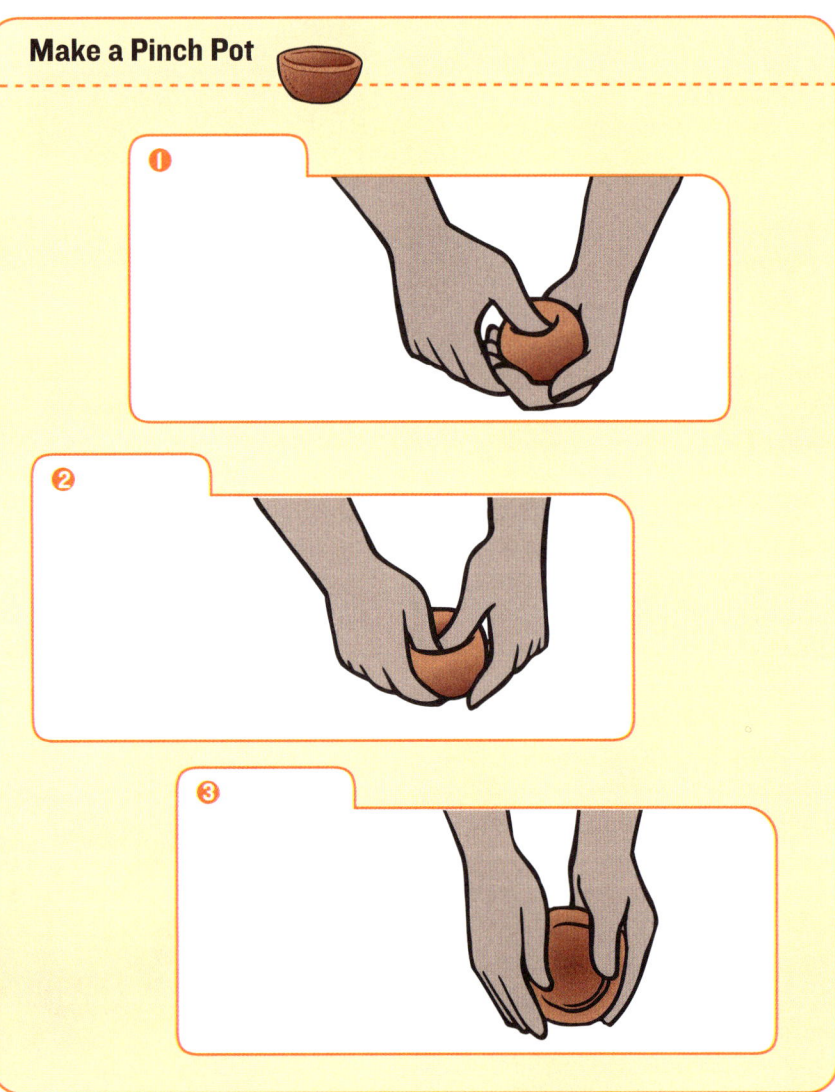

## 2. Coil Up!
Make a piece of pottery, using the coil method. Rub the clay between your palms into snakelike coils then layer the coils on themselves to make a cup or container. Join and smooth the coil layers.

## 3. Handle with Care
Learn how to handle clay with care. Show that you know how to:

- Store moist, unused clay and reclaim pieces of unfired, used clay for future use.
- Wedge clay properly to insure that your piece does not explode in the kiln.
- Store a work in progress properly.
- Use the slip and score method to attach two pieces of moist clay together.

## 4. Time for Tiles
With the help of illustrations, your leader, or another adult, decorate squares of clay with stamps, patterns, graffito (decorating on clay by scratching to the surface below), burnishing, filigree, carving, or modeling. If you can, visit museum collections displaying works of clay and ceramics from other cultures and countries.

## 5. Fuel and Fire
Visit a professional potter's studio, or invite a potter or ceramist to a group or troop meeting. Ask about her craft. Include questions about how to use a kiln, the oven used for hardening clay.

## 6. Grin and Glaze It!
Decorate bisqueware (fired and unglazed ceramic clay). Ask your leader, teacher, or crafts supply salesperson about the effects of underglazes, glazes, or overglazes; the colors of each glaze when they dry; and the opaqueness or shininess of the glaze. Experiment with different glazing techniques: dip, sponge, or paint. Then glaze a piece. Follow instructions so that your glaze will not stick to the kiln shelf and so that lids will not stick to pots during the glaze firing. *Note:* If you want to use your bisqueware as a serving piece for food, it must be glazed at least on the inside in order to be safe.

## 7. Bas-relief
Bas-relief is a form of sculpture that partially sticks out from a flat surface. Create a three-dimensional figure from a plaster block by pouring plaster onto a flat surface, such as a cookie sheet. Remove the plaster when it has hardened and carve a design into it. Then make a bas-relief plaque by rolling out a slab of clay over the plaster mold, making sure the clay goes into the parts you've carved out. Let the clay dry and separate it from the plaster. Decorate with acrylic paints if you like.

## 8. Dream Decorator
Look at modern examples of ceramics and pottery by visiting department or specialty stores with a friend, troop, or family members. Which of these would you use in a room or space in your dream house?

## 9. Pass on the Knowledge
Help a younger Girl Scout or friend make pottery using any one of the methods described above. Arrange to display the results.

## 10. Folk Pottery
Find two or three examples of folk sculpture or pottery at a museum, online, or in magazines. Look for examples from a variety of cultures and places in this and other countries. Observe how pieces from Africa or Asia, for example, are different from those of Central America and the United States. If possible, get pictures or reproductions of the works you are describing. Label them by their titles, dates, and places of origin.

## Create and Invent

# "Collecting" Hobbies

**The key to a lifetime of collecting fun is to enjoy looking for and building a collection of items you love.**

## 1. Building Your Collection

Before starting a collection, ask yourself the following questions. Write down the answers and discuss them with your family or other adult.

- Is the hobby fun?
- Can I afford it?
- Do I have the space for it?
- Is it something that will not harm the environment?

## 2. Share Your Collection with Others

One of the best parts about having a collection is sharing it with others. Arrange, display, or mount your collection so that you are able to show it to others.

## 3. Meet Other Collectors

Find out what clubs, organizations, Web sites, or magazines are out there for people with your hobby. If possible, meet and talk with other collectors, or exchange e-mails to discuss your collection. Be sure to follow the Online Safety Pledge you'll find on the Girls Only Web site *www.gogirlsonly.org*.

## 4. Be the Expert About Your Hobby

Part of the fun of a collecting hobby is being an expert about what you are collecting. Learn more about the items in your collection.

## 5. Organize a Hobby Fair

Get your collecting friends together and show off all of your collections at a hobby fair. Invite your fellow collectors to display their collections in small booths or stations in your school, in your backyard, anyplace!

## 6. Organize Your Hobby

Organize your collection, including the name or classification of each object. List when you acquired the object, how much it cost or where you found it, and something special about each item.

## 7. Go on a Treasure Hunt

Go on a hunt for pieces to add to your collection. Depending on your hobby, you could attend a flea market, street fair, or auction; take a walk on the beach; dig through your family's old letters; or go to an antique or collector's shop.

## 8. Collect for the Community

Sometimes collecting isn't just a hobby, it's a community service. There are many ways to help others by collecting. Collect clothes and donate them to a charity, feed the hungry by organizing a food drive and collecting canned goods, or keep your local park clean by collecting trash. These collections are not meant to be kept or put on display; they're more useful when given away.

## 9. Collecting Globally

Find out whether the items in your collection would be different if you lived someplace else. Do you have a shell collection? Would your shells be different in Mexico, for example, or in Indonesia? If possible, add to your collection with items from other countries.

## 10. Generation to Generation

Sometimes grandparents, parents, or aunts and uncles will hand down their collections. Some collections are in families for years and years. Perhaps your family has a tradition of collecting. Ask members of your family if they collect anything. If they do, what do they collect and how long have they been doing it? Did someone in the family hand the collection down to them? Offer to help carry on the tradition by contributing to the collection, or share with them the things you've learned about collecting.

## Create and Invent

# Creative Solutions

**You know more than you think. And this badge will prove it. Stretch your mind in many directions—find creative solutions to everyday problems.**

### 1. The Chinese Tangram

The tangram is a puzzle made of seven geometric pieces: five triangles, one square, and one rhomboid (parallelogram). The seven pieces can be arranged to create over 300 forms of people, animals, flowers, boats, etc. Make your own tangram puzzle out of paper, cardboard, poster board or wood (see illustration). Then use it to create at least five different things. There are only two rules: 1) Use all seven puzzle pieces on a flat surface. 2) Pieces should touch but not overlap. Make copies of the seven geometric pieces, and work with other girls to see what they can create with the tangram.

## 2. Change Directions

Change your routine for a week. Breaking your routine can help you see things in a new way. Pick one or two things you do the same way or at the same time every day—where or when you do your homework, the way you get dressed, the first thing you do in the morning, the last thing you do at night. Think of a different way, a different time, or a different order of doing each thing. Then make the changes and see if you feel any different.

## 3. Ordinary Items, Extraordinary Uses

Here are ordinary items people use every day: paper clip, rubber band, toothbrush, flashlight, safety pin, bandage, socks, plain white unlined paper. Select three of the items and think of seven unusual ways they can each be used. Have a contest with friends. Set a timer for 45 seconds. Who can come up with the most uses for any one item in that time? Pick another item and reset the timer. Who wins this round?

## 4. Historical Insight

Find out about one of the women listed below who helped solve a problem in her society. Find a way to share her achievements with others.

Clara Barton
Ida B. Wells
Sarah Winnemucca
Rachel Carson
Dolores Huerta
The Trung Sisters
Fannie Farmer
Juliette Gordon Low
Jane Addams
Bessie Coleman
Susan B. Anthony

## 5. Alternative Solutions

With a group of friends, select two stories, fairy tales, films, TV shows, or plays that you have all seen or read. Discuss the story line and the major character and her conflict in each. Come up with three or four other solutions to each situation.

## 6. How Others Solve Problems

People are often hired for their problem-solving ability. Speak to at least one person who frequently has problems to solve on the job. The person you talk to could be, for example, an engineer, manager, plumber, computer software designer, teacher, or carpenter. Ask that person to identify one problem she has had to solve and how she solved it.

## 7. Local, National, and Global Problem Solving

With your friends, family, or Girl Scout troop, come up with a list of ten local, national, or global problems. You might list things like environmental pollution, crime, or overcrowded schools. A local problem could be your community center's need for a basketball court. Then, select *one* item from your list and come up with three ways to help your community (or the larger society) deal with that problem.

## 8. Shipwrecked on an Island

You are shipwrecked on a tropical island and have no idea when you will be rescued. The island is uninhabited but there is a stream of fresh water. If you could have one person and five items (but no boat) with you, who and what would you choose? Why? What choices would your friends or family make? Are they similar to yours?

## 9. Coded Language

With a friend or two, invent your own coded language. Create an alphabet using signs, symbols, pictures, or even letters from the English alphabet. You could add some foreign words to represent other words or phrases. Write a message using your secret code. Be sure to make a dictionary that explains your coded alphabet.

## 10. Create a World

The year is 2040. You are mayor of the first international town on the newly colonized planet, Zepton. The people who have come there from different places, races, and religions, want to create a society of peace and harmony. Describe the laws you would create and what else you would do to achieve such a society.

# Create and Invent

# Dance

Try your hand at many dance styles and steps. Step, tap, and whirl your way through the activities for this badge.

## 1. Watch Their Moves

You can learn a lot about dance by watching how people (and animals) move. Watch two of the following and use your observations to choreograph or design an original dance:

- A group of young children playing
- Animals in a zoo, such as monkeys, elephants, birds, seals, and reptiles
- People on a crowded bus or train, some on their way to or from work
- Dancers rehearsing in a yoga, ballet, or modern dance class
- An athletic team warming up and playing a sport

## 2. Moods and Moves

Watch how people move when they are sad, happy, angry, or lost in thought. Use mood and movement to portray a story or scene through dance.

## 3. Step, Stamp, Stomp!

Tap dance—sometimes called dancing on the "souls" of your feet—is a form of dance that accents fancy footwork. With the help of a tape, books, or a class, learn three of these basic tap dance steps: step, stomp, scuff, brush, and leap. Practice on your own or with a buddy. Wear tap shoes or shoes with hard soles.

## 4. Dance Watcher

Attend a dance performance, watch one on TV, or observe a dance class. How do the dancers' movements match the music? Do the costumes make it more interesting? What did you like most?

## 5. Dance Around the World

Explore the dance of a country other than your own. Not sure where to start? There are Latin dances such as the *cha-cha*, *rumba*, *tango*, *merengue*, and *salsa*; the Spanish *flamenco* dance; folk dances, such as the Polynesian *hula*, Israeli *hora*, Russian *kazatzka*, Polish *mazurka*, and Italian *tarantella*; High Life jazz dances of West Africa; and classical Indian or Indonesian dances. Learn the steps of at least one of those dances well enough to teach it to a friend or group.

## 6. Lines and Squares

In line dancing, dancers are arranged in a line, side by side. Each person performs intricate steps to the beat of music. In square dancing, groups of eight form a square, with each person with a partner, in starting position. A square dance "caller" calls out the patterns to perform and all the partners follow. In your troop or group, attend or put together your own square dance or line dance. Invite friends and family of all ages.

## 7. Country and Western Dancing

Country dancing is fast-paced and musical. Some of the dances that make up country dancing, such as kicker dancing, cowboy dancing, and Western dancing, can be done in couples or as line dances. "Partners" dress in cowboy fashion, from boots to hats. Create a country and western theme dance event, with décor and food to match.

## 8. Belle of the Ball

Ballroom dances have steps that make up a "figure." Once the figure is learned, ballroom dancers work at repeating the figure more gracefully or with added steps. Learn one classic ballroom dance, like a waltz, fox trot, or box step.

## 9. Dance Through the Decades

Swing dancing peaked during the "Big Band" era in the 1940s and 1950s. Rock and roll in the 1950s and 1960s introduced new dance forms, as did disco music in the 1970s. Do some dance research. Ask older relatives and other adults about the dance forms of their youth—were they 50s swingers? 60s twisters? 70s disco queens? Hold a theme night with your troop or a family dance night.

## 10. Dance Party

With your troop, group, or others, hold a dance party. Choose a place that is safe, spacious, and won't be too loud for the neighbors. Try to involve all of the guests in the dancing. If one of the guests has a physical disability, think of ways to include her. Pick someone to act as disc jockey ("DJ") and select and arrange all the tapes and CDs. Be sure to test the sound system ahead of time.

## Create and Invent

# Discovering Technology

How does a computer do what it is supposed to do? How does a CD store all that music? What makes a car run? To figure out the answers to those questions, you have to understand technology. Technology is the science of the way things work. Do some exploring into the past and future of technology.

### 1. Just for Practice
Use a software program to build or design something, or map something.

### 2. All Things Digital
Chips aren't just in cookies! They are in computers, clocks, coffee makers, cars—even toys. With your troop, group, friends, or family, divide into two teams. Each team creates a list of 20 things that have a computer chip in them. Swap lists. Each team then searches for the items. When you meet again, see who has found the most items.

### 3. Find the Inventions
There are lots of hobbies and activities you can do that use technology. Do the "Test Yourself: Find the Inventions" activity in the "Create and Invent" chapter of your *Junior Girl Scout Handbook*.

### 4. Outdoors Technology
Read the sports section of the "Be Healthy, Be Fit" chapter and the "Let's Get Outdoors" chapter of your *Junior Girl Scout Handbook*, or in this book. Find examples of the uses of technology outdoors and in sports activities.

## 5. Technology to Wear
Visit an artisan who makes useable or wearable art, such as jewelry, clothing, or pottery. Find out what technologies are used and how those technologies (specific tools, machinery, materials) have changed through history. Find out if the technologies have been adapted or improved upon by different cultures. Discuss the differences between a product made by an artisan and a product that is made by a machine.

## 6. The Inner Workings
Under the guidance of an adult, pick an item and learn how to put it together, take it apart, care for it, or make simple repairs to it. Some suggestions:

- Hook up and care for a computer and its various hardware attachments, including the printer.
- Hook up and care for a sound system, including the speakers.
- Take care of and change a battery in an electric toothbrush, a watch, clock, or kitchen appliance.
- Maintain a bicycle, including the tires, moving parts, and brake system.

## 7. Tools to Make Life Easier
With the help of an adult, compare the following items to their simpler counterparts. Which item is more useful? Which is easier to use? Discuss your findings with your group or peers.

- An electric screwdriver vs. a manual screwdriver
- An electric can opener vs. a manual can opener
- A flashlight vs. a candle
- A computer vs. a pencil
- A car vs. a horse and wagon
- Man-made fleece vs. wool

## 8. Recycling Technology
Where do garbage and recycled products go? How do you get rid of obsolete machines? Find out how things are recycled in your community by doing one of the following:

- Visit a recycling center or landfill facility and find out what materials are recycled and where they go.
- Pick a product, such as a toy, a piece of clothing, a personal computer, motor oil, or a car. Find out what the options are for recycling or disposing of this product in your community—other than a trip to the landfill. Find a way to encourage your family or community to recycle.
- Find at least three products made from recycled materials. (You can check out catalogs, the Internet, or your local mall for ideas.) Compare those products with products made from non-recycled materials in terms of price and usability.

## 9. The Future Is Here
Investigate a new or developing type of technology that looks exciting to you. Some examples: computer sensory recognition (voice, handwriting, or optical), distance learning, nanotechnology (microscopic machines), gene therapy, or robotics. What are the strengths of the technology? What are its drawbacks? How might you use it in your life? When will it be practical (in terms of cost, ease of use, and safety) or is it practical already? If possible, visit a technology fair, trade show, or showroom for a company that specializes in technology. Or visit a museum that focuses on technology, investigate products online, or in technology related magazines.

## 10. Then and Now
Discover how technology has changed the way things are done. Pick at least three careers and find out how technology is used in each of them. Has technology changed the jobs, or the way the jobs are performed? Share your findings with your troop or group by role playing, participating in a panel discussion, or hosting a discussion by people in those professions.

Create and Invent

# "Doing" Hobbies

"Doing" hobbies are activities that you like to do—singing, playing games or sports, cooking, taking pictures, gardening, painting, bird-watching, reading, or playing an instrument. Once you find a doing hobby that "fits," you'll spend hours having lots of fun.

## 1. Handmade Especially for You
Use your hobby to make a gift for someone. If you sing, you can sing that person a song. If you read, you can read a story to that person.

## 2. The Right Fit
Ask yourself these questions about your hobby and discuss the answers with an adult family member or other adult.

- Is it fun?
- Can I afford it?
- Do I have space for it?
- Where will I do it?
- Can I do it alone or with others?
- Do I have time for it?
- Are there safety or environmental factors to consider?

## 3. Learning a "Doing" Hobby
Practice your hobby. Demonstrate or try to teach your hobby to others.

## 4. Hobbies in the Past
Learn something about the history of your hobby and about others who share your hobby.

## 5. Your Hobby: A Possible Career
Sometimes the skills you learn from your hobby are skills you will use in a future career. Find out about three kinds of careers that are related to your hobby. How are they different? How are they the same? Can you see yourself in one of them?

## 6. Do Your Hobby with Others
Participate in an activity with other people who also share your hobby. For example, sing with a musical group, hike with your troop/group members, play an instrument in a band, join a bird-watching club, or go to a garden or flower exhibit.

## 7. What in the World Are You "Doing"?
What do people do as a hobby in other countries? Choose a country other than the U.S. and find out about a hobby that's popular there. You can use the Internet or your local library to get information. Or ask someone who has lived in or traveled to that country to tell you what she/he knows about hobbies in that area. If possible, try the hobby yourself.

## 8. Give Back
Sometimes your hobby will allow you to do something for your community or the environment. For example, if your hobby is gardening, volunteer to help plant flowers at your local park. If you like to read, read out loud to a senior citizen who has trouble reading the small print of the newspaper. Find a way to "give back" to your community through your hobby.

## 9. Hobby Together
Find out about organizations and clubs that promote your hobby. If you have a hobby, there is probably a club for it. For example, there are clubs for sports (with members from beginners to experts), reading, knitting, and photography.

## 10. Find a New One
Many activities in your *Junior Girl Scout Handbook* would make great hobbies. Find an activity that interests you and find out more about it as a potential hobby.

## Create and Invent

# Drawing and Painting

**Capture your creativity using paint, a pencil, a pen, or a mouse.**

- Pastels
- Paints 
- Chalk 
- Crayons 
- Felt-tip Markers/Ink Pens 
- Colored Pencils

## 1. Media Savvy

Explore different types of media: paints, crayons, pastels, chalk, felt-tip markers, ink pens, colored pencils, charcoal, or computer programs for drawing and painting. Choose three types of media and make three different pictures of the same thing using a different medium each time. How does the use of different media change the picture?

## 2. Primary—Secondary

Learn the primary and secondary colors. Practice mixing primary and secondary colors to make new colors. Make a picture that uses the colors you have created.

## 3. No Brushes

Experiment with two different painting techniques. You can try: finger painting, where you use your fingers instead of brushes; sponge painting, where you use sponges or pieces of sponge instead of brushes; string painting, where you dip string in paint and make a design on your paper with the wet string; or spatter painting, where you put a toothbrush in paint and knock it against a small screen or hard edge to "spatter" the paint on paper.

## 4. What's Your Line?

Make two pictures that show different uses of line. Experiment with pencils, felt-tip markers, crayons, or pieces of chalk to get different kinds of lines: thick, thin, straight, curved, broken, vertical, horizontal, and diagonal. Color in between the lines if you choose.

## 5. In Shape

Use shapes to make a picture. Look at an object or scene and try to find the basic shapes: triangle, circle, square, rectangle, etc. What shapes would you use to make a human being? What shapes would you use to make a flower?

## 6. Shades of Color

Create two pictures showing many shades of the same color. What do darker shades do? What do lighter shades do? How can you use color to make something appear closer or farther away in your picture?

## 7. It's How You Look at It

Find out about perspective. Look at something far away. Measure it with your fingers or a ruler. How big is it? What happens if you move closer to the object? How can you show this on paper? Draw or paint a picture in which you use perspective.

## 8. On the Wall

Murals are pictures painted on walls. Murals usually tell a story in a series of scenes and may be painted by groups of artists. Decide with your group what the design of your mural will be. Sketch it out on a piece of graph paper. You can make a mural using a long roll of white paper or butcher paper. First, cover the floor with newspapers. Then, stretch your paper on top of them. Next, block out parts of the mural on the rolled out paper using your sketch as a guide. Each painter may be responsible for her own section or painters can work together on each part before starting on the next.

## 9. On Your Own

Create an art gallery or art show where you can display your work and those of others.

## 10. Women Who Paint

Read an article, watch a TV show or video, or look online and find out about a woman artist. How did she get involved in the arts? How has she achieved success?

## Create and Invent

# Folk Arts

Folk arts are the arts of everyday people, like you and your friends or family. They include dance, song, stories (folk tales), crafts, and even special foods that reflect the history and tastes of a particular group of people. Add color to your life with folk arts.

### 1. Family Portrait
Before the days of instant and digital cameras, painters often traveled around, stopping to make pictures of families wherever they were asked. Often, they were asked to include details that were important to the family. Draw or paint a picture of yourself or your family as an artist might have done it before cameras were invented. Include some things that are dear to you and your family, such as family heirlooms (valuable objects handed down from generation to generation), favorite hobbies, toys, books, or collections.

### 2. A Picture Tells a Thousand Thoughts
Look at some old photographs of your family or other people. Examine the poses, clothes, and facial expressions. Do they seem different from what you see in pictures taken recently? What do the pictures tell you about the people and their lives? Write captions or a short story about the pictures.

### 3. Tell a Story
Practice the art of storytelling. If possible, get together with a local storyteller or children's librarian and ask how she/he keeps an audience interested. Find a fairy tale, myth, or legend that you like. Practice telling it out loud, as you would if you were rehearsing a part in a play. Retell it, or part of it, to a group, perhaps at a special ceremony or event.

### 4. Fancy Feet
Learn a folk dance. Teach a friend or troop members some folk steps and dances.

### 5. Traditional Art
Learn an art form that was traditional for girls 75 years or more ago. Complete a small project using that art form.

### 6. What Toys Tell Us
Find pictures of old children's toys or games, or visit a museum, historical house, or antique store. Talk to grandparents or older relatives who grew up in the pre-electronic age about the toys they played with as youngsters.

### 7. Folk Arts Around the Globe
Look for examples and pictures of traditional folk arts from at least three countries. Do a folk art project either by following written instructions or by doing what someone teaches you.

### 8. A Feast of Folk Crafts
Work on a large folk art project that requires lots of helping hands, such as a taffy pull, a kite flying festival, or a troop quilt.

### 9. Fresh and Original
Create a new folk art product, using handmade or store-bought items. Some examples are adding enamel paint designs to old pottery or dishes, making scented candles or soaps, making paper, or adding decorative items (beads, buttons, ribbons, etc.) to clothing. As with any project, use non-toxic materials that meet safety standards.

### 10. Time Travel
Visit a place near you where antiques, historical crafts, or collections of folk art are on display. You might visit museums, antique stores, or places designated as historic landmarks. Find out how items on display were used in the past.

Create and Invent

# Jeweler

Make and design your own necklaces, pins, bracelets, or other ornaments. All types of materials can be used.

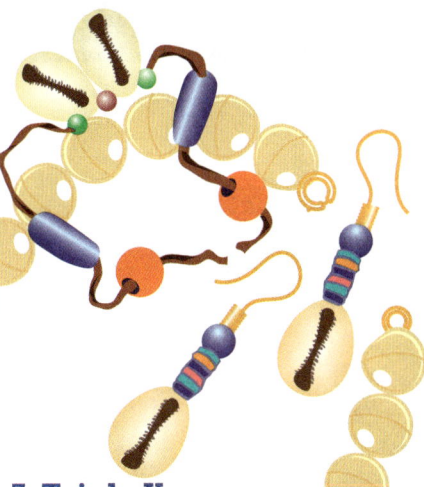

## 1. Jewelry from Everyday Objects

Make a piece of jewelry using materials that are not precious metals or gems. You might make a pin, a necklace, a bracelet, or a hair ornament. Some ideas for materials are:

- Handmade beads: Form beads from papier-mâché, clay, colorful magazine pages, wrapping paper, or aluminum foil.
- Hardware: Use hardware "findings" such as screws, nuts, washers, wire, and chains.
- Paper: Paint or draw designs on pieces of paper. Several pieces can be joined with cord or thread, or glued together.

You can protect and harden the finished designs with a clear varnish or clear nail polish. Safety pins can be glued to backs to make pins, holes can be punched to attach pieces to necklaces, and hairpins or barrettes can be attached to make hair ornaments.

## 2. Macramé

Knot string and other cords into decorative patterns. Interweave beads, sanded pieces of wood, and shells to create unique macramé jewelry. See the "Create and Invent" chapter in your *Junior Girl Scout Handbook*.

## 3. Jewelry from Other Lands

Learn about the jewelry of four different cultures (for example, from an American Indian culture or a culture from Europe, South America, or Africa). Or look at an ancient culture, such as early Egypt or Asia. Describe the materials and styles used, and their customs and traditions for wearing jewelry. If possible, find pictures of the type of jewelry worn in each culture.

## 4. Jewelers' Skills

Learn about the different jewelry-making techniques of soldering, casting, hammering, and molding. Can you describe a situation when each might be used, or find a picture showing an example? If possible, visit an artist who uses one or more of those techniques to make jewelry.

## 5. Take a Tour

Visit a museum or gallery exhibit of jewelry. Take an organized tour of the exhibit or ask someone knowledgeable to explain the work. Be sure to bring a notebook and sketch any designs you'd like to remember!

## 6. Something Natural

Make a piece of jewelry out of organic material (something found in nature). You can combine a variety of colors, shapes, and textures by using shells, stones, seeds, and other materials you could find on an outdoor scavenger hunt. Look at the section about swaps in the "Adventures in Girl Scouting" chapter in your *Junior Girl Scout Handbook* for ideas about jewelry made from rocks and from flowers.

## 7. Triple Up

Make an item of jewelry that combines at least three different elements. For example, you can combine leather laces with wire and stones. Come up with other interesting combinations.

## 8. Store Your Gems

Make a box for your jewelry. You can decorate a small cardboard, metal, or wooden box with decoupage, or decorate a small basket. Add decorative touches with pieces of discarded jewelry, pearls, beads, or shells. See the "Create and Invent" chapter in your *Junior Girl Scout Handbook* for information about decoupage.

## 9. True Gemstones

Learn about one type of stone or mineral used in jewelry. For example, you might choose to learn more about your birthstone. Does the stone or mineral have any special meaning? Are there any legends or myths about its special power?

## 10. Get the Message?

Find out about the symbolism of different kinds of jewelry, such as wedding bands or friendship bracelets. Make a piece of jewelry to give to someone else as a symbol of your friendship.

## Create and Invent

# "Making" Hobbies

"Making" hobbies are activities in which you create something. See the list of crafts in the box for some of the "making" hobbies. Start now to learn about the world of crafts. Choose a craft and try the activities.

*My scarf is almost finished.*

## 1. Choose Your Craft

Before starting any hobby you need to see if it will fit into your lifestyle. Ask yourself these questions and discuss the answers with an adult family member or your troop or group leader.

- Is this hobby fun?
- Can I afford it?
- Do I have time for it?
- Do I have room for it?
- Are there any environmental concerns?

What craft meets your needs?

## 2. Practice Your Craft

Check with experts and in craft books, or surf the Web for ideas and instructions. Go to craft and variety stores or check around the house for supplies. With adult help if needed, make at least three examples of your craft.

## 3. Re-Craft

Practice your craft using a material you've never used before. Make at least one example of the new craft. Show your new craft item to others and explain what you have learned about using different materials.

## 4. Where and When

Learn more about your craft by looking at global and historical examples. Try finding global examples at craft fairs and museums, in books, and by surfing the Web. Look for historical examples at antique shows, flea markets, and museums, and in books. Discuss what you learned with your troop, group, or family members. If possible, show some examples of global and historical crafts to others.

## 5. Make a Recycled Craft

Try making craft items from things you normally throw away. Look in craft books or on the Web for ideas on how to use egg cartons, juice lids, packing peanuts, or other items. You can make a craft that you are familiar with or choose a new craft entirely.

## 6. Make a Craft with a Nature Theme

Many crafts have nature themes. Learn how to use nature in crafts. Make a craft item with a focus on plants and animals. Here are some examples:

- A print made with leaves
- A mosaic made from eggshells
- A basket made of plant materials

## 7. An Honor

Your craft project is being placed in the "Museum of Modern Crafts." Write a description of the piece that will appear in the museum. Include details of tools, materials used, and other interesting information.

## 8. Your Own Gift Wrap

After you have made several craft items, you might want to give some away as gifts. Design your own gift wrap and wrap up your homemade gifts.

## 9. Crafty Cash

Find out more about people involved in the crafts business. Visit a crafts person where she works or have her come to your troop or group meeting to share information about her job. If that is not possible, find information about professional crafts people in books or magazines or on the Web. Share the information that you learn with your troop, group, or family.

## 10. Safe Crafts

Help protect yourself and others while you are practicing your craft by making a Craft Safety Checklist. Think about the tools and supplies involved in making crafts. Brainstorm with others to come up with a list of at least eight to ten safety guidelines. Start your list with these two safety rules:

1. Store sharp tools in a safe place. Never leave them on the floor.
2. Use aerosols in a well-ventilated area, never in a small, closed room.

Write down your Craft Safety Checklist and keep it for future reference.

## Types of Crafts

Knitting
Crocheting
Embroidery
Sketching
Photography
Weaving
Sewing
Jewelry making
Painting
T-shirt design
Pottery
Basket weaving
Tole painting
Macramé
Decoupage
Wreath making
Mosaics
Woodworking

## Create and Invent

# Math Whiz

Math is used everywhere: to make change, follow a recipe, build a table, figure out how far it is to the next town—even to the next galaxy! Become a math whiz and you can do anything.

## 1. Math Hunt
How many daily examples of math can you and your friends think of? There are checkbooks to balance, measurements to use for recipes, tips to calculate, grocery charges to add. Set a timer for three minutes. Who can think of the most math-related daily activities?

## 2. Your Numbers Are…
Measure yourself in five different ways. The length of your arm or leg, the length of your stride, and the amount of cereal you put in your bowl are just a few of the ways you add up. Come up with your own! See the chart on page 235 to convert your measurements into metric.

## 3. Shape Up
Look for geometric shapes around your home, school, playground, or other area. You can check floors, walls, doors, windows, leaves, flowers, or other items. Find out the names of the shapes you don't already know.

## 4. Calculate Your Flight Time
Choose a destination that you would like to visit anywhere in the world. Using a world map with a distance key, figure out how far the place is from your hometown. How long would it take you to drive there? Fly there?

## 5. Make It Count
Can you tell how many jelly beans are in a jar without counting every one? Have an adult or older friend fill a jar with jelly beans or other small candies. Make sure she carefully counts how many are put in, records the number, and keeps it somewhere safe (no peeking). Then you and your friends try to guess the number in the jar. How did each of you come up with your number? What's the correct answer? Who was closest?

## 6. Make a Math Puzzle
Draw a square divided into nine equal spaces (3x3). Put a penny on each square (nine pennies). Two players take turns removing one penny at each turn. A player must always leave at least one penny in each row or column. The last person to play wins. If a player takes a penny that makes a column or row empty, she loses. Play at least 10 games. Try to discover a strategy for winning the game.

## 7. Predictions
Make a prediction, such as, "I think that between 2:00 and 3:00 p.m., one out of every five people walking down the street will be wearing jeans." Make a plan to check your prediction. Then carry it out. Compare your prediction with the results.

## 8. Make Your Own Code
Assign the letter "A" a number value. If A=7, B would equal 8, E would equal 11, and so on. Write out a "secret message" for a friend, using equations to substitute for each letter. For example: If A=7, E=11, L=18 and P=22, you could spell out the word "apple" by writing: 3+4, 10+12, 2x11, 23-5, 22÷2. Send your friend a message and see if she can unravel your meaning. Don't forget to share the key to the code with her!

## 9. Scale It
Visit a playground and measure or estimate the height, length, and width of several pieces of equipment. Then, using what you have learned, create a model, or drawing of it. Decide what your scale will be and note it on your model.

## 10. Just the Stats
Pick your favorite sport and find five examples of how math principles are used in the game.

## Create and Invent

# Ms. Fix-It

**Learn how to do basic repairs by doing the following activities. You'll be a Ms. Fix-It in no time.**

### 1. Call for Help
Find out what you should do when faced with each of these emergencies. Learn when you can help and when it is best to call for help and leave the area until the emergency is over.

- You smell gas.
- The smoke alarm or security system turns on accidentally or won't shut off after an emergency is over.
- A toilet or sink gets clogged.
- The thermostat won't shut off or fails to turn on the furnace.
- A washing machine is overflowing.

### 2. It's Electric!
Learn more about how to handle and fix electrical problems properly. Do at least three of the following:

- Have someone show you what to do if the lights go out while you are home alone.
- Show that you know how to follow three or more safety rules when using electricity.
- Look at the electrical panel box where you live.
- Find out about fuses and circuit breakers and how to change or reset them.
- Find out how to turn off the electricity in case of flood, storm, or other emergency.
- Know how and whom to call in your community or in your building (owner, superintendent) in case of an emergency.

### 3. Flash
Keep a flashlight in your repair kit or in an easy-to-reach spot in your home. Learn how to change the battery and the light bulb.

### 4. Fix a Faucet
A washer is a small disk with a hole in the middle. It can be made of metal, rubber, or plastic. A washer is placed beneath a nut or at a joint. Its main job is to prevent leaking. A common place to find a washer is in a faucet. Find out what fixtures in and around your home require washers. Then, learn how to replace a washer that is broken or worn out. Keep some spare washers in your repair kit for future use.

### 5. A Simple Fix-It
Call a plumber for major plumbing problems, but you can solve some common problems involving a toilet yourself. Review the inner workings of the toilet tank. With the lid off, flush the toilet and watch how everything works. Learn the names of the parts, some of the common problems, and how to do the repairs.

Pliers

## 6. Conserve Energy
Conserving energy not only helps your parents reduce the cost of utilities, but it is also good for the environment. Do at least one of the following to help conserve energy in your home:

- Find out what changes you could make in your home that would help save water.
- Learn how to weather-strip your windows and doors.
- Find out about energy-efficient light bulbs and install them in the lights of your home.

## 7. Hang It Up
Show your ability to hang an item on a wall. Learn about the different types of walls and what types of fasteners are best used for each.

## 9. Repairs Within Your Community
Use your knowledge of basic repairs to help others. Find a community organization that could benefit from your "fix-it smarts," or help a senior citizen who needs to make some repairs at home.

Hammer

## 10. Read All About It
Read the operating instructions that came with a major appliance. What are three common problems that appliance may have? How do you fix them? *Hint:* Look at the troubleshooting section in the instruction booklet.

Saw

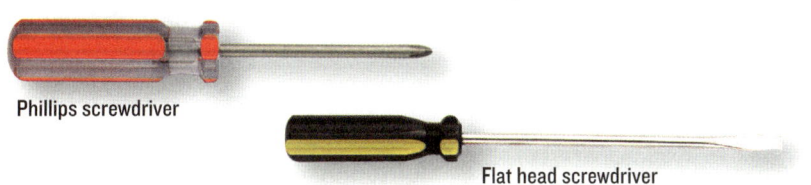
Phillips screwdriver

Flat head screwdriver

## 8. Out and About the Home
There are things inside and outside your house or apartment that may require some repair work. Ask an adult for assistance and do two or more of the following:

- Help paint or refinish a piece of furniture.
- Tighten the screws to the handles of your kitchen cupboards and drawers.
- Help fix a crack or hole in a wall, sidewalk, or driveway.
- Help with some painting, papering, or other repair to your walls.
- Help rewire a lamp or replace the cord on an electrical appliance.

Sandpaper

Awl

## Create and Invent

# Prints and Graphics

You can make a print or design out of almost anything you see. Use them to decorate paper, fabric, clothing—even Web pages.

## 1. Rubbed the Right Way
Make three different rubbings—you can use anything that's got a raised or engraved design. Place a blank sheet of paper over the surface. Rub back and forth with a piece of crayon, chalk, or pencil. Experiment. Repeat patterns and make designs with different objects.

## 2. Stamp Designs
Make your own stamp. Cut a design into a soft object like a potato, eraser, or sponge. Press the design into a shallow plate of water-based paint or an ink pad and then stamp it onto paper.

## 3. Nature's Prints
Find a natural object, such as a leaf or a piece of bark. Press one side of the object into an ink pad, or paint one side with water-based paint, and place it on a piece of paper. Place another sheet over the object and press on it firmly with your fingertips. Lift the top sheet of paper and the image of the object will be revealed. Use paint, markers, or colored pencils to complete your design.

## 4. Stencil Fun
Create a stencil. Draw a design on a piece of stiff paper and then cut out the design. Place your stencil onto another piece of paper. Using paint, markers, or colored pencils, color over the design. Overlap your designs or try this on other materials like fabric or wood.

## 5. Silk Screening
Learn about silk screening. Create a design that can be easily silk-screened. Print your design.

## 6. Graphic Design
Try your hand at using graphic design software. Create a design and print it up.

## 7. Eye For Design
Use one of the print or design techniques in this badge to create some stationery, cards, or wrapping paper.

## 8. Help By Design
Use your print-making skills in a service project. You can make note cards or stationery for an organization, programs for an event, or posters for a community center.

## 9. Decorating with Prints
Create a suitable mat and frame for one of your prints to use in your home or give as a gift. Or use one of your print designs as a wall hanging.

## 10. Book Design
Design the page of a book, including choosing the font, creating an illustration, and adding a border.

## Create and Invent

# Puzzlers

**Mazes, crosswords, math tricks, magic. All these involve working with puzzles. Test your brain power by solving or creating puzzles.**

### 1. A Maze with a Theme
Design your own maze on paper. Give your maze a theme, such as "Help the Bird Find Her Nest" or "Show Sue How to Get to the Beach." Add pictures to make it more interesting. Make copies of your maze and ask at least two other people to solve it. Ask them what they think could make the maze easier or harder.
OR
Create a walking maze on the ground, using tape or chalk, for others to test their skills. Or visit a garden or cornfield that has a maze you can navigate.

### 2. Crossword Puzzler
Pick a topic and make up your own crossword puzzle. Be sure you have at least five clues across and five clues down. You can use graph paper or a computer software program to help lay out your puzzle. Have a friend or family member try to solve your crossword.

### 3. Do You See It?
Optical illusions "trick" your eyes. You may see one thing, while someone sees another, or, something may seem to be something that it is not. Look at the optical illusion above. What did you think when you looked at it? Try out optical illusions on your family or friends.

# PICARIA

## 4. Picaria

Picaria is a game played by the Zuni people of the southwestern part of the United States. It is thought that the first form of this game was created by Arabian people who lived in Northwestern Africa. They introduced the game to people who lived in Spain hundreds and hundreds of years ago. Spanish travelers brought the game with them to the United States more than 400 years ago.

### What You Need

- A game board. The board may be drawn on the ground, stone, or on wood.
- Six counters (pebbles, bottle caps, leftover game pieces)—three for each player.

### What You Do

You need two players. Each player has three counters of one color. You move your counters on the diagonal lines attempting to make "three-in-a-row" where the lines intersect.

1. Players take turns putting counters on the game board.
2. Neither player can put a counter in the center spot until all six counters have been put on the board.
3. When the players have taken turns getting all six counters on the game board, the next player may move a counter along a line to the next empty intersection to try to make a row of three counters.
4. Jumping is not allowed.
5. The first person to get three-in-a-row wins.

There are eight ways to do this. Set a time limit. If no one makes a row of three in the given time, the game ends in a tie. Play another version of this game from Ghana and Nigeria called *Achi*, with each player using four counters instead of three.

## 5. It's in the Cards

Learn and perform three card tricks that use mathematical or logical thinking. See if your audience can figure out how you did your tricks.

## 6. It's Magic

Become an amateur magician. Learn three magic tricks. You can refer to a book or a kit, or ask someone to help. Practice each trick and then perform them for others. Ask if anyone can solve the trick. Or attend a magic show and learn how at least one of the tricks was done.

## 7. The Game of Nim

Play the game of Nim, described below, several times with another person. If you are playing with a group, change partners after each game. Figure out strategies that might help you win. Here's how to play:

1. Put nine pennies in three rows, with four pennies in one row, three in the next, and two in the last row.
2. The two players take turns removing pennies using these rules: A player can take away pennies from only one row during a turn. The player can take as many pennies as she likes from the row, but must take at least one.
3. The player who takes the last penny is the winner.

## 8. Scramble

Word scrambles are a type of puzzle. For example, the letters "nanaba" can be unscrambled to spell the word "banana." Choose a topic, such as sports, books, or Girl Scouts. Scramble the letters of five or 10 words on that topic. Copy your puzzle and try it out on your family, friends, or troop. See who can unscramble the most words in two minutes.

## 9. Word Search

Make up a word search using a piece of graph paper or a grid that you create. Chose a theme and a title that reflects the words that can be found, such as weather, school, or seasons. Include at least ten words in your search. Ask friends or family to find the hidden words.

## 10. One Dollar Words

In this math puzzle, each letter of the alphabet represents an amount of money. A = 1 cent, B = 2 cents, C = 3 cents, and so on. Find at least three words that are worth exactly $1.00. Ask your friends and family members to join in the fun, and see who can come up with the largest number of $1.00 words in a week.

## Create and Invent

# Sew Simple

**Improve your wardrobe. Redecorate your room. Make a gift for the holidays. How? By sewing! You can make things for yourself or others when you learn to sew by hand or with the latest technology. It's Sew Simple.**

### 1. Hands Down
Try your hand at hand sewing. Some stitches to try are:

- Running stitch
- Hemming stitch
- Slip stitch
- Catch stitch

Need help? Ask someone who can sew, take classes at a fabric store or community center, or look through sewing books or sewing Web sites.

### 2. A Stitch in Time
Using written instructions and someone to guide you, explore machine stitching on a sewing machine. Try your hand at one or more of the following:

- Basting stitch
- Zig-zag stitch
- Seam stitching

### 3. Foot Fun
Decorate your socks. You can stitch fabric to the upper cuff of your socks or add lace. You can even embroider a cool design on them.

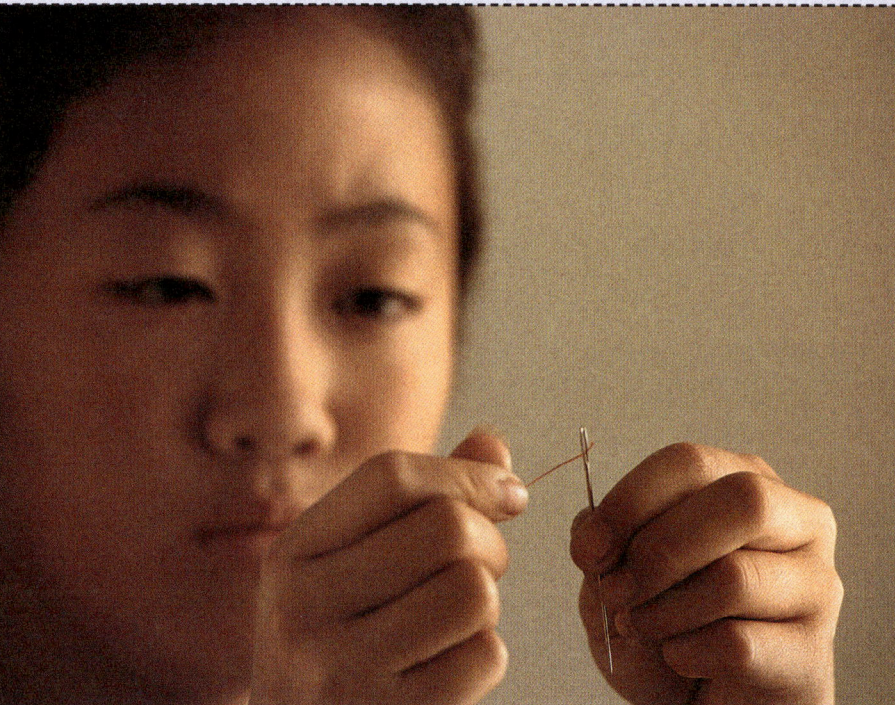

### 4. Program It
Many sewing machines contain mini-computers. They can be programmed to sew decorative stitches. Learn how to program a design on the sewing machine, then try to make the design.

### 5. Pick a Pattern
What do you want to make? Look through a pattern book and pick one out. In addition to style, look at:

- The number of pieces to put together
- Extras like interfacing, zippers, or elastic waists
- The type of fabric recommended by the pattern company
- The amount of fabric needed

These will help you pick patterns that are easy enough to complete, and challenging enough to keep you interested.

\* See page 235 for the metric conversion chart.

### 6. A Perfect Fit
Use the diagram on a pattern envelope to figure out your size. Have a friend or family member measure you every place you see a solid line on the diagram. Figure out your size according to that diagram.

### 7. Sew for Service
Choose some items to make for people in need. Baby quilts and baby clothing are welcome at women's shelters and some newborn units at hospitals. "Ditty" bags can help residents of a homeless shelter keep their belongings close by. Many sewing clubs work on group service projects. Find out what you can do.

### 8. Hospital Helpers
Children going through radiation treatment or chemotherapy often lose their hair. With a group, make "cancer caps" for them to wear until their hair grows back. Be sure to use really soft fabric. Designs are available online or at sewing stores around the country. Donate your caps to a hospital in your area. You can make and sign cards to go with the caps.

### 9. Find the Fabric
Fabrics have difference widths, textures, colors, and designs. Visit a fabric store to see the differences. What fabrics do you like? How much fabric will you need to make a particular item? What's the cost?

### 10. Sew a Puppet
1. Trace the puppet pattern pieces onto tracing paper. Then cut out four hands and two faces. Fold the tracing paper and place the straight side of the body pattern even with the fold of the tracing paper. Cut two folded bodies.
2. To make the puppet out of fabric, use the tracing paper as a pattern and make the same cuts on fabric around the tracing paper pattern. You may need to pin the paper pattern in place.
3. Match notch 1 on each hand piece to notch 1 on each arm and sew them together along the dotted line. Put the right sides of the body and hands together and sew, leaving the bottom edge open. Turn the body right side out so that the seams are on the inside of the puppet body.
4. For facial features, paint or sew on buttons or pieces of fabric onto the face, being careful not to sew through to the back of the head.
5. Sew the head along the dotted line, leaving 2 inches* open
6. Sew the front part of the head to the front of the puppet's body using a backstitch or running stitch. Do the same with the back side. Leave an opening for your fingers to come from the body into the neck opening.
7. Add lace, rickrack, ribbons, and applique as decoration.

**Puppet pattern**

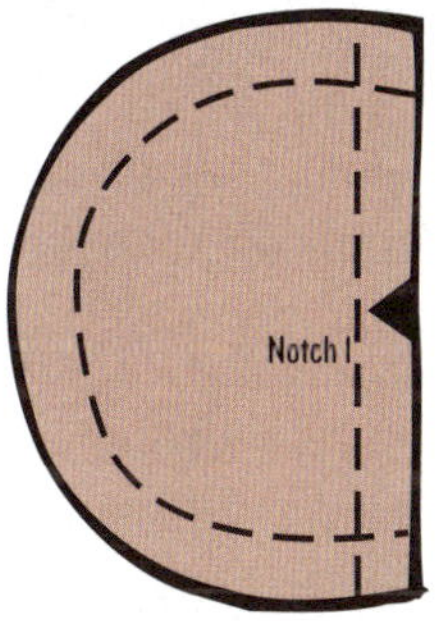

Hand 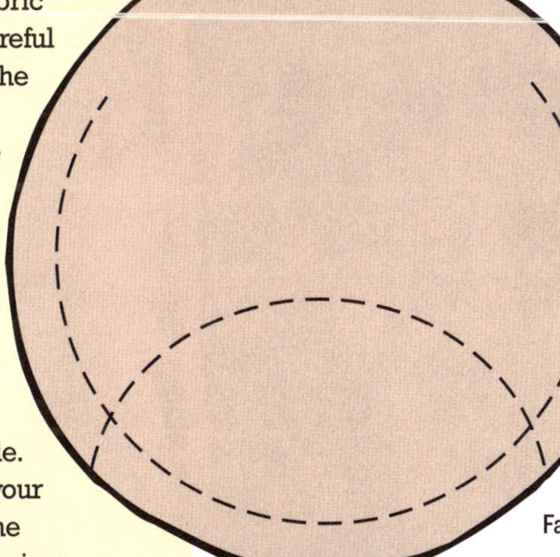 — Face 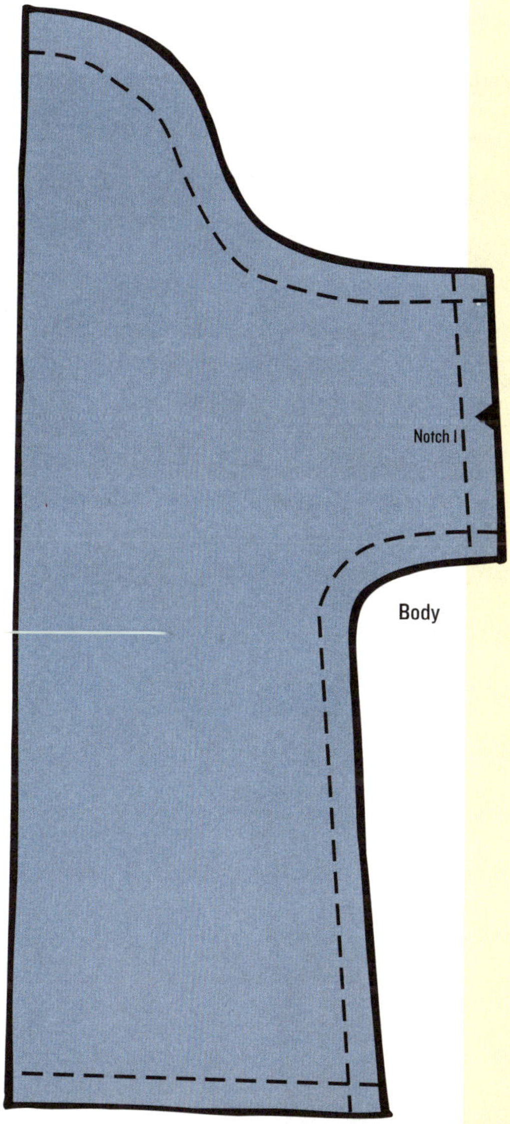 — Body (Notch 1)

You might want to use your puppet to help a Brownie Girl Scout earn her "Puppets, Dolls and Plays" Try-It.

## Create and Invent

# Theater

Do you picture yourself center stage? Or are you the behind-the-scenes type, happy to design and build costumes or sets for a production? Find out all about creating, preparing for, and performing a show.

### 1. Make a Mask
Create a mask to be used in a skit you create.

### 2. Character Traits
A play has a lead character, supporting characters, and extras. Read a play and choose a character that you would like to play. Show that you understand your character by describing the following:

- The character's personality (Is she fun-loving, moody, independent, caring?)
- The character's behavior (Does she do kind acts? Does she plot revenge?)
- What other people think of your character (Do they look up to her? Do they want her to leave town?)

### 3. Character Charades
Write types of characters on pieces of paper and place them in a bowl. Each person picks a character and, without talking, acts it out until the group correctly guesses who or what it is. Create a real or a unique character. Some examples: a skier, an elephant, a clock, a camper, a detective, a cyclist, or a plane.

### 4. Mirror Mimic
Try to "mirror mimic" with someone else. One person is the leader. The other person plays the mirror and copies everything the leader does. Take turns being the leader. For example, you can make large circles with your hands, move side to side or up and down, knock on a door, comb your hair, climb a ladder, dance, or brush your teeth.

### 5. How You Say It
Say "I did it" five times, expressing a different emotion each time. For example, say it with pride, guilt, fear, happiness, surprise, or horror.

### 6. Mix It Up, Make It Up
Using basic materials (pieces of fabrics, yarn, newspapers, sheets, old clothes, costume jewelry, etc.), design your own costumes and props for a performance.

### 7. The Changing Faces in Theater
Take a trip to a makeup counter or to a place where theatrical makeup is sold. Watch a demonstration. Then make up one complete face for a special character, such as a man, a clown, or an animal.

### 8. Belt It Out
Make sure you're loud enough to be heard. Put your hands on your waist. As you inhale, your waist should expand against your hands, pushing them out. As you exhale, your waist should deflate, like a balloon. Breathe like this three or four times. How far out can you get your hands? As you exhale, say, "Ahhh." Have a friend time you. How long can you hold that "Ahhh?" Try again, only this time go for volume. How loudly can you say "Ahhh?" Try again, going for both volume and time.

### 9. Theater Around the World
Find pictures, make a drawing, prepare a booklet, or do a dramatic presentation of a style of theater from another part of the world.

### 10. See It Live!
Attend a play, a theatrical performance, a dinner theater, or a school or community production.

## Create and Invent

# Toymaker

**TOYS!** You have them. You use them. You share them and you trade them. Now you can do more than just play with toys. You can make them.

## 1. It's Your Design
Create a toy of your own design in one of the following categories: rolling toy, spinning toy, balancing toy, stuffed toy, mechanical toy, musical toy.

## 2. Toys Around the World
Find out about toys in other countries or in several cultures in the United States. Check out library books and Internet sites for information. Create a simple toy that you discovered.

## 3. Toys Through History
Investigate the history of toys. What were some of the earliest kinds of toys? What kinds of toys did your grandparents and great grandparents play with? If possible, visit a museum or historical society to see a collection of toys. What kinds of materials were they made from? Learn how to make one of these toys and make it.

## 4. Make a Doll House
Make a doll house for yourself or a younger child. Use wood, foam board, or heavy cardboard. You can make furniture from wood, clay, cardboard, plastic, or papier-mâché. Decorate the walls and floor of your house with wallpaper, paint, or other materials.

## 5. Make a Board Game
Find out what makes a good board game by playing several different kinds. Then decide upon a theme for a game of your own. Decide how players will move, make up rules, and create the board. Try your game out with friends and family.

## 6. Challenge the Imagination
Create a brainteaser game, toy, or puzzle. It could be a mechanical puzzle, a mathematical game, a string game, a computer-created puzzle, or a trivia game. Play it with family or friends.

## 7. Design an Educational Game
Many games help you learn while you are having fun. Create a game that helps someone learn something new.

## 8. Toy Safety
Talk to an adult about toy hazards. Do a toy hazard check at home, at a nursery school, or at a day care center. Share your findings with adults and children and help develop a plan to eliminate toy hazards.

## 9. Toy Recycling
Help collect toys and fix them up for kids who would benefit from them. You could help out with an existing toy drive in your community or start one in a group.

## 10. Trash It!
A "trash toy" is made from anything that might be thrown away. Ask your family to save some things they would usually toss out. Boxes, milk cartons, cans, egg trays, string, buttons, shells, and newspapers are just a few of the things you might use. Let your imagination run wild and see what kind of trash toy you can create. Will it be a set of musical instruments? A wheeled toy? Stilts? Share your toy with your troop, group, or others.

## 10 Toy Hazards to Avoid

1. Toys left on stairs.
2. Toys with small parts for children under three.
3. Toys for an older child in the hands of a younger child.
4. Toys with sharp points or rough edges.
5. Uninflated or broken balloons for children under eight.
6. Toys with heating elements for children under eight.
7. Sports equipment without protective gear.
8. Broken toys.
9. Toys not played with properly (hitting, throwing, etc.).
10. Any toy used without sensible supervision.

[Reprinted courtesy of Toy Manufacturers of America]

## Create and Invent

# Visual Arts

Works of art follow rules and patterns. Understanding them can help you appreciate the beauty of art and improve your own artwork.

### color wheel

- yellow
- yellow-orange
- orange
- red-orange
- red
- red-violet
- violet
- blue-violet
- blue
- blue-green
- green
- yellow-green

### 1. Color Wise
Find out about primary and secondary colors. Make a color wheel and explain it to others. What are complementary colors? Practice mixing colors to make new ones. Create a picture using all the colors on a color wheel and some of the new colors that you created.

### 2. Color Your Mood
Using color, create a picture that shows a feeling or emotion. You can try:

- Happiness
- Sadness
- Surprise
- Joy
- Calm

### 3. Black and White
Make a design or picture using only black and white. Look for examples of drawings, advertisements, and photographs that are in black and white instead of color. Share some of these with others. See if you can figure out why the artist or photographer chose to use black and white instead of color.

### 4. One Color, Many Shades
You can make many shades of the same color. Look at something that is mostly one color. Notice that light and shadow can change the basic color into different shades. Make a picture of something that is mostly one color. Some examples are a hill full of trees that are many shades of green, buildings in a city that are many shades of brick red or gray, or snow on fields that are many shades of gray and white.

### 5. Still Life
Collect a variety of objects with unusual and interesting shapes, such as shells, rocks, or jewelry. Place them on a blank piece of paper and trace around them using a pencil or black ink pen. Remove the objects and complete your design, adding more black, white, or color.

### 6. Art Bridges
Have you ever thought about art as a way to build bridges across cultures? Each country or culture has its own history and style of art. Find examples of artwork you like from other cultures and try to make an example of your own.

### 7. Design It
Look for design in everyday objects. Find different designs in nature (such as a spider web) and different designs that are made by people (such as a skyscraper). Make a drawing of one of the designs you see.

### 8. On the Move
Draw or paint a person, an animal, or an object in motion, perhaps a boat sailing or a dog running. What did you do to show movement?

### 9. Tour It
Visit one or more places where you can see many types of visual arts. You could visit a museum, an art exhibit, an art gallery, a gift shop, a department store, a card shop, an art collector's home, an artist's studio, or an advertising agency, or a graphic design studio. If possible, visit a place where you can see the artist at work.

### 10. Put It in Perspective
See how perspective works by looking at a few works of art that show things looking smaller in the distance. Then draw your own picture using the first rule of perspective: As two parallel lines move away from you—as in railway tracks or highways—the lines get closer and closer together. Eventually, the lines may touch at a point in the distance. After that point, you can't see the lines any further.

## Create and Invent

# Write All About It

**Can you imagine yourself writing books, TV shows, radio scripts, song lyrics, magazine articles, or content for the Internet? Try sharpening your writing skills with the activities in this badge.**

### 1. Write from the Start
Writers watch and record what they see and hear in the world. And the more they practice writing, the better they become. Start your own writer's notebook. For one week, write at least five minutes every day. Record conversations, ideas, and images that surround you. You can describe people you see, places you go, and events that happen.

### 2. Story Starters
Create three different story starters—opening lines of a story, play, or poem that help writers get going. Then, pick one of the story starters and continue! Write for 15 minutes or more. Can't think of any of your own? Try one of these:

- Aisha and her best friend hadn't spoken for days...
- "Did you see what Shawna brought to school?" Kim asked Johanna as they ran to their next class...
- She was home alone when she heard a strange tapping at her window...

### 3. Memoirs Are Memories
Memoirs are people's written memories of their lives. Try your hand at writing a memoir. Think about an event that meant a great deal to you. It can be something that happened a long time ago, or last week. Use your words to capture the sounds and smells of the event, as well as what happened. What characters (people or animals) were involved? Having trouble getting started? Try starting with "The day I..." or "How I..." or "When I was ___ years old..." Even "I remember..." will get you started.

### 4. How to How-To
How-to writing explains how to do something. Pick a skill or hobby you are good at and write instructions that tell someone else how to do it. It can be a cooking recipe, how to operate a video player, how to fold your sleeping bag—anything! Give your how-to to a friend and ask her to follow your instructions. Did you forget anything important?

### 5. True Fiction
Fiction is writing that comes from your imagination. Many fiction writers use a real event as a starting point, then make up the rest. Use these hints to write your own story:

- Figure out what things happen in your story (this is called the plot). Your story needs to have a beginning, middle, and end. Usually the actions build to a climax (the high point of a story), which is usually near the end.
- Before you start writing your story, describe your main characters in a notebook. Jot down ideas or make sketches of them. Include details so that your characters seem different from each other. (Remember, characters can be animals, too.) When you start to write your story, look at your descriptions to help you figure out what a character might do or say.
- Describe your setting. Does your story take place on a farm? In a city? On a beach?
- Make your story have a point. Why should someone bother to read it? Will the characters change? Will they learn something important?

### 6. Group Writing for Laughs
With a group of friends, write a fun story. The first person writes down one sentence and shows it to the second person. That person writes one sentence and shares only that sentence with a third person. When everyone has had a turn, read the whole story aloud.

### 7. Play It Out!
Playwriting takes special skills. Not only do you write down the words the characters will speak, but you also have to remember to describe the people's actions! Look at a play or script to learn about the format for playwriting. Then, write a short play, using that form as a guide. Perform your play or read it aloud, asking friends to play each part.

### 8. Author! Author!
Some writers write ads, news stories, reports for companies, even handbooks for Girl Scouts! Try to talk to writers in your community about their work. What type of training did they have? What is their typical day like? How much are they paid? What do they like least about their writing jobs? What do they like most?

### 9. A Pocket Full of Poems
Free verse or rhymed poetry. Haiku or concrete poetry. Limericks or sonnets. There are many different kinds of poems. Find out how to write three different types of poems. Then pick one and try your hand at two or three examples.

### 10. Good News
To write a news article, reporters must cover the "five W's": Who, What, When, Where and Why. Some would also add "How." Practice using the five W's to write a news story about something that's happening in your community or Girl Scout troop. If you like, see if your local newspaper will publish your story.

## Create and Invent

# Yarn and Fabric Arts

Macramé, crocheting, knitting, weaving, embroidery, and batik and fabric dyeing are some ways to use textiles, fibers, and yarns in artistic and practical ways. Have fun and improve your home, your clothes, or your wardrobe—even your mood.

# Knots

**Overhand**

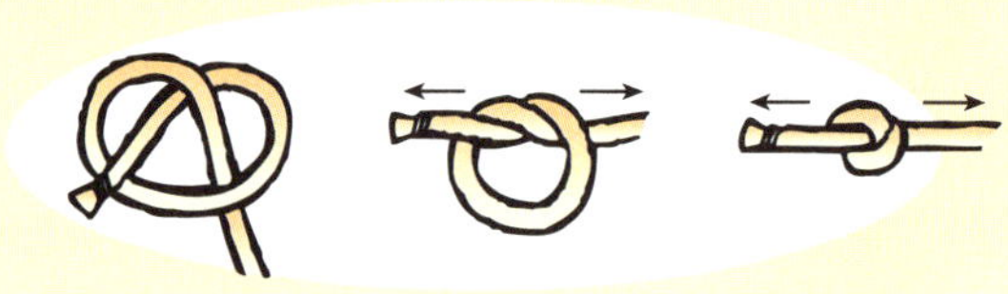

**Square**

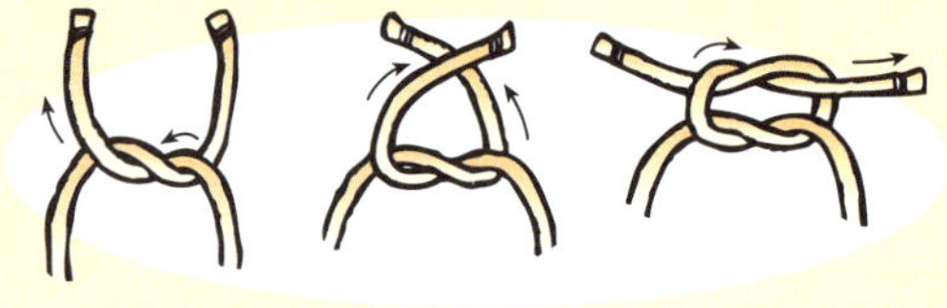

**Half hitch**

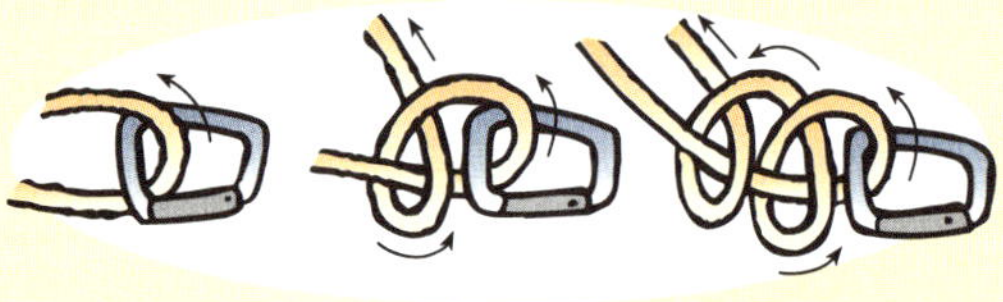

**Sheepshank**

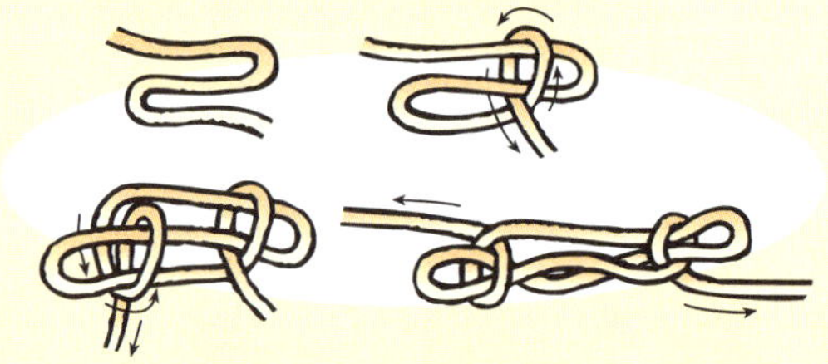

**Clove hitch**

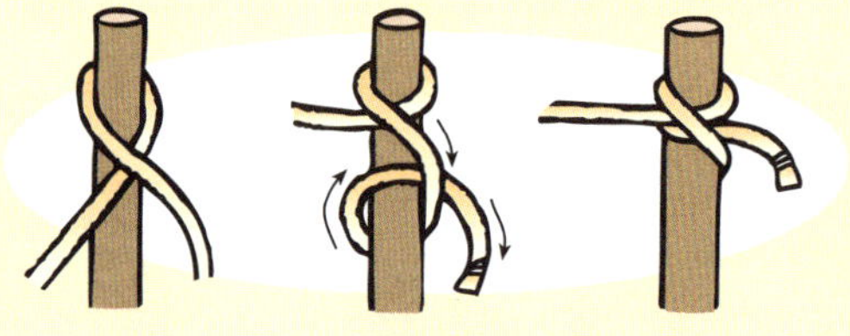

**Granny**

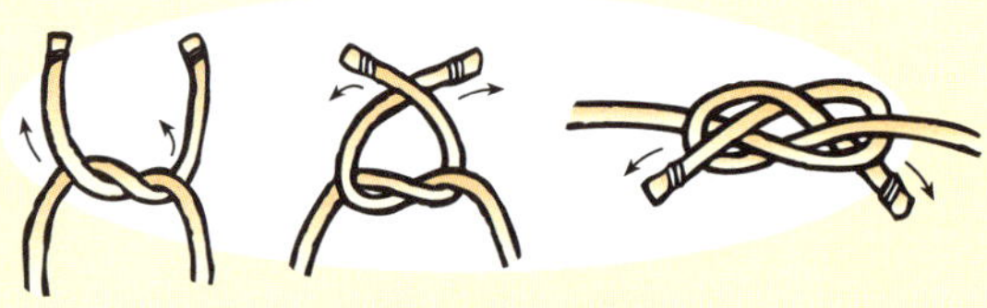

# Stitches

**Cross Stitch**

**French knot**
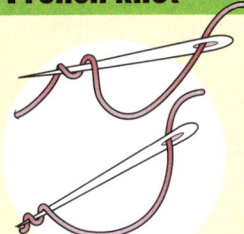

**Back Stitch**
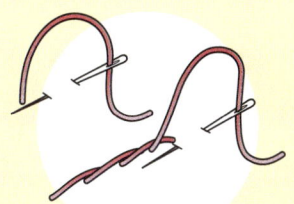

**Chain stitch**

**Satin stitch**
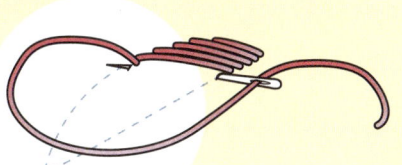

**Blanket stitch**
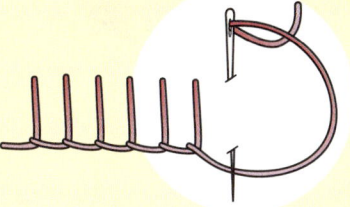

## 1. Dye It
Use dyes or tints to decorate a small object like a scarf, T-shirt, or pillowcase.

## 2. Weave On
Learn how to weave and do one of the following: Weave something on a cardboard loom; weave a tapestry on a cardboard or other type of loom; make and thread a simple loom (such as back-strap or flat frame), then demonstrate how to use it and weave something on it; make a belt with finger weaving, tube weaving, or some other type of narrow weaving; create a basket in a woven, coil, braided, or twining technique.

## 3. Famous Fabric Masterpieces
Find examples of fabric arts displayed in a museum in your area or in a virtual museum online.

## 4. Knots
Learn how to make the following knots:

- Overhand
- Square
- Granny
- Half hitch
- Sheepshank
- Clove hitch

## 5. Knot Project
Do a simple macramé project: belt, plant hanger, bookmark, or place mat.

## 6. Knit On
In knitting, learn how to cast on, knit, purl, and cast off. Make a scarf, cap, afghan square, or other small item.

## 7. Crochet On
In crocheting, learn to start a chain, single crochet, double crochet, tie off, or end. Crochet a scarf, cap, afghan square, or other small item.

## 8. A Stitch in Time
Learn how to do each of the following embroidery stitches:

- Chain stitch
- Cross stitch
- Satin stitch
- French knot
- Blanket stitch
- Back stitch

Complete a small embroidery project.

## 9. Fabrics of the Past
Find out about a fabric art that was traditionally done by women in earlier times.

## 10. Fabrics 'Round the World
Find out about fabric arts that are traditional to a particular culture or country.

# 9 Explore and Discover

# Aerospace

**Do airplanes, kites, and space shuttles interest you? If so, you'll love the activities in this badge. Not sure? Try them out and find out how amazing the aerospace field is.**

## 1. Paper Airplanes
Make and fly three different designs for paper airplanes.

## 2. Test Flight
Put together a simple model glider or make your own out of balsa wood. Can you make your glider fly straight, stall, loop, bank right, and bank left?

## 3. Go Fly a Kite
Make and fly your own kite. What type of wind makes the kite fly best? What can you try to make the kite better?

### How to Make a Kite

Take a sheet of thin paper and cut a square shape. Decorate the paper with magic markers. Use drinking straws as the supports of your kite like this:

Attach your string or cord as shown. Find an open place away from poles and power lines and try flying your kite.

## 4. Think Sky High
Visit an airport, an airplane cockpit, a control tower, a space center, an aerospace museum, or a planetarium.

## 5. Models Away!
Attend a radio-controlled or control-line airplane event or a model rocket launch. Find out how much time and money it takes to build a model.

## 6. Shoot for the Stars
Watch a space launch in person, on television, or on the Web. Find out what kind of space vehicle or satellite was launched and why.
OR
Visit NASA's Web site www.nasa.gov and find out what missions are underway or planned for the future. Be sure to check out the "NASA Kids" link.

## 7. Contact!
Talk to some older people in your community about air travel before 1960. Not sure where to start? Ask about: early aircraft, barnstorming, dirigibles, coast-to-coast travel, Amelia Earhart, a Powder Puff derby, and military flying by women during the two World Wars.

## 8. Space Flight Spinoffs
The science and technology used in exploring space have many applications here on earth. Find out about one of the following. If possible, try the product or talk to someone who uses it in her life.

- Dehydrated foods—food from which water has been removed, first developed for astronauts (such as yummy ice cream!).
- The infrared thermometer—an ear thermometer that uses the technology developed by scientists to measure the temperatures of stars and planets.
- An advanced heart pacemaker—a miniature device designed to keep a human heart beating, uses long-life batteries developed for space flight.

## 9. Up, Up, and Away!
Put on an air show and invite other groups to participate. Try one of the following:

- Have races for different kinds of model aircraft, such as gliders and airplanes. Give awards for different achievements, such as longest flight, best stunt, or most accurate flight.
- Hold a kite-building workshop.
- Host a kite-flying festival.

## 10. Women Flying Sky High
Do you have the right stuff to be an astronaut? Go online www.quest.arc.nasa.gov/women/intro.html and see what it takes!
OR
Visit the home page of the Ninety-Nines www.ninety-nines.org, an international organization for women pilots, and be sure to check out the section on "Women Pilots Today."

*Explore and Discover*

# Computer Fun

**The computer is a great tool for doing schoolwork and hobbies. Computers help you work faster and "smarter." Knowing how to use a computer is essential in most jobs now and into the future. This badge will help you prepare.**

monitor at or below eye level

hands and wrists straight and relaxed

proper chair to support back

feet resting comfortably on the floor

## 1. Get Set Up
If you have a computer at home, this is a must! Read about how to "stay tuned up" in the "Explore and Discover" chapter of your *Junior Girl Scout Handbook.* Evaluate your computer ergonomics. Create a healthier work environment for yourself and for others who use the computer. Read the Online Safety Pledge in the "How to Stay Safe" chapter of the handbook and make sure you and your family sign it.

## 2. Just the Basics
Learn how to do basic computer operations. Demonstrate your ability to do the following: create a document using a word-processing program, save a document, add numbers or bullets to a list, use the spell-check function, print out stored information.

## 3. Computer Artist
You can be an artist using the computer. Use graphics or photo software to do one of the following:

- Create an illustration or design that can be saved and inserted into a document or used as a screensaver.
- Learn to rotate, crop, size, sharpen, and brighten a photo from a scanned or digital file.

After you have your picture, you could use it as a screensaver, illustrate something you have written, or use it in a larger product, such as a quilt or memory book.

## 4. Desktop Publishing
Create a newsletter on your computer. Include a theme, a banner headline, columns, text wrapping, clip art or pictures, boxed text, and page numbers. Save it and print it for others to read.

## 5. Fun and Games
Help put on a demonstration of computer games and software for your troop or a group of younger girls. Select the games or software for content, the age of the participants, educational value, and enjoyment.

## 6. Review the Products
Be a computer software reviewer. Pick out at least two software programs to review that were written for kids. Compare your evaluation with that of the experts in a software review magazine. How are the reviews the same as or different from yours? Would you use reviews to help choose software? Why or why not?

## 7. Get Practical
Use a software program to do something that will save you time, teach you something, or get organized. Check out additional ideas for this activity in the section about getting connected in the "Explore and Discover" chapter of your *Junior Girl Scout Handbook*.

## 8. What's Available?
Visit a computer store. Compare different kinds of personal computing systems. Ask someone to help you determine the basic options for a family computer, including printers and other hardware. Don't forget to compare the costs. Decide which system would be the best for you.
OR
Read at least three computer magazines. Decide what information would be helpful to your family if you were going to purchase, upgrade, or expand the usefulness of a computer.

## 9. On the Job
Interview four different people and find out how they use computers in their jobs.

## 10. Comparison Shopping
Find out about the different products that people use to conduct business, stay connected, or hook up to the Internet when they are away from their offices.

## Explore and Discover

# Globe-Trotting

**If you enjoy finding out about new places, dream of taking vacations in exotic locations, or want to help save the environment anywhere in the world, this badge is right for you.**

### 1. Picture It
Every country's architecture is influenced by climate, the types of available materials, the number of people in an area, and the amount of space available. Use an encyclopedia, magazines, videos, art books, or the Internet to find out about the types of architecture found in three very different places (for example, polar regions, desert communities, and a big city). Then sketch out the different designs, or create collages of photographs that show the differences in architecture.

### 2. Toot Your Own Horn
Is your community a tourist destination? If it isn't, could it be? Is the geographical setting dramatic? Are there cultural or historical sites that tourists could visit? Most communities have features that can lure visitors—like a spot where a famous moment in history occurred, a lake for fishing or swimming, or natural resources such as sulfur baths, geysers, or volcanic rock. Create a poster, a travel brochure, or a presentation highlighting your community's unique features.

### 3. Read All About It

Read two or three short stories, or a book in which the setting (time and place) influences the plot. Some examples are Jean Craighead George's *Julie of the Wolves,* which is based in Alaska in the early part of the 20th century; Madeleine L'Engle's *A Wrinkle in Time,* in which the characters move beyond the real world; and books by Laura Ingalls Wilder, which take place on the Western frontier. How does the setting influence the plot and the way the characters live and act? Now create your own opening to a story that takes place in a country other than the one you live in now. You can write it down on paper or act it out with friends.

### 4. Just a Drop

Water is vital to life: nothing can live without it. Yet, lots of people live where drinkable water is limited, or almost nonexistent. One thing these people do is collect water during a rainstorm, and save it to drink, cook, and wash with later. During the next rainstorm, put out a big pot or bowl. How much water did you collect? Now consider how long it would take you to collect enough water to use in a day. Keep track of how many cups of water you drink every day, and how much water you use for cooking, cleaning, washing clothes, and bathing. (You can estimate how much is used in washing clothes and bathing.) What is the total? How many pots of water would you need to take care of your daily needs? Could you cut back on the amount of water you use?

### 5. Be Aware— Be Prepared!

Volcanoes, tornadoes, floods, earthquakes, hurricanes, fires, and droughts: every location has its challenges. Pick one of these natural phenomena and find out:

- What causes it?
- What can be done, if anything, to prevent it?
- What can be done to prepare for it?
- Where is it most common?
- What types of assistance do people need if the phenomenon occurs in their community?

### 6. Map It Out

Pick a country and become an expert on it. What are its major rivers, mountain ranges, and other geographical features? What climate does it have? How does the climate affect what kinds of trees or plants grow there? How does it affect what farmers can grow there?

### 7. Dear Diary . . .

Re-create the life of an explorer. Research how the person traveled and got fresh food supplies and water. What instruments of navigation were used? What was the explorer searching for? Why did the explorer leave home? Create a diary as if you were this person. Make diary entries for one week.

### 8. Is Anybody There?

Investigate three ways that people in different parts of the world use technology to keep in touch. How common are these forms of technology in your community? How do they work? What are the advantages and disadvantages of these forms of technology?

### 9. We're All Connected

Find out about a career in which people need to know about countries other than the United States. Get information from the Internet, a book, or a magazine. Some examples of careers to look into are importer, buyer for a store, travel agent, travel writer, or stockbroker. How does knowledge of other languages and cultures help in these careers?

### 10. It's All Yours

Do you love the mountains, or would you rather be at the ocean? Create a geographical locale that's perfect for you. What features will it have? What will the weather be like? What types of plants and animals will there be, and how many people will live there? Create a picture book "photo album" of this ideal locale to share with your troop, friends, or family. Does such a place really exist? Find out.

## Explore and Discover

# Let's Get Cooking

**Making your own meals can be lots of fun. Stirring, beating, mixing, baking—learn safe ways to prepare delicious, healthy meals with these fun activities.**

### 1. Keeping It Clean

When preparing and eating food, keep your hands squeaky-clean! Believe it or not, bacteria can cling to the natural oil on your hands. Want to see? Take two apple pieces. Wash one apple piece and then wipe it with dirty hands and place it in a sealed jar. Label the jar "dirty hands." Now wash your hands. Take a second apple piece and wash it, then wipe it with your clean hands. Label this jar "squeaky-clean." After one week, look at both apple pieces. Are there any differences? How does this experiment demonstrate the importance of washing your hands?

### 2. When in Doubt, Throw It Out

Talk with a dietician, a health educator, or a restaurant owner and find out: How long can you keep different kinds of leftovers before they become dangerous to eat? How long can you keep a picnic lunch out of refrigeration? What actions can you take to keep your food safe?

## 3. Have It Your Way

With a group of friends, create your own *healthy* fast-food restaurant. Develop a menu, set the prices, and design the look of the restaurant. Don't forget to give it a great name. Assign jobs like hostess, waitress, or chef. Decide where people will be able to find this restaurant. Then stage your "grand opening." Invite people to come to your "restaurant" and try some of your creative dishes.

## 4. Something for Everyone

Not everyone has the same access to healthy food. Tragically, more than one billion people worldwide are underfed. Collect food that can be donated to shelters or to another organization that could benefit from additional food. Make sure you include nutritious food that won't go bad, such as canned goods, juice boxes, dried fruit or fruit rolls, packaged cereals, and pastas.

## 5. The Perfect Egg

Eggs are a great source of protein and can be prepared in many different ways. Create a recipe in which eggs are used. Need inspiration? You might look at cookbooks with recipes from other countries. *Note:* Although eggs taste good and are good for you, they can be dangerous if you don't cook them properly. You can limit the threat of these harmful bacteria by making sure that eggs are fully cooked. Uncooked eggs are one reason not to taste cookie dough or cake batter before it's been baked!

## 6. New Wave Chef

Microwaves, electric grills, rotisseries, and other appliances help make cooking fast and fun. Select an appliance and, with an adult's help, try out a recipe that lets you use it.

## 7. Tasty Treats: Fruit Surprise

Here is a great way to make a tasty treat for you and your friends that doesn't involve cooking.

**What You Need**
- 1 cup* container of fruit-flavored yogurt
- 1 cup* of whipped cream or whipped cream substitute
- 4 mini pie crusts (pre-cooked)
- Fresh berries or other fruit

**What You Do**
1. In a bowl, mix the fruit-flavored yogurt and the whipped cream.
2. Scoop the mixture equally into each of the four pie crusts.
3. Decorate the pies with the fresh berries or other fruit.
4. Refrigerate for 15 minutes. Then, devour!

Now it's your turn: Create your own no-cook recipe.

## 8. Mix It Up

Blender drinks are fun, quick, and easy to make. When you use healthy ingredients, the drinks can also boost your energy. Hold a blender party. Invite each guest to bring a recipe for a vegetable or fruit drink and all the ingredients it requires. Be sure to plan ahead, so you'll have everything you need. Experiment with combinations of fruit, milk, yogurt, juice, honey, and natural flavorings to create a variety of drinks. Select fruits such as blueberries, strawberries, melon slices, peaches, pineapple, or bananas. Also try tropical fruits such as kiwi, mango, and papaya. For vegetable juices, try combining carrots, celery, and tomatoes.

## 9. Food Around the World

With your Girl Scout troop or group, eat your way around the world. Start in the U.S. and trace a path around the globe—in any direction. Each girl chooses a country on the "trip." She then finds a healthy recipe from that country to share with the troop. What can you learn about a culture from a recipe and its ingredients?

## 10. The Big Change

With the help of an adult, take a recipe that you find in a cookbook and make it healthier. For example, you can change the ground beef in a meat sauce to ground turkey or chicken. If you are baking, try substituting a half cup* of applesauce for a stick of butter. Try tofu in your cooking as a healthy source of protein. Be creative and have fun!

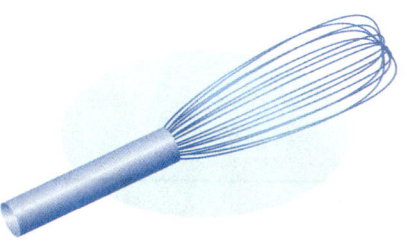

* See page 235 for the metric conversion chart.

*Explore and Discover*

# Making It Matter

**Engineers take scientific knowledge and make useful things from it, such as cars, bridges, and computers. Practice being an engineer with this badge.**
*Note:* **More activities about this topic are available in the** *Junior Girl Scout Leader Guide Book.*

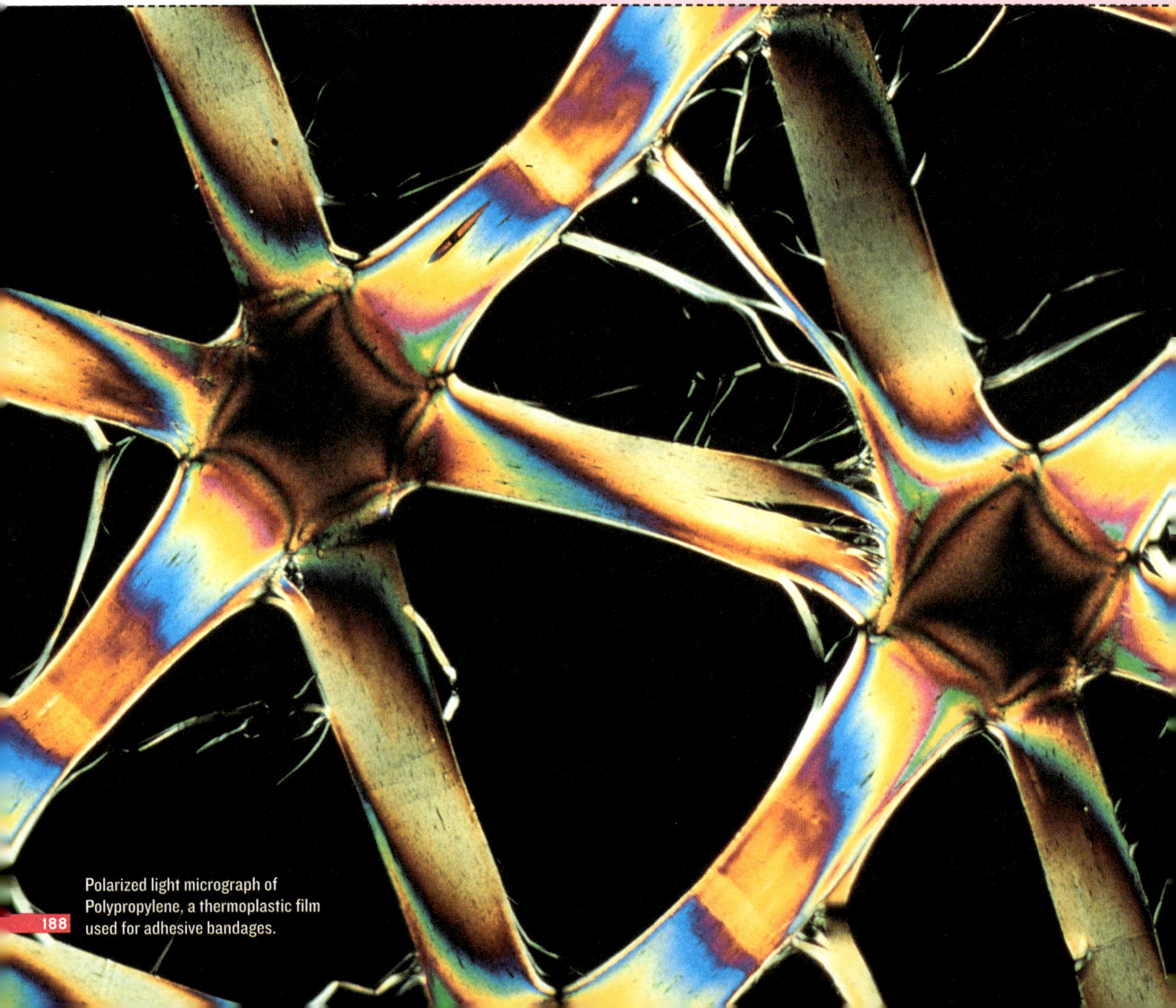

*Explore and Discover*

Polarized light micrograph of Polypropylene, a thermoplastic film used for adhesive bandages.

## 1. Making a Polymer

Many of the products you use every day are made of plastics. Plastics are a type of material called a polymer—a chemical compound of chain-like molecules. Parts of cars, clothes, CDs, sneakers, and many, many other things are made of polymers. Here's a chance to make your own polymer.

### What You Need
- Borax (available in the laundry section of a grocery store)
- Water
- A measuring cup
- A tablespoon*
- White glue
- A plastic cup

### What You Do
1. Dissolve 1 tablespoon* of borax in 1/2 cup* of water.
2. Put 1 tablespoon* of white glue and 1 tablespoon* of water into a plastic cup and stir. When the glue and water are mixed well, add 1 tablespoon* of the borax solution and stir. What happens?

## 2. Polymer Possibilities

By adding different ingredients, engineers can change the look, feel, and behavior of a polymer. Here's how you can make different polymers with different properties. You need the same materials as in activity 1, plus: salt, sugar, baking powder, coarse corn meal, and a 1/2 teaspoon* measuring spoon.

### What You Do
1. Dissolve 1 tablespoon* of borax in 1/2 cup* of water.
2. Put 1 tablespoon* of white glue and 1 tablespoon* of water into a plastic cup and stir. Add 1/2 teaspoon* of salt and stir until the salt is dissolved. Then add 1 tablespoon* of the borax solution and stir. What happens?
3. Repeat Step 2 using sugar, baking powder, and corn meal instead of salt. How do the polymers compare?

Find other plastic objects. Compare their different properties—hard, soft, stretchy, bouncy, textured, or clear.

## 3. Making Connections

Electrical engineers work with circuits and electricity. From light switches to electrical generators, engineers keep the juices flowing. Here's your chance to wear an engineer's hat—find out how a doorbell works by making your own.

### What You Need
Each of these items can be found at any electronics store:
- A 9-volt battery
- A 24- or 26-gauge copper wire
- A push-button switch
- A 9-volt buzzer

### What You Do
Follow the diagram below to attach the wire to the buzzer, switch, and battery, making an electrical circuit. When you push the button, you should hear your doorbell "ring." Can you think of other things in your home that work like this?

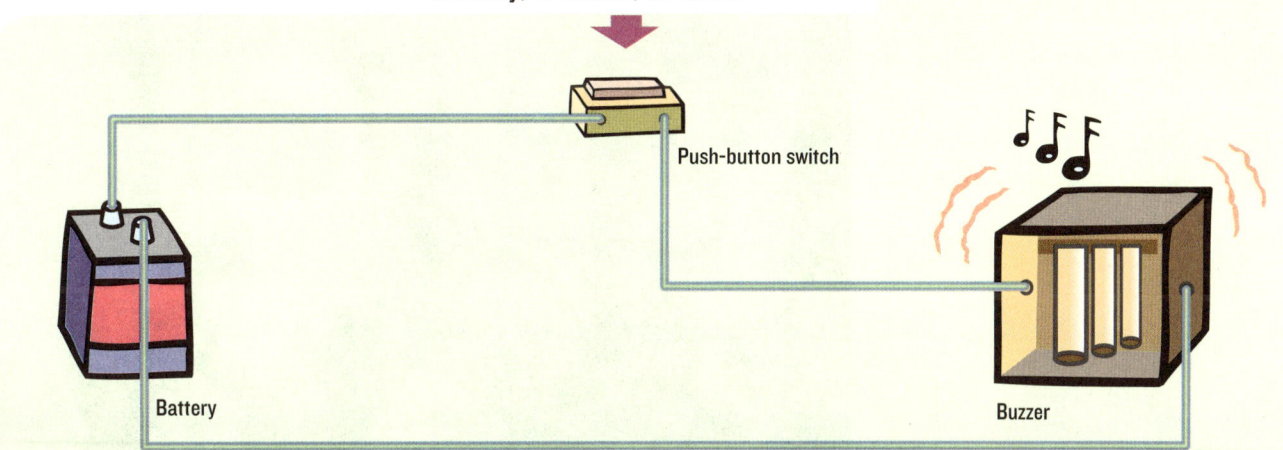

* See page 235 for the metric conversion chart.

## Explore and Discover

# Making It Matter

### 4. Moving Parts

Find out the role of bearings in machines (such as your family car or a pair of roller skates) by doing this simple experiment.

**What You Need**
- A coffee can or similar type of can (empty or full)
- A lid that fits over the bottom part of the can
- A pencil (preferably without a point)
- Plasticene clay (available at toy and hobby shops)
- Marbles

**What You Do**
1. Make a dumbbell-like object by placing equal-sized balls of clay on each end of the pencil.
2. Center one end of the pencil on the lid, and then attach it to the lid with the clay.
3. Place the lid on the bottom of the can. Can you make the lid turn on the end of the can? How well does it turn?
4. Now, remove the lid from the can. Place the marbles on the top of the can.
5. Put the lid back on top of the can, this time over the marbles. Try making the lid turn on the end of the can. What happens? Why? Can you find an example of using bearings to help something turn in a "machine"?

### 5. Materials and Structures

Civil engineers design highways and bridges. Knowledge of building materials is needed in order to meet the load demands. Here's an engineering challenge—try to build a structure from which you will hang a cup, using the following materials:

- Old newspaper (if rolled up tightly, it can become a surprisingly strong building material)
- Tape
- String
- A plastic cup
- A cupful of small rocks or gravel

Can you fill the cup with rocks or gravel without its tipping over?

### 6. Engineering in Action

Visit a factory, water- or sewage-treatment plant, recycling center, waste-to-energy incinerator, power plant, or construction site. Do engineers work there? If so, interview someone about her job. Find out what role engineers played in the design of the facility.

### 7. Label Check

Look at ten different products around your house—check the kitchen cupboard, the cleaning supplies, and perhaps your craft supplies. What chemicals can you find, listed as ingredients of the products? Which products require you to take special safety precautions when handling and disposing of them? What are those precautions?

## 8. Base-ic Facts

Is it an acid or a base? Find out by making your own pH tester. First you'll want to read the section about pH in the "Explore and Discover" chapter of your *Junior Girl Scout Handbook*.

**What You Need**
- A radish (or red cabbage juice)
- Baking soda
- A measuring cup
- A tablespoon*
- Vinegar or lemon juice

**What You Do**
1. Scrape the skin of the radish into a glass of water. Use your fingernail or a dull knife edge. Scrape enough to turn the water into a pinkish color. (Or add enough cabbage juice to turn the water pinkish.) The pinkish water is the "tester."
2. Dissolve 1 tablespoon* of baking soda in about 2/3 cup* of water.
3. Put 1 tablespoon* of this solution into a clean cup.
4. Put 1 tablespoon* of vinegar or lemon juice into another cup.
5. Add a few drops of the pH tester to each cup.
6. What happens? Gently pour the contents of one cup into the other cup. What happens then?

## 9. Reverse Engineering

Reverse engineering is when you take something apart to see how it works. Find an old simple appliance (such as a hair dryer, toaster, blender, or clock) that is ready for the scrap heap. (Check with the owner for permission to use it.) Carefully take the appliance apart, keeping track of what part came from where. Try to explain how you think the appliance might work. Then, try to put it all back together again. *Note:* An adult should be present during this activity. *Do not* plug the machine in to see if it works after taking it apart and putting it back together again.

## 10. Use Computers to Design

Engineers use CAD (computer-assisted design) to test how things they have designed will work before they actually build them. Find out more about computer-assisted design by talking to people who use it in their jobs or by doing online research. See if you can find a Web site or software that allows you to build a model on the computer and test it.

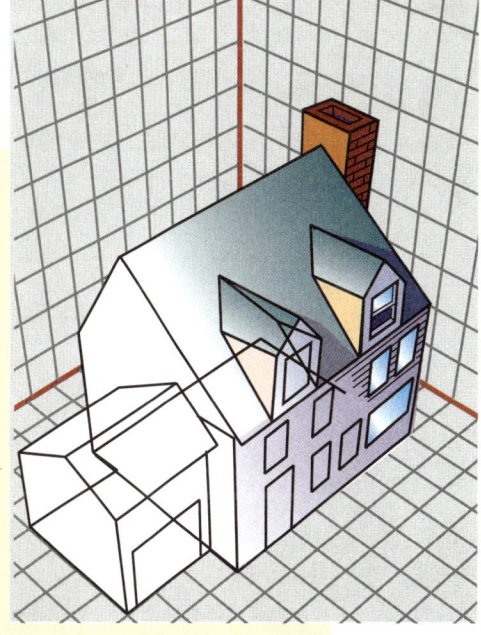

*Explore and Discover*

# Making Music

**A musician is someone who creates art with musical instruments. Try your hand at one or more instruments. Is the musical life for you?**

### 1. A Family Affair
All instruments belong to different family groups. For example, a clarinet is made of wood, so it belongs to the woodwind family. Choose an instrument family and learn what the members of that family do.

### 2. A New Sound
Design a brand new instrument. How is it played? What does it sound like?

### 3. Practice, Practice, Practice
The best way to master any instrument is to practice. However, practicing the same thing over and over can be boring. Keep things interesting. Not sure how to start? Try learning two new songs. Or play a song—or scales—backwards. Another idea would be to create your own silly songs.

### 4. Compose Yourself
Write a simple melody of at least eight measures for an instrument. Write down your piece using symbols for notes, key, tempo, and dynamics. Try to teach someone to play your newly composed piece.

### 5. Musical Roots
Many pieces of music have interesting stories behind them. Pick a piece of music and find out about the following: What was the composer like? What other pieces did she or he compose? When was the music composed? Why was it written? Does the piece of music tell its own story?

### 6. Be a Conductor
One of the most celebrated musicians on the stage is the conductor—and she or he doesn't even play an instrument! A conductor guides the musicians through the music by keeping the count, telling various sections when they start or stop, and telling the musicians if they should play softly or loudly. Choose a piece of your favorite music, and learn how to conduct the piece. Use something for a baton, such as a wooden spoon or chopstick, and keep the beat. When should the piece be played loudly? When should it be played more softly?

### 7. Music with a Theme
Select one of these themes and play music that matches it, for an audience of friends or family: the sea, a river, a busy urban area, a forest, a mountain range, a field or meadow, a circus or festival, a march or parade.

### 8. On Stage
Using your musical skills, take part in a performance in a Girl Scout ceremony, an individual recital, a group performance, or a community musical event.

### 9. Opera, Anyone?
Watch an opera or operetta on television, or attend an opera in person. Listen for the story. How much of it is sung? How much is spoken and in what language? How are the voices related to the characters (for example, why does a soprano sing a certain role rather than a bass)? Who composed the opera, and when did she or he live?

### 10. The World and Its Influence on Music
Throughout history, composers have written songs about significant world events. Some of these pieces were written in celebration. Find out about two pieces of music that were influenced by historical events. Play or sing them for your troop or group and explain what influenced the composers to write them.

## Explore and Discover

# Music Fan

**Find out about classical, jazz, rock, rap, folk, pop, country, or gospel music with this badge.**

## 1. Express Yourself
Design your own music awards. With a group of friends, decide on at least five categories you want to recognize. You can make up your own, such as the best single female singer. Ask at least five people to come up with the best in each category. Play the winning selections at a party.

## 2. Listening to Something New
Listen to at least two types of music that are new to you—either live or recorded.

## 3. Sharing Music
Perform! Sing, play an instrument, or produce a performance for others to see. Stage your performance for an audience of at least ten people.

## 4. Found Music
Make your own simple musical instrument, using common objects found around the house. Your instrument might be one that produces a sound if you move it through the air, shake it, or hit it with another object. Pick one favorite song that you can accompany with your instrument.

## 5. What's a Song Made Of?
Choose a recorded song that you like and listen to it several times. What instruments do you hear: drums, bass, guitar, violin, saxophone, others? How many singers are there? Do some of them sing backup?

## 6. Folk Songs from Afar
Every culture has its own folk songs. Some have been translated into English; others are widely sung in their native languages. Learn a folk song from two different cultures.

## 7. Careers in Music
You don't have to know how to play an instrument to find a job where music is important. Interview someone with a career that involves music, such as a sound engineer, a music critic, a composer, or a music teacher. Find out why that person chose music as a career. How did she learn her job? What does she enjoy about her career? Write up your interview and share it with your troop, friends, or family.

## 8. Music: Insight to History
It's fun to look back and listen to music that was popular in another time. Find two songs that were written during another period of history. What does this music tell you about that period? Is that music still sung or played today?

## 9. Nature's Call
Not all music is made with instruments or human voices. There's nature's music—for example, a frog croaking, the wind in the trees, rain falling on the roof, birds chirping. These sounds, when strung together with no talking, can be very relaxing "music." Go for a hike through the woods, or a walk in the park. Bring along a hand-held tape recorder and make your own recording of the sounds of nature. Be careful not to talk while you are taping.

## 10. Dance Time
Create a dance to a tape or CD that you've chosen.

## Explore and Discover

# Oil Up

**Oil is both an energy source and a raw material that is used to make many of the things you use each day. Learn more about this interesting, slippery substance.**

### 1. A Day's Work
Learn what rescue workers or scientists do to try to save animals that have been affected by an oil spill. Read a story, watch a TV show or video, or use the Internet to get information.

### 2. Fossil Facts
Create a display that shows how plants and animals from millions of years ago became the oil used today.

### 3. Where in the World?
Design a map that shows where most major oil deposits around the world are located.

### 4. Around the World
Pick one country other than your own that supplies the world with oil. Find out about the people who live there. What are their customs? What languages do they speak? If you were to visit there, what would you want to see?

## 5. Make and Clean Up an Oil Spill

Oil is often prepared and shipped thousands of miles (or kilometers) before it reaches your home, school, or local gas station. An oil spill is always a risk. Find out why oil spills can be so difficult to clean up. To see what it's like to make and clean up an oil spill, pour some cooking oil in a bowl or pan of water. Try different ways of getting the oil out of the water.

- Try to gather it all in one place using a string.
- Try to skim it off with a spoon.
- Try to soak it up with paper towels or cotton balls.

What else can you use? What works best?

## 6. How Does an Oil Spill Affect a Beach?

Use sand and water to build a "beach" in a foil pan. Put a block of wood, rock, feather, furry fabric, leaf, or a twig in the sand. Pour vegetable oil in the water and make waves to wash the oil up onto the beach. What happens? Try removing the oil from the objects on the beach using the techniques listed in activity 5 for an oil spill.

## 7. Ten? Twenty?

How many careers are involved in finding oil, getting it out of the earth, moving it from place to place, making fuels from it, producing chemicals and other products from it, and preventing and cleaning up oil spills? Read an article or Web page, or watch a TV show or video about jobs in the fields of geology, engineering, ship building, or environmental protection.

Oil spills are dangerous to animals. This bear's fur has been coated with oil from an oil spill.

## 8. Oil Drop

Pretend you are a drop of oil. Create a comic book or skit that explains what happened to you after you were removed from the earth. How were you transported? Where were you taken? What changes did you go through? Where are you now?

## 9. Come Clean

Visit a service station when it's not very busy. How many spots of oil or grease do you see on the ground? Ask the service station manager how he or she cleans up oil and gasoline spills. How does the person dispose of the used oil when the oil in a car is changed? What does the service station do to prevent spills?

## 10. It's in What?

If fewer petroleum products were used, the chances of oil spills would be reduced. To the right is a list of products that are made from petroleum. Keep a log for one week of which petroleum products you use and why you are using them. At the end of the week, look at your chart. What can you personally do to cut down on petroleum usage?

## Petroleum Products

Fabrics made of synthetic fibers
Most "wrinkle-free" clothes
Plastic bags, containers, pails
Food packaging
Vinyl house siding
Interior and exterior paints
Toys
Video and audio tapes
CDs (music and computer)
Costume jewelry
Detergents
Rugs, carpets

Methane for heating
Propane for camp lighting, barbecue grills
Automotive gasoline and aviation fuel
Diesel fuel
Home heating oil
Finished lubricating oils
Wax
Varnishes, alcohols, solvents
Prescription drugs, plastic intravenous (IV) bags, and sterile syringes
Computers, cellular phones, and fax

Asphalt
Baby oil
Lip gloss
Skin lotion
Jet fuel
Petroleum jelly
Charcoal lighter fluid
Paraffin wax
Paint thinner

## Explore and Discover

# Rocks Rock

**You might not spend a lot of time thinking about rocks. But rocks hold up roads, your house, and your town. Find out what types of rocks are in your area and how they've held up over the years. To earn this badge you must do activity 1.**

Erosion on a beach

Rock collecting

Turtle fossil

### 1. Be a Rock Hound!
Start a rock collection. Go exploration hike to see how many different kinds of rocks and minerals you can find. Before you go, consider what equipment you might need. Take safety precautions! And don't collect any samples from an area where collecting stones is prohibited. If removing a rock will make an impact on the environment, *don't take it home*! Instead, photograph or observe the stone where you found it, so others will get to see it later.

### 2. Geo Hunt
Search for clues in your community or in a place you visit that shows one or more of the following:

- Where a glacier had been
- Where a volcano had erupted
- Where erosion had happened
- Where water once covered the area
- Where the earth has shifted

Discuss, describe, or show others what you have found.

### 3. What Type Is It?
Each rock you collect will fall into one of three major categories: igneous, sedimentary, or metamorphic. Which types are yours? Use books, Web sites, or maps to help you figure out which types of rocks you've gathered.

### 4. Soil Sense
Discover what makes up soil. Collect two soil samples, each sample from a very different spot. Spread each soil sample out on a light-colored sheet of paper, and use your senses.
- *Look:* Are the grains large and easy to see? Medium? Or small? Are there any stones in the soil? Is the overall color of the soil light, medium, or dark?
- *Smell:* What does it smell like? Wet some of the soil and rub it between your fingers and smell it again.
- *Touch:* What does it feel like? Sandy soil feels rocky or pebbly. Clay soil feels sticky. A loamy soil feels gritty.

## 5. "Geo" Careers

Can you imagine yourself working with dinosaur bones? How about with precious stones? Or have you ever pictured yourself being an expert on volcanoes, the ocean floor, or faraway planets? Believe it or not, all of these careers have backgrounds based in geology (the study of rocks). To learn more about possible geology-related career choices, complete the match-up activity below. Pick one career that you'd like to learn more about.

**Career Choice**
1. ___ Lapidarist
2. ___ Hydrologist
3. ___ Geological oceanographer
4. ___ Paleontologist
5. ___ Astrogeologist
6. ___ Seismologist
7. ___ Vulcanologist
8. ___ Mining engineer

**Definition**
a) Studies where water is found on earth and the effects of water on or below the surface
b) Studies and creates maps for other bodies in the solar system
c) Cuts, polishes, and engraves precious stones
d) Studies how to extract natural resources such as gold, coal, diamonds, and oil from the earth
e) Investigates the shape and the material of the sea floor and the history of the sea sediment and rocks
f) Studies fossils (forms of life from the past)
g) Studies earthquakes
h) Studies volcanoes

Answers: 1c, 2a, 3e, 4f, 5b, 6g, 7h, 8d

## 6. Wipe Out Erosion!

Erosion is the wearing away of rocks and soil by air, wind, and water. Hook up with a group that is trying to fight the effects of erosion in your area. Some activities to look into could be:

- Planting dune grass to help keep the sand along the shore from being blown out to sea. Small, wooden fences can also be used to create artificial sand dunes. These methods keep the beach where it should be—on the beach!
- Maintaining trails, which could include helping to build terraces or steps along steep paths. Terraces and steps make it harder for rainwater to wash straight down a hill, so less soil is removed when it rains.
- Helping to build a walkway over marshy wetland areas.

## 7. Around the Globe

Volcanic eruptions, geysers, earthquakes, and tsunamis (tidal waves) have had tremendous impact on people around the world. Pick one of these phenomena, and find out a place where it affected people and what those effects were.

## 8. The View from Above

Find photographs of the earth taken from a high altitude. Photos that were taken from a plane or satellite would be best. Use these photos to locate:

- Major oceans
- Land areas
- Mountain ranges
- Fault lines
- Volcanoes
- Farmland
- Rivers, lakes, and other inland waterways
- Other features of interest

## 9. Fossil Fun!

Fossils can be formed in different ways. A fossil may be the image (known as an "impression") that an object leaves in stone, which becomes the "mold" for that object. Make your own "fossil" by pressing a leaf, rock, skeleton, bone, or dead insect into some soft plaster of Paris and allowing it to harden. Look carefully to see the details made in the impression when the item is removed. If you can, go on a fossil hunt.

## 10. Weathered or Not . . .

To discover firsthand the effects of weather on the land, do one of the following:

- Go for a walk in your neighborhood and look for chips, cracks, and rough areas in a sidewalk. Think about how these might have happened. How has nature helped cause these changes in the sidewalk?
- Discover what happens when water gets into cracks and spaces in rocks and then freezes. Fill a small plastic container with water, put the top on, and then freeze it. What happens to the container? What does this mean for areas where there is water that freezes?
- Acid rain affects different types of stone in different ways. Visit a cemetery and notice the different types of stone used to make the headstones. Or walk around your neighborhood and check out buildings made from different types of stone. Notice how the lettering, statues, carvings, and/or corners are worn away. What conclusions can you draw from your observations?

## Explore and Discover

# Science Discovery

**Scientists ask questions and find answers. Put your own investigative powers to the test. Experiment!**

Inside a kaleidoscope

## 1. Chemical Appearing Act

Discover how you can use a chemical reaction to make an artistic design. Sometimes, when chemicals react with each other, colors change.

### Starch Solution

Mix 4 tablespoons* of cornstarch in 1 cup* of lukewarm water. Or save the cooking water from boiled potatoes or pasta and let it cool.

### Iodine/Alcohol Solution

Mix 1 tablespoon* of tincture of iodine in 1 cup* of rubbing alcohol. This solution will have a yellowish-brown color.

### What You Need
- White paper
- Newspaper
- A wide paintbrush
- An artist's thin paintbrush
- Starch solution (see the directions)
- Iodine/alcohol solution (see the directions)

### What You Do
1. Dip the thin brush in the starch solution and do a simple drawing of an animal or flower.
2. Tape the corners of your paper to newspaper to keep it from curling. Starch solution is colorless, so when it is dry, nothing will show on the paper. (The sun or a hair dryer can make it dry more quickly.)
3. Dip the wide brush into the iodine/alcohol solution and, taking care not to rub, gently stroke over the original painting. Observe what happens. Why do you suppose there is a change?

Try some other activities using this chemical reaction: send a secret message, make a treasure map, put on a magic show for younger children or your family.

As with all science experiments, use caution with chemicals and the heating process.

## 2. Light and Reflection

Make a simple kaleidoscope.

### What You Need
- A shiny picture postcard
- Tape
- Colored cellophane
- White tissue paper
- Scissors

### What You Do
1. Fold the postcard, with shiny side in, lengthwise into three equal sections.
2. Tape the postcard (now a triangular tube) so the seam doesn't leak light.
3. Cut small pieces of colored cellophane. Cut two pieces of the tissue paper 2 inches* larger than the end of the tube.
4. Place the cut cellophane between the two pieces of tissue paper and tape the layers around the tube.

### How to Make a Kaleidoscope

A kaleidoscope relies on reflected light to create its special effects. Hold it up to the light and shake. What do you see?

\* See page 235 for the metric conversion chart.

## Explore and Discover: Science Discovery

Collecting and testing ocean water off the coast of California.

### 3. Water Tricks
Try these water tricks:

- Make a needle float on water. You will need a source of clean water, a bowl, and a needle. You might need a few tries. Why do you think the needle floats?
- How many drops of water can you get to stay on the top of a penny? You will need a penny and an eyedropper. Try this activity a second time and put a dab of soap on your finger. Then touch the water. What happens when the soap meets the skin of water molecules on your penny? Any idea why?

### 4. Can't Live Without It
Using newspapers, magazines, telephone books, or the Web, search for people, things, places, and issues that are science-related. Make a collage of what you find. Turn your collage into a poster, a book cover, or an illustration for a special event having to do with science.

### 5. Act Like a Scientist
Do two of the following things that an archaeologist, botanist, or geologist might do in her work:

- Make a drawing of something you find outdoors—either natural or people-made—and record your observations about it, as well as where and when you found it.
- Identify at least five different kinds of trees, flowers, or animals.
- Classify five rocks as to whether they are igneous, metamorphic, or sedimentary.

## 6. Become a Scientist

More men enter the fields of science and technology than women do. Interview or visit with a woman who is a scientist and find out how she got interested in her field, who encouraged her to pursue science, where she gets information, and which people are most supportive to her in her job.

## 7. It's a Hands-On and Happening Place

Visit a hands-on science or natural history museum, participate in a museum sleep-in, or participate in a science fair or event sponsored by your school, Girl Scout council, or community.

## 9. See What?

How is your brain challenged by optical illusions? Look in your library or on the Web for some optical illusions that you can share with your troop or your family.

## 10. Here's the Rub

Discover how speed is affected by friction by trying this experiment.

**What You Need**
- A cookie sheet, plastic tray, or piece of wood that is at least 18 inches long*
- A small toy car with wheels
- Different substances that can be put on the surface of the sloping track you will create, such as water, oil, sand, or carpeting. (This could get messy, so do it outdoors or somewhere else that can be easily cleaned up.)
- A stopwatch

**What You Do**
1. Tilt your ramp (e.g., cookie sheet) with your hands.
2. Time your car's descent, without anything on the slope, and record the results.
3. Now put something on the ramp such as the water or oil. Predict whether you think the car will move more slowly or more quickly down the ramp. Run the time trial again and record the results.
4. Continue testing with each of your substances. Share your findings with other people. How could you use this information when riding in a car or riding your bike?

## 8. Environmental Observer

The Stream Health Checklist tells you what to look for, smell, and touch to determine how healthy a stream is. Use the checklist to make an environmental report card for a stream or to develop your own checkpoints for an area you want to explore.

This checklist may be photocopied.

# Stream Health Checklist

[G] Good    [F] Fair    [P] Poor

☐ **Variety of stream animals** (fish, snails, insects, worms, and other living creatures). The greater the number of types, or species, the healthier the stream.

☐ **Available shade** Shade is good for water temperature.

☐ **Stability (lack of erosion) of stream bank**

☐ **Turbidity of water** (amount of stuff suspended in the water) Does water appear cloudy or clear? Clear is good.

☐ **Smell of water** (smell can indicate pollution).

☐ **Signs of runoff from surrounding land** Runoff can pollute and take away oxygen.

☐ **Amount of garbage along the stream**

*See page 235 for the metric conversion chart.

## Explore and Discover

# Science in Everyday Life

**Science is everywhere—in a spider web, a ray of light, even a pile of dirt! Observe and discover the exciting world of science that is around you every day.**

## 1. Tools of the Trade

Interview a doctor or dentist and find out about the different ways science and math are used in her work. Ask for a demonstration of science at work. For example, have your blood pressure taken or find out how tooth decay can be prevented.

## 2. Catch the Beat

Your heart flexes as many as 100,000 times a day pumping blood throughout your body. What a machine! Learn to take your pulse when you are sitting and at rest. (Ask someone to show you the arterial pulse points on your wrist or on either side of your neck.) Figure out the beats per minute (count the beats for 15 seconds and multiply that number by 4) to determine your resting heartbeat. Now, find what your heartbeat is after doing two of the following: jumping, standing, dancing, or running in place for 30 minutes each. Be sure to bring your heartbeat back down to resting between each activity.

Grand Canyon

## 3. Natural Geometry

Spiders are some of nature's best weavers, and the thread they use is remarkably strong. Observe some webs outdoors. Look for differences in the patterns done by different spiders. Sketch a web or capture a spider-web print on black paper. Use a gentle mist of glue or silver spray paint (under adult supervision) to spray the web. Then, "capture" the web against the paper and snip the threads that are holding it in place.

## 4. Forces of Nature

Try to imagine how long it took the Colorado River to carve out the Grand Canyon. Combine time and powerful forces, such as water and gravity, to create erosion by doing one of the following:

- Build a "mountain" with soil outdoors or observe a pile of earth at a construction site over a period of time. What are some of the patterns of erosion that develop?

- Experiment with water flow as a force of erosion at the beach, in a sandbox, or at a "stream table" in a science museum. What are some patterns that develop? Can you change them by diverting the water?

- Soak some bean seeds overnight and place them in a plastic film canister with a moist cotton ball (or a piece of a cotton T-shirt. Put the lid on and leave it for a week. What happens? How does the result exhibit a force of nature?

## Explore and Discover

# Science In Everyday Life

### 5. Science Fiction?

Authors of science fiction have often correctly anticipated new technology and social changes in their writings about the future. Write a science fiction short story, skit, or musical about life in the year 2075. What will life be like? What will have become better? Worse? Below, can you match the writer to her or his prediction or plot device?

| Author (Book) | Prediction |
|---|---|
| ☐ 1. George Orwell (*1984*) | a) Satellites |
| ☐ 2. Isaac Asimov (*I, Robot*) | b) Submarines |
| ☐ 3. Jules Verne (*20,000 Leagues Under the Sea*) | c) Interactive television |
| ☐ 4. Mary Shelley (*Frankenstein*) | d) Heart transplants |
| ☐ 5. Ray Bradbury (*The Martian Chronicles*) | e) Telepathy |
| ☐ 6. Arthur C. Clark (*2001 Space Odyssey*) | f) Communicating with dolphins |
| ☐ 7. Marion Zimmer Bradley (the Darkover series) | g) Mechanical body parts |
| ☐ 8. Madeleine L'Engle (*A Ring of Endless Light*) | h) Robotic ethics |

Answers: 1c, 2h, 3b, 4d, 5g, 6a, 7e, 8f

## 6. Color Mixing

Is mixing different-colored lights different from mixing different-colored paints? Tape some squares of white paper up in a dark hallway. Use flashlights with red, blue, and green cellophane (the primary colors of light) taped over them, and shine different combinations of light on the paper. Record the secondary colors you get with each combination. You can also experiment by shining the lights through different-colored water in clear glasses, or through colored glass or marbles. What happens when you combine a primary color of light, such as blue, and a secondary color like pink? Now do the same thing mixing the primary colors of red, yellow, and blue on paper using paint. What happens when you mix secondary and primary colors?

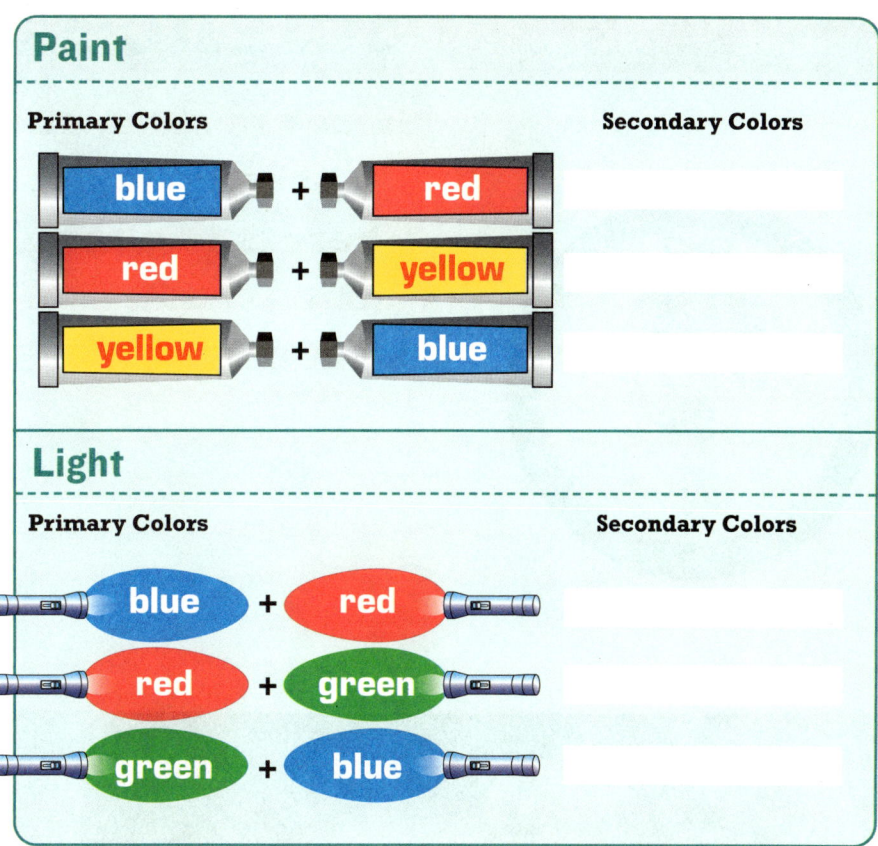

Continue experimenting with paint colors, and create a picture or design that contains at least 15 or more colors that you have mixed. Which of these predictions have come true?

## 7. Rockin' Along

Go on a geology walk! Find evidence of a changing earth brought about by water, wind, weather, plants, animals, and gravity. Look for:
- Crystals in stone or soil
- Decaying plant life
- Erosion on a hillside
- Evidence of changes brought about by people
- Examples of weathering on buildings or statues
- Loose rocks at the bottom of a hill
- Material deposited by water
- Rocks formed by compression
- Rocks smoothed by water

## 8. How Much Time?

Time has always been an important unit of measurement. People have invented many different ways to measure time. Find out about early time-keeping tools. Create your own simple instrument that marks the passage of time.

## 9. Here Today, Still Here Tomorrow?

Pick an item that you use often. Find out how it has changed since the time it was first invented. Draw or design a model of what you would like to see it become in another 25 years, or create a replacement for its function. Some items to think about are a radio, a wristwatch, a computer, a book, money, medicine, or a fast food.

## 10. The Key, Please

Choose a group of living things you can observe, such as birds, mammals, reptiles, amphibians, flowers, or trees. Use a simple identification book or field guide to find the names of seven different species in that group. Learn the key characteristics of each species that can help to identify it. These might include what it looks like, where it lives, and how it behaves.

*Explore and Discover*

# Science Sleuth

Here are some questions you can ask or investigate, just like a scientist. There isn't always a "right" or "only" answer—that's the challenge of sleuthing.

## 1. What's Vibration Got to Do with It?

Make a simple musical instrument that you can tune. Here are some ideas: bottle pipes (blowing across the top of water bottles), glass chimes (using a spoon against water glasses), comb kazoo (using tissue paper), drum (using plastic stretched across a cup), shaker (a container with dried beans), *maraca* (using a shaker with a handle), or idiophone (using your fingers to rub around the rim of crystal wine glasses). Listen to the pitches of the sounds and experiment with ways to change the pitches and add more notes. Then, try to explain how the sound is created using vibration, or play a simple melody.

## 2. The Science of Papermaking

How many kinds of paper can you find around your house? Compare the differences in color, texture, absorption, and composition. Create a paper-testing lab and choose different types of paper that are best for wiping up spills, painting, writing in ink, and writing in pencil.

## 3. Crystal Quest

What do ice, diamonds, rock candy, quartz, and snowflakes have in common? Crystals, of course! Grow your own crystals by following the recipe below. (It will take at least 2-3 days for the crystals to grow.)

**What You Need**
- Epsom salts
- Water
- Small saucepan
- Large spoon
- Pipe cleaner
- Food coloring
- Pencil
- Clear plastic cup

**What You Do**
1. With the help of an adult, boil the water in the saucepan, take the pan off the burner, and place it on a hot pad.
2. Using the spoon, slowly add the Epsom salts a little bit at a time, stirring constantly. Keep adding the salts until no more will dissolve or mix in.
3. Pour the solution into the plastic cup, almost up to the top.
4. Follow illustrations 4 and 5. Wrap the pipe cleaner around the pencil so that it hangs over and into the cup. Curl the end so that the crystals will have a good place to grow and suspend it in the solution.

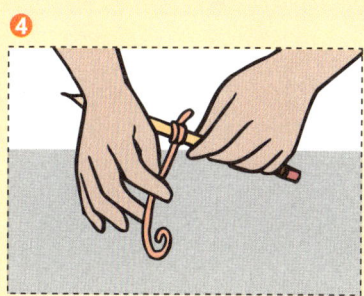

## Explore and Discover

# Science Sleuth

### 4. When Is Silver Green?
Find out what happens to different kinds of metals when they are exposed to air (oxidation) and weathering. Compare iron, silver, copper, and brass. Find at least five examples of metals, indoors or outdoors, that have undergone some kind of surface changes.

### 5. You Can't Escape Your Identity
With the help of a police officer, private investigator, or other professional, dust for and lift a fingerprint. Try comparing your fingerprints to someone else's and note the differences and similarities. Find out what other evidence, such as DNA from hair or skin samples, can be used to identify a person or a vehicle. The FBI uses seven main characteristics in fingerprint identification: the loop, arch, whorl, tented arch, double loop, central pocket loop, and accidental. Here are illustrations of the three most common. Can you find them in your fingerprints?

### 6. Water Questions
Have you ever seen a bug walking on water and wondered how it does it? Sometimes things look impossible to do, but if you know your science, there might be an answer. Here are some challenges to try with your friends, family, or troop members. Do at least two of the following:

- Move water from one container to another without pouring it.
- Use water to show how that air exists, exerts pressure, and takes up space.
- Make something heavier than water float.
- Cause a plant to drink water indoors without watering it, as shown in the "Incredible Slurping Plant" activity in the Explore and Discover" chapter of your *Junior Girl Scout Handbook*.

### 7. Read the Directions— But How Does It Work?
Find out how to hook up a computer to the Internet, a VCR to your television, or a music system to speakers. Demonstrate to another person how all the parts and pieces link to each other and what each piece of equipment does.

### 8. Seeing the Light
Your eyes can only see a portion of the light that is there—the white light. With technology, you can see other kinds of light on the spectrum, such as infrared or X-ray. Each type of light has its own signature pattern that can be seen when it is separated with a prism. Try separating light. Use a crystal or prism to separate natural light. Then separate light that is created by technology. Can you record the signature of a regular light bulb? The sun? A fluorescent bulb? Are there any differences?

arch pattern

whorl pattern

loop pattern

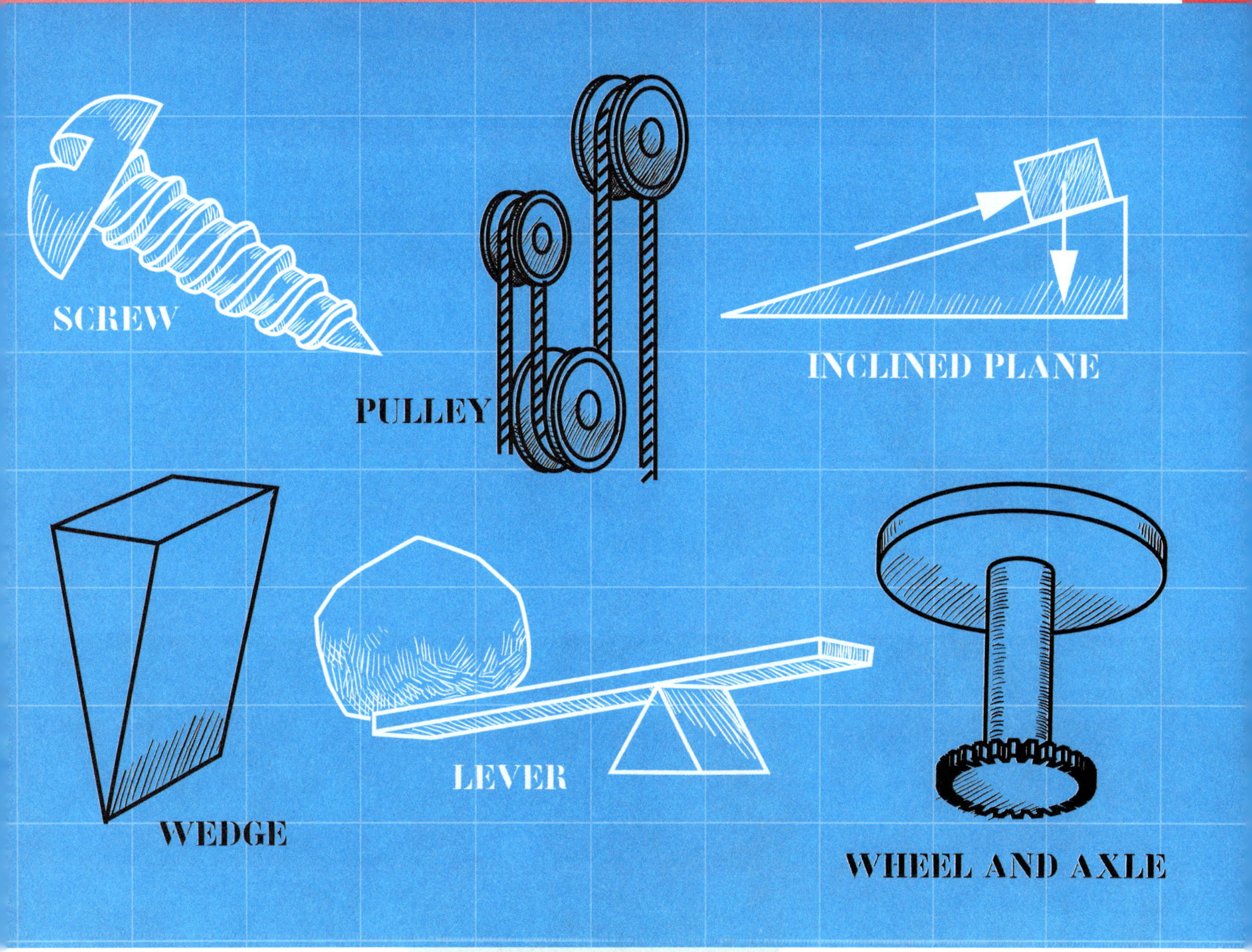

SCREW

PULLEY

INCLINED PLANE

WEDGE

LEVER

WHEEL AND AXLE

## 9. It's in the Genes

Genes "tell" each cell in your body how to develop. In the future, scientists may be able to anticipate and cure illnesses by mapping individuals' genes. Find out about a disease or condition that is believed to be linked to genes. Discuss the following with your troop, family, or another adult:

- In what situations would you want to know about your genes? In what situations would you not want to know? Why or why not?
- Do you think others should have access to information about your genes? Why or why not?

## 10. What Is a Simple Machine?

A machine is a device that helps use a force to move something and do work. See the six simple machines above. Do one of the following:

- Participate in a scavenger hunt where you find two examples of each of the machines, one indoors and one outdoors.
- Use at least three simple machines to put together a piece of equipment that will perform a job.
- Create a complex machine that combines two or more simple machines.

### Explore and Discover

# Sky Search

**The sky is filled with planets, stars, moons, satellites, and more. Instead of just gazing up at the sky, why not learn about what you're looking at? It starts with this badge.**

"Orion The Hunter" constellation

## 1. Mapping the Skies
Learn how to use a star map. Obtain or make such a map for your stargazing location that adjusts to the time and season when you are observing stars.

## 2. Constellations
Constellations are stars that appear to be in groups when looked at from Earth. If you were to travel in a spaceship, you would find that most stars that look close together are actually billions of miles apart. Learn to identify at least five of the constellations seen from Earth.

## 3. Direction, Please
Learn about the North Star and why it has been used for navigation throughout history. Help others locate the North Star. Use the North Star to find two constellations or asterisms (part of a constellation).

## 4. Planets
Learn which of the nine planets are visible to the naked eye. Try to locate at least one of these during a stargazing adventure. If possible, use a telescope to help you see better detail. Write down what you discover.

## 5. Connect the Dots
Learn stories from two or more ancient cultures—such as Greek, Norse, American Indian, Pacific Islander, or Chinese—that were used to explain what was seen in the sky.

## 6. Tools of the Trade
Learn the parts of a telescope and how to use one. If possible, use a tracking telescope or look through telescopes with different magnifications.
OR
Visit a large observatory and learn what kinds of telescopes are used there. What do astronomers learn by using telescopes?

## 7. Time for the Moon
Learn more about the moon—its phases, age, names of features—and then take a closer look. The best time to observe the moon is when the moon is partially lit, around the "quarter" phases of the moon. Use binoculars or a small telescope to help you see the valleys, ridges, mountain ranges, and craters on the moon.

## 8. The Sky Is Falling!
Learn about meteors, meteorites, meteor showers, and comets. Find out when meteor showers may be visible in your area. With an adult, arrange a meteor-watching party and count the number you see in an hour.

## 9. Star Stamps
Address an envelope to yourself or a friend, including your solar system and galaxy address. Draw a stamp on your envelope that celebrates an event in space exploration. Write a letter and include a map to your favorite planet.

## 10. Mission: Space
Learn about a current mission in space. What is the purpose of the mission, and how is information recorded and sent back to Earth? If possible, follow the mission over a period of time and visit a Web site that describes the mission and shares pictures or data.

**Eagle nebula**

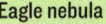

Stages of a lunar eclipse

"Leonid Fireball" meteor

### Explore and Discover

# Water Wonders

When you look at a globe, you can see why Earth is called "the water planet." Water gives life, but it also carries diseases and destruction. Learn more about the world of wet and wonderful water.

### 1. It's in a Cycle
Water is the ultimate in recycling. Show your understanding of the water cycle. What happens at each step of the cycle—evaporation, transpiration, condensation, and precipitation? *Hint:* Don't forget the role of the sun in providing energy.

### 2. The Water You Drink
Find out where your drinking water comes from. Is it from an aquifer, spring, river, reservoir, or another source? What is done to the water to make it safe to drink?

### 3. Not Enough?
Find out about an area of the country or world that has too little water. Learn why the area is so dry, how the people who live there are affected, and what is being done about the problem?

### 4. Life Underwater
Visit a place like an aquarium, fish hatchery, zoo, or pet store and look closely at the aquatic animals. Find three different animals that live all or part of their lives underwater—like fish, frogs, turtles, snails, sea lions, or beavers—and learn how their adaptations allow them to live in water.

- How do they move?
- How do they breathe?
- How do they protect themselves?

### 5. Water Food Chain
Find out about a water ecosystem's food chain by doing one of the following in a body of fresh water or salt water.

- Drag a plankton net in the water and observe what you capture, using a magnifying glass or a microscope.
- Take a bottom sample from a marsh. Place it in a white dish or pan. Look for signs of life.
- Look under rocks, in a pool, in a stream, or in a tide pool. What do you see?

In each case, find out what would make a food chain that would include the animals you observed. Would *you* have a place in such a food chain?

### 6. A Balanced Life
Set up a fresh- or salt-water aquarium. Balance the numbers and kinds of living things with a healthy food and water supply.

### 7. Water Work
Visit a place where water has been put to work, such as a sewage- or water-treatment plant, an irrigation control center, a mining operation, a power plant, a fish hatchery, or a physical therapy center. Find out where the water comes from, how it is used, and what happens to it afterwards. What kinds of jobs can you observe at the facility? What things do the people do? How did they learn how to do them?

### 8. Fixing It Up
Help with a project to improve a water-related habitat. You might participate in a shoreline clean-up, do plantings to filter water, fill gabions (a wire basket that holds rocks) along banks to prevent stream erosion, or construct and put up birdhouses or nesting platforms. The water's the limit!

### 9. Just Add Salt
Find out how salt water and fresh water are different. Do at least two experiments to find out which:

- Boils first
- Freezes first
- Yields crystal
- Makes better soapsuds
- Makes floating easier

> **Recipe for Salt Water**
>
> Mix 1 cup* of water with 1 tablespoon* of salt until the salt is completely dissolved, or dip a bucket in the ocean!

### 10. Water Comparisons
Conduct a water taste test with others. Taste several different kinds of water (tap water and different brands of bottled spring and mineral water) and rate each on a scale of 1 to 5 (5 is the best tasting). What did you find?

*See page 235 for the metric conversion chart.

## Explore and Discover

# Weather Watch

**Wouldn't it be great to be able to predict the weather? You'd never get caught in a rainstorm without an umbrella! Weather affects your life everyday. Learn to predict and plan ahead with this badge.**

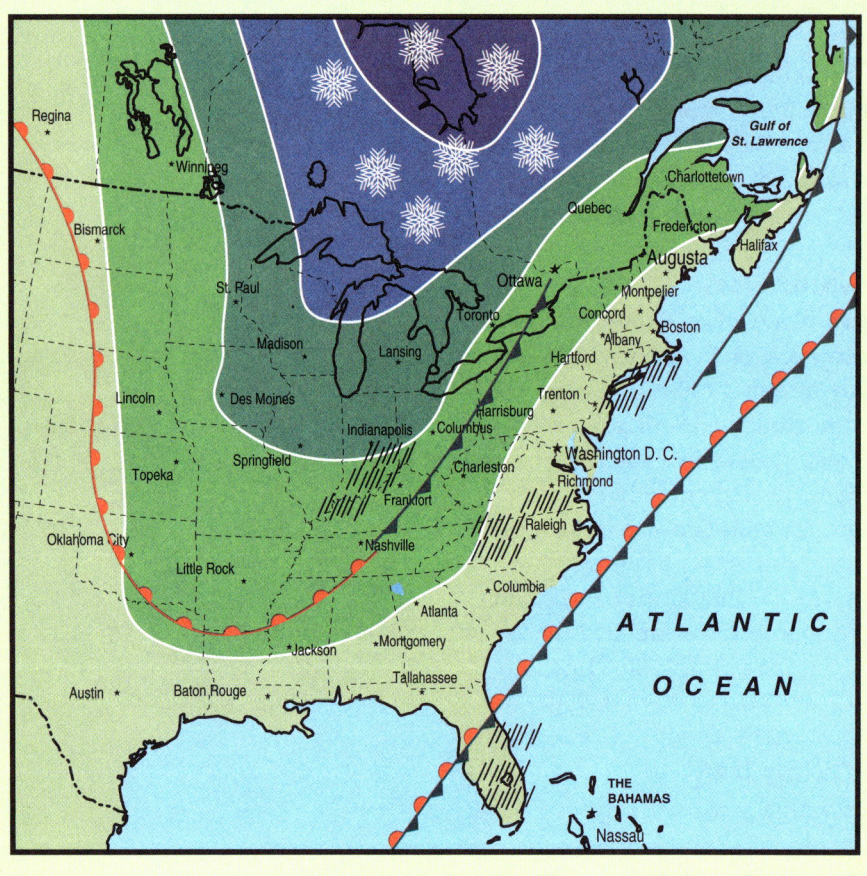

### 1. Weather Maps
Learn to read a weather map printed in a newspaper. Look for places where it's raining, or places where it's hot or cold. Predict the weather in your area using the maps and information given.

### 2. Visit a Weather Station
Visit a weather station, or interview a weather reporter or meteorologist about weather forecasting. Find out what kinds of equipment are used to watch and predict weather, why weather stations are useful, how the data about weather are interpreted, and how accurate weather predictions usually are.

**Where to Find Weather Stations**
- Airports
- Military installations
- Television stations
- U.S. Weather Service facilities
- Federal and state agencies responsible for public lands

## 3. Become a Cloud Watcher

Pay special attention to clouds for a week. Find out what kinds of clouds you are watching and what kinds of weather usually go with them. Then, make a cloud chart by drawing pictures or gluing magazine photos of cloud types on a piece of paper. Label each type of cloud (such as cirrus, cumulus, nimbus, and stratus) and use your chart to help predict the weather for a week. How accurate were you?

Cirrus clouds

Nimbus clouds

Cumulus clouds

Stratus clouds

## 4. Build a Weather Instrument

Find directions for building an instrument that helps you predict the weather, such as an hygrometer (measures changes in humidity), a barometer (see box), an anemometer (measures wind speed), or an alcohol thermometer (measures temperatures). Then build it.

## Build Your Own Barometer

**What You Need**
- A balloon
- A large baby-food or similar-sized jar
- A heavy-duty rubber band
- A drinking straw
- A piece of cardboard

**What You Do**
1. Cut a large section from the balloon and stretch it tightly over the mouth of the jar.
2. Wrap the rubber band around the balloon so it stays put.
3. Cut the end of the drinking straw into a point.
4. Lay the straw across the top of the jar.
5. Glue the non-pointed end of the straw to the center of the balloon.
6. Fold the piece of cardboard so that it will stand up next to the jar.
7. Mark where the pointed end of the straw touches the cardboard.
8. Draw a line and label the line number 5.
9. Draw another ten lines (five above and five below the number 5 line) on the cardboard. They should each be three millimeters* apart from one another. Write the numbers 0-10 on the lines. Make sure the straw is pointing at number 5.

Watch what happens to the straw over the next week. Check your barometer at approximately the same time every day. What is the weather like when the straw points to a lower number? What is the weather like when it points to higher numbers?

\* See page 235 for the metric conversion chart.

## Explore and Discover

# Weather Watch

**5. Weather Smarts**
Find out about weather-related emergencies that your community might face, such as hurricanes, tornadoes, flash floods, or lightning storms. Create a family plan for each emergency situation that could occur in your area. Include an emergency number to call for local or state weather reports. Then do one thing that will help your family be better prepared for a weather emergency.

Hurricane from space

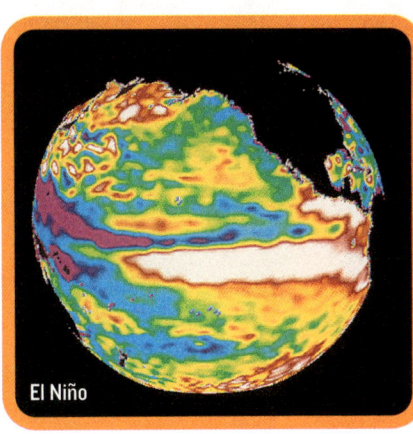
El Niño

## 6. Weather Trends
What's all the talk about global warming, La Niña, El Niño, and holes in the ozone? Find out more about one of these major weather trends. How is it affecting the climate and quality of life in your part of the country or another part of the world? What, if anything, can you or your community do to learn to live with the changes in weather cycles?

## 7. Weather Games
Make a game about weather. You can make a card or board game, a word game, or an active game. Share this with others.

## 8. Help Others Be Weather-Prepared
Help to run a weather-safety booth at a community event. You can make posters or distribute safety tips for weather emergencies common to your area. At your booth, include some hands-on learning for kids.
OR
Help an older neighbor prepare a kit for use in a weather emergency.

## 9. Paper Spirals and Frontal Systems
How do you make a paper spiral spin without blowing on it? Cut the spiral out of paper using the pattern below. Put a small hole through the center using a large needle. Tie a knot in a 6- to 8-inch-long piece of string and thread it through the hole.* Hold the spiral very still above a lamp. Be patient and wait a few minutes. What does the spiral do? Do you know why? A front has come through. When two air masses of different temperatures meet, the boundary between them is called a front. The colder air sinks and the warmer air rises. This movement often causes rainy weather and storms.

## 10. Make Your Own Weather
With the help of an adult, try making your own rain cloud.

### What You Need
- Very hot (but not boiling) water
- A large piece of plastic wrap
- Matches
- Ice cubes
- A clear liter plastic bottle cut down to be about 6-8 inches tall*

### What You Do
1. Cut a piece of plastic wrap large enough to drape over the top of the bottle.
2. Put several pieces of ice on the plastic wrap and set it aside.
3. Fill the bottle 1/3 full with the hot water.
4. Light a match and throw it into the bottle.
5. Quickly place the plastic wrap with ice on top of the bottle.
6. Wait and watch to see a rain cloud appear.

What is the cloud that is formed? It isn't smoke. It's water droplets forming on the smoke particles. The water vapor rises from the hot water and when it gets to the cool air near the ice, the vapor cools and begins to sink, condensing into water droplets. This forms a cloud. Droplets that form on the underside of the plastic may become so heavy that they fall as rain.

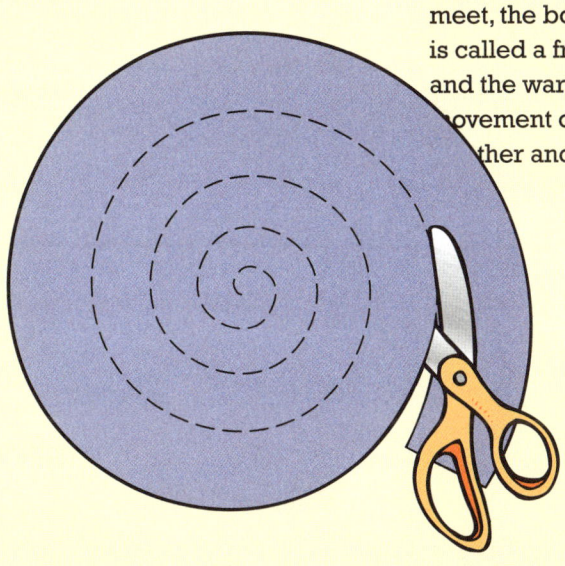

* See page 235 for the metric conversion chart.

# my Badge RECORD KEEPER

| | Name of badge | List the activities you did | Date badge completed |
|---|---|---|---|
| 1 | | | |
| 2 | | | |
| 3 | | | |
| 4 | | | |
| 5 | | | |
| 6 | | | |
| 7 | | | |
| 8 | | | |
| 9 | | | |
| 10 | | | |

| | Name of badge | List the activities you did | Date badge completed |
|---|---|---|---|
| 11 | | | |
| 12 | | | |
| 13 | | | |
| 14 | | | |
| 15 | | | |
| 16 | | | |
| 17 | | | |
| 18 | | | |
| 19 | | | |
| 20 | | | |

# my Badge RECORD KEEPER

| | Name of badge | List the activities you did | Date badge completed |
|---|---|---|---|
| 21 | | | |
| 22 | | | |
| 23 | | | |
| 24 | | | |
| 25 | | | |
| 26 | | | |
| 27 | | | |
| 28 | | | |
| 29 | | | |
| 30 | | | |

| | Name of badge | List the activities you did | Date badge completed |
|---|---|---|---|
| 31 | | | |
| 32 | | | |
| 33 | | | |
| 34 | | | |
| 35 | | | |
| 36 | | | |
| 37 | | | |
| 38 | | | |
| 39 | | | |
| 40 | | | |

# Index to BADGES

| Title | Page | | Title | Page |
|---|---|---|---|---|
| **Across Generations** | 40 | | **Art in the Home** | 130 |
| **Adventure Sports** | 68 | | **Art to Wear** | 134 |
| **Aerospace** | 180 | | **Becoming a Teen** | 30 |
| **Architecture** | 128 | | **Being My Best** | 32 |
| **Art in 3-D** | 132 | | **Books** | 136 |

BADGES ARE SHOWN AT ACTUAL SIZE

| Business-Wise | 10 |
| Camera Shots | 138 |
| Camp Together | 92 |
| Car Care | 58 |
| Careers | 12 |

| Caring for Children | 42 |
| Celebrating People | 44 |
| Ceramics and Clay | 140 |
| Choice Is Yours, The | 60 |
| "Collecting" Hobbies | 142 |

225

# Index to BADGES

| | |
|---|---|
| Communication | 46 |
| Computer Fun | 182 |
| Consumer Power | 34 |
| Cookie Connection, The | 8 |
| Court Sports | 70 |
| Creative Solutions | 144 |
| Dance | 146 |
| Discovering Technology | 148 |
| "Doing" Hobbies | 150 |
| Drawing and Painting | 152 |

BADGES ARE SHOWN AT ACTUAL SIZE

| | |
|---|---|
| Earth Connections | 94 |
| Eco-Action | 96 |
| Environmental Health | 72 |
| Field Sports | 74 |
| Finding Your Way | 98 |
| First Aid | 62 |
| Folk Arts | 154 |
| Food Power | 76 |
| Frosty Fun | 100 |
| Fun and Fit | 78 |

227

# Index to BADGES

| | | |
|---|---|---|
| Girl Scouting Around the World | 2 | Healthier You, A — 80 |
| Girl Scouting in My Future | 4 | Healthy Relationships — 48 |
| Girl Scouting in the USA | 6 | High on Life — 64 |
| Global Awareness | 14 | Highway to Health — 82 |
| Globe-Trotting | 184 | Hiker — 102 |

BADGES ARE SHOWN AT ACTUAL SIZE

| Badge | Page |
|---|---|
| Horse Fan | 104 |
| Horse Rider | 106 |
| Humans and Habitats | 16 |
| It's Important to Me | 36 |
| Jeweler | 156 |
| Lead On | 18 |
| Let's Get Cooking | 186 |
| Local Lore | 50 |
| Looking Your Best | 38 |
| "Making" Hobbies | 158 |

# Index to BADGES

| | |
|---|---|
| **Making It Matter** 188 | **Ms. Fix-It** 162 |
| **Making Music** 192 | **Music Fan** 194 |
| **Math Whiz** 160 | **My Community** 52 |
| **Model Citizen** 20 | **My Heritage** 54 |
| **Money Sense** 22 | **Oil Up** 196 |

BADGES ARE SHOWN AT ACTUAL SIZE

 **On My Way** 24

 **Outdoor Cook** 108

 **Outdoor Creativity** 110

 **Outdoor Fun** 112

 **Outdoors in the City** 114

 **Pet Care** 56

 **Plants and Animals** 116

 **Prints and Graphics** 164

**Puzzlers** 166

**Rocks Rock** 198

231

# Index to BADGES

| | | |
|---|---|---|
| **Safety First** | 66 | |
| **Science Discovery** | 200 | |
| **Science in Everyday Life** | 204 | |
| **Science Sleuth** | 208 | |
| **Sew Simple** | 168 | |
| **Sky Search** | 212 | |
| **Small Craft** | 118 | |
| **Sports Sampler** | 84 | |
| **Stress Less** | 86 | |
| **Swimming** | 120 | |

BADGES ARE SHOWN AT ACTUAL SIZE

| Theater | 170 | Water Fun | 122 |
| Toymaker | 172 | Water Wonders | 214 |
| Traveler | 26 | Weather Watch | 216 |
| Visual Arts | 174 | Wildlife | 124 |
| Walking for Fitness | 88 | Winter Sports | 90 |

# Index to BADGES

BADGES ARE SHOWN AT ACTUAL SIZE

 **World Neighbors** 28

 **Write All About It** 176

 **Yarn and Fabric Arts** 178

 **"Our Own Troop's" Badge** VIII

**Your Outdoor Surroundings** 126

**"Our Own Council's" Badge** IX

## Girl Scout Badges

Badges shown in the badge book chapters are shown larger than actual size.

Actual size:

1 1/2" in diameter

Shown in chapters:

# METRIC Conversion

## CUSTOMARY TO METRIC

| Customary | | Metric |
|---|---|---|
| 1 inch (in) | = | 2.54 centimeters |
| 1 foot (ft) | = | .3 meters |
| 1 yard (yd) | = | .9 meters |
| 1 mile (mi) | = | 1.6 kilometers |
| 1 acre | = | .4 hectares |
| 1 quart (lq) (qt) | = | .9 liters |
| 1 gallon (gal) | = | 3.6 liters |
| 1 ounce (avdp) (oz) | = | 28.4 grams |
| 1 pound (avdp) (lb) | = | .5 kilograms |
| 1 horsepower (hp) | = | .7 kilowatts |

## METRIC TO CUSTOMARY

| Metric | | Customary |
|---|---|---|
| 1 centimeter (cm) | = | .39 inches |
| 1 meter (m) | = | 3.3 feet |
| 1 meter (m) | = | 1.1 yards |
| 1 kilometer (km) | = | .6 miles |
| 1 liter (l) | = | 1.1 quarts (lq) |
| 1 cubic meter (m3) | = | 284.2 gallons |
| 1 gram (g) | = | .04 ounces (avdp) |
| 1 kilogram (kg) | = | 2.2 pounds (avdp) |
| 1 kilowatt (kW) | = | 1.3 horsepower |

## UNITS OF LENGTH AND MEASURE

### Length

| 12 inches | = | 1 foot |
|---|---|---|
| 36 inches or 3 feet | = | 1 yard |
| 1760 yards or 5280 feet | = | 1 mile |

### Liquid Measure

| 8 ounces | = | 1 cup |
|---|---|---|
| 16 ounces or 2 cups | = | 1 pint |
| 32 ounces or 4 cups or 2 pints | = | 1 quart |
| 64 ounces or 4 pints or 2 quarts | = | 1/2 gallon |
| 128 ounces or 16 cups or 8 pints or 4 quarts | = | 1 gallon |

## TEMPERATURE CONVERSIONS

### From Fahrenheit to Celsius

To convert from degrees Fahrenheit to degrees Celsius, subtract 32 degrees from the temperature and multiply by 5/9.

### From Celsius to Fahrenheit

To convert from degrees Celsius to degrees Fahrenheit, multiply the temperature by 1.8 and add 32 degrees.

# my JUNIOR GIRL SCOUT MEMORIES

## YOUR JUNIOR GIRL SCOUT MEMORIES

You might want to take some time to fill in your Junior Girl Scout memories before you move on to Cadette Girl Scouts. Look back from the other side of the bridging rainbow. Remember all of the fun things that you have accomplished as a Junior Girl Scout.

Encourage your friends to join you as you become a Cadette, or wait for them on the other side if they are younger. Say good-bye to being a Junior, and hello to the world of Cadette Girl Scouting!

I have been a Junior Girl Scout during these years: _____

My favorite activities were:

_____
_____
_____
_____

My favorite field trips were:

_____
_____
_____
_____

My favorite service projects were:

_____
_____
_____
_____

I felt like a leader when I:

_____

_____

_____

I am proudest of:

_____

_____

_____

The adults I met in Girl Scouting were:

_____

_____

_____

I had fun when we:

_____

_____

_____

The words I would use to describe my Junior Girl Scout experience are:

_____

_____

_____

The girls I met as a Junior Girl Scout were:

_____

_____

_____

# NOTES

# AUTOGRAPHS

# AUTOGRAPHS

# my FRIENDS

| Name | Address | Phone | E-mail |
|---|---|---|---|
| | | | |
| | | | |
| | | | |
| | | | |
| | | | |
| | | | |
| | | | |
| | | | |
| | | | |
| | | | |
| | | | |
| | | | |
| | | | |

| Name | Address | Phone | E-mail |
|------|---------|-------|--------|
|      |         |       |        |
|      |         |       |        |
|      |         |       |        |
|      |         |       |        |
|      |         |       |        |
|      |         |       |        |
|      |         |       |        |
|      |         |       |        |
|      |         |       |        |
|      |         |       |        |
|      |         |       |        |
|      |         |       |        |
|      |         |       |        |
|      |         |       |        |